The British Prime Minister

Also by Anthony King

The British General Election of 1964 (with David Butler)
The British General Election of 1966 (with David Butler)
Britain Says Yes: The 1975 Referendum on the Common Market
The New American Political System (editor)
Both Ends of the Avenue: The Presidency, the Executive Branch and Congress in the 1980s (editor)

The
British Prime Minister

SECOND EDITION

Edited by

Anthony King

MACMILLAN

First edition 1969
Reprinted 1974
Second edition 1985
Reprinted 1986

Published by
Higher and Further Education Division
MACMILLAN PUBLISHERS LTD
Houndmills, Basingstoke, Hampshire RG21 2XS
and London
Companies and representatives
throughout the world

Typeset by
Wessex Typesetters Ltd
Frome, Somerset

Printed in Hong Kong

British Library Cataloguing in Publication Data
The British Prime Minister.—2nd ed.
1. Great Britain. *Prime Minister* 2. Great
Britain—Politics and government—1979–
I. King, Anthony, *1934–*
354.4103'13   JN405
ISBN 0-333-38827-5
ISBN 0-333-38828-3 Pbk

Contents

Acknowledgements

The author and publishers wish to thank the following who have kindly given permission for the use of copyright material:

The American Political Science Association and Professor Richard E. Neustadt for his article 'White House and Whitehall'.

Tony Benn for his lecture 'The Case for a Constitutional Premiership'.

Kenneth Berrill for his Stamp Memorial Lecture.

Andre Deutsch Limited for 'Richard E. Neustadt interviewed by Henry Brandon' extracted from *Conversations with Henry Brandon*.

Bernard Donoughue for his article 'The Conduct of Economic Policy 1974–79'.

Fontana Paperbacks for 'Prime Ministerial Government', part of R. H. S. Crossman's 'Introduction' to *The English Constitution* by Walter Bagehot.

G. W. Jones for 'The Prime Minister's Aides' published in *Hull Papers in Politics*, No. 6, University of Hull.

A. D. Peters & Co. Ltd on behalf of G. W. Jones for his article 'The Prime Minister's Power' in *Parliamentary Affairs*, 1965, published by The Hansard Society.

Weidenfeld (Publishers) Limited and Michael Joseph Limited for extracts from *The Governance of Britain*, 1976, by Harold Wilson.

Acknowledgements

Introduction: The Textbook Prime Ministership

Pity the poor textbook writer. He is working on a book on British politics and government. He would like to include a chapter on the prime ministership. After all, the prime minister is universally reckoned to be the most powerful single individual in the British system of government, and in 1985 the office has been held for six years by Margaret Thatcher, a person of quite extraordinary personal force. To write about British government without focusing on the prime ministership would be like writing about modern aviation without focusing on jet propulsion.

Thus motivated, our writer turns to the only sources he can turn to – the existing specialist literature on the subject. A textbook cannot of its nature be based on large quantities of original research; it has to be based mainly on the more detailed work of others. What does the writer of textbooks find when he turns to the specialist literature on the British prime ministership? The short answer is: 'very little'. Biographies and memoirs abound, but works by academic political scientists are few and far between. All of the books on the prime ministership can easily be held in one hand; the books on the prime ministership and the cabinet together can easily be held in two hands. The article literature is similarly meagre, as the shortness of the Bibliography at the end of this present volume makes clear. The contrast between the paucity of writing on the British prime ministership and the richness and variety of the work on the American presidency could hardly be more striking. The average academic interested in American politics has in his office at least two long shelves of books concerned with the United States presidency – and that excludes biographies and memoirs.

It is worth pausing to emphasise just how thin the British

literature is. Carter's *The Office of Prime Minister* (1956) was a solid enough work in its day, but it was based entirely on secondary sources and is now nearly 30 years out of date (details of the Carter book, and of the others cited here, will be found in the Bibliography beginning on p. 258). Benemy's *The Elected Monarch* (1955) was likewise solid, but did not claim to be much more than a textbook aimed at secondary school pupils. Berkeley's *The Power of the Prime Minister* (1968) was a polemical essay rather than a thorough scholarly treatment, while Blake's more recent *The Office of Prime Minister* (1975), although full of interest, is based on a short set of lectures and runs to only 67 pages. The treatment in all of these volumes is historical to a greater or lesser extent, with the result that William Gladstone and Stanley Baldwin loom just as large as Harold Macmillan (and much larger than, say, Harold Wilson). No book specifically on the prime ministership has been published in the past ten years. For the time being, the best general discussion is probably that of Richard Rose in 'British Government: The Job at the Top' (1980). This can usefully be read in conjunction with the materials that follow here.

Why, one asks, is the academic literature on the prime ministership so thin? Part of the answer lies, of course, in the intrinsic difficulty of conducting research into an office that is at once so powerful and so inaccessible. Prime ministers are not about to allow inquisitive academics to wander unimpeded through the interconnecting rooms of 10 Downing Street, or to sit in on cabinet meetings. Even interviews with top politicians and officials can be time-consuming and hard to arrange. Similar factors also affect students of the American presidency, but at least American academics do not have to surmount quite such high barriers of official secrecy and reticence. It is also the case that the resources of British political science are very limited. There are only about 1,000 teachers of political science in the United Kingdom (compared with something like 12,000 in the United States), and of this already small number only a fraction are students of British government as distinct from political theory, Chinese government, international relations or whatever.

Not surprisingly under the circumstances, many of the most interesting things that have been written about the prime ministership have been written by people who have worked in Number 10 or else have served in the cabinet. Five of the chapters in this book – those by Harold Wilson, Bernard Donoughue, Richard Crossman, Tony Benn and Kenneth Berrill – are by present or former practitioners of government, and the two chapters by Richard E. Neustadt are by a man who was given an entrée into Britain's governing circles in the early 1960s partly because of his association with President Kennedy.

Whatever the explanation for the lack of scholarly interest in the British prime ministership, the results have been unfortunate, and the rest of this introduction should be read as a series of warnings (implicit as well as explicit) to the would-be student of this fascinating subject.

In the first place, to survey the textbook literature on the prime ministership is to survey a remarkably uniform landscape. Because the volume of research on Number 10 is so limited, and because important additions to it are made so rarely, textbook accounts of the premiership are typically based almost entirely on other textbook accounts of the premiership. The same materials are endlessly recycled, like clothes in a slow-moving washing machine, churning on and on. The same episodes – the Attlee government's decision to build the atomic bomb, Sir Anthony Eden and Suez, Harold Macmillan's 'night of the long knives' in 1962, Harold Wilson's resistance to the devaluation of sterling – are referred to again and again, as though, out of the thousands of decisions taken by British government since the Second World War, only a handful are of real significance.[1]

Old arguments are also rehashed. Several writers devote a good deal of space to discussing the issue of the size of the cabinet, even though the cabinet's size has varied only within narrow limits since 1945 (between 18 and 23) and even though no prime minister since 1945 has probably spent more than half an hour, at most, thinking about the subject.[2] Several textbooks similarly devote a number of paragraphs to Winston Churchill's 'overlords' experiment of the early 1950s, even though the experiment was not a success and no prime minister in the ensuing three decades has seriously thought of repeating it.[3] Even the language of the textbooks is repetitious. The same metaphors are used again and again, typically being drawn, for some obscure reason, from either ecclesiastical architecture ('the cabinet stands at the pinnacle of government') or Egyptian tourism ('the structure of the government machine can be likened to a pyramid with the prime minister at the apex'). The phrase *primus inter pares* (first among equals) is solemnly – and endlessly – discussed, although it must be evident by now that, as an analytic device for exploring the relations between prime ministers and their cabinet colleagues, it is so vague as to be completely useless.[4]

The paucity of materials on the prime ministership has had another unfortunate effect on the textbooks on British politics. Whatever one's views in the debate about 'prime ministerial government' (see chapters 7 and 8 below), no one denies the central importance of the prime ministerial office in the British scheme of things. In the Thatcher era it would be bizarre to claim that the prime minister cannot play a major part in influencing – indeed moulding – events. And the textbooks readily acknowledge the prime minister's importance. Yet, for the reasons just mentioned, most of them devote very little space to Number 10 and those who inhabit it. Few of the textbooks contain a whole chapter on the prime ministership, and most contain fewer than a dozen pages on the subject. To take an example at random, Norton's *The British Polity* (1984) is one of the best books in the field, but only six pages are given over to the prime ministership, rather less than the amount of space that is devoted to the House of Lords.[5] The cumulative effect is to create the impression in the reader's mind that the prime ministership is actually less important than it is made out to be. The prime minister becomes a bit of a blur – an odd thing for the prime minister, of all people, to be.

Academic neglect of the prime minister in terms of quantity might not matter especially if it were not associated, in addition, with rather low standards in terms of quality. Writers of textbooks are at a disadvantage; they cannot generate much in the way of new materials themselves, and in the case of the prime ministership they have few new ideas and little fresh research to draw on. It is therefore understandable that they are apt to become a bit slack. They advance propositions without testing them against reality. The result is that the reader, confronted by any textbook statement, however bland and uncontroversial it may appear, needs to ask insistently 'But is it true?'

Consider, for example, the following seemingly innocuous assertion:

> Some members of the party have such status that their inclusion [in the cabinet] is almost automatic: thus, Harold Macmillan had to give senior posts to R. A. Butler and Selwyn Lloyd; Lord Home had to appoint R. A. Butler, Edward Heath and Reginald Maudling; Harold Wilson had to appoint George Brown, James Callaghan and Patrick Gordon Walker.[6]

Not much, one might think, to disagree with there – and Harold Wilson's reluctant inclusion of Tony Benn in the Labour cabinet of 1974 is another case in point. But in fact the number of counter instances is far too large to be shrugged off. Enoch Powell had a very large following in the Conservative party of the late 1960s, but Edward Heath kept him out of his 1970 administration. Barbara Castle had been a prominent member of Labour's National Executive Committee (NEC) for more than 20 years by 1976, often standing at or near the top of the poll in the constituency section; but James Callaghan had no compunction about excluding her from his incoming administration. Edward Heath in 1979 was a former Tory leader and prime minister, still with a broad basis of support in the Tory party; but Margaret Thatcher was determined to keep him out, and she did. In other words, on closer examination the seemingly innocuous statement turns out to be true only by definition or else not true at all. One is prompted to think more carefully about the circumstances in which prime ministers do, and do not, include specific individuals in their administrations.

Or consider another case, also in connection with the prime minister's prerogative of hiring and firing. Another textbook writer says:

> Aside from some celebrated exceptions, PMs have rarely proved 'good butchers', a quality that Clement Attlee

deemed necessary for any occupant of the office. The PM's powers are exercised more often in the reshuffling of cabinet posts than in dismissing holders of those posts.[7]

Again, the statement sounds innocuous. But is it true? There have been nine prime ministers since the war, two of whom, Sir Anthony Eden and Sir Alec Douglas-Home, served for less than two years. Of the remaining seven, at least four were very good butchers indeed. Attlee had few inhibitions about dismissing ministers whom he considered incompetent or whom he thought had misbehaved – witness, for example, his peremptory sacking of Hugh Dalton following a harmless budget leak in 1947. Macmillan was the man who sacked six members of his cabinet on one night. Callaghan not only excluded Barbara Castle from his government but effectively forced out Roy Jenkins. Margaret Thatcher between 1979 and 1984 fired Norman St John-Stevas, Mark Carlisle, Sir Ian Gilmour, Lord Soames, David Howell and Francis Pym, at least two of whom, Gilmour and Pym, were held in high esteem by many on the Conservative back benches. Even Wilson, who was undoubtedly reluctant to fire people, nevertheless did so on a number of occasions; Douglas Jay, for example, was sacked in 1967 for resisting the overtures that the prime minister was making towards the European Economic Community. The 'celebrated exceptions' thus turn out to be more like the norm. Again, one is prompted to think more carefully, and systematically, about the circumstances in which prime ministers do, and do not, let people go.

This last case also draws attention to another weakness in many of the textbook accounts: their tendency to see the premiership in excessively static terms – to talk, for example, about '*the* powers of *the* prime minister'. The prime ministership, however, is a highly dynamic office. The people who hold it vary widely in temperament, in operating style, and in the purposes to which they wish to put the office. The same prime minister in the course of a single term of office is likely to find that changed political circumstances affect his or her capacity to influence events (the badly battered Harold Wilson of 1967–69 was a very different prime minister from the triumphant Wilson of 1964–66, just as Eden post-Suez bore little resemblance to Eden pre-Suez). And prime ministerial involvement also varies widely from issue to issue. Moreover, the political context within which Labour prime ministers operate is strikingly different from the one in which Conservative prime ministers have their being. Beloff and Peele in *The Government of the United Kingdom* (1980), and Barber in *British Politics in Perspective* (1984), are among the few textbook writers who emphasise this variety and fluctuation.[8]

Reference was made earlier to the extent to which the writers of textbooks – almost inevitably in the absence of research – recycle one another's examples, arguments and even phrases. For the same reason, most of them also deal with the same specific topics, with the result that important aspects of the prime ministership are dealt with not at all or only in passing. A subject, once omitted, tends to stay omitted.

A good example of this tendency concerns the British prime minister's control over the structure of government – which is separate from, and in its way just as important as, the prime minister's ability to hire and fire individual ministers. In most countries, the structure of government departments is determined by statute, and the head of government can reorganise departments only with the consent of the legislature. In Britain, by contrast, the first two provisions of the Ministers of the Crown (Transfer of Functions) Act 1946, state:

(1) His Majesty may by Order in Council provide for the transfer to any Minister of the Crown of any functions theretofore exercisable by another Minister of the Crown.
(2) His Majesty may by Order in Council provide for the dissolution of the Government Department in the charge of any Minister of the Crown and the transfer to or distribution among such other Minister or Ministers of the Crown as may be specified in the Order of any functions theretofore exercisable by the Minister in charge of that Department.[9]

In practice, these sweeping powers are exercised only by the prime minister who, in addition, can of course determine the size, composition and remit of all cabinet committees as well as (within limits) the cabinet itself. The academic literature, however, is largely silent on this aspect of prime ministerial power.[10]

Another important omission, or at least partial omission, concerns the prime minister's control over senior appointments in the civil service. It was said during Harold Wilson's time at Number 10 that the individuals he chose – and, more important, the type of individuals he chose – to run major government departments would determine the style, and perhaps some of the policies, of British governments for years to come. Likewise, one of Margaret Thatcher's more significant legacies looks like being a whole generation of permanent secretaries and deputy secretaries, not necessarily sharing all of her substantive views but probably sharing her general approach to problems of public sector management. Most of the textbooks refer briefly to the prime minister's role in the making of senior civil service appointments, but they do not draw attention to the importance of the subject, or set out in any detail exactly what the prime minister's role is.

As a final example of a topic slighted in the literature one might cite prime ministerial involvement in foreign affairs and the affairs of the EEC. Suppose that a prime minister resigns or retires during his or her term of office and is replaced by another prime minister of the same party, as Harold Macmillan was replaced by Sir Alec Douglas-Home and Harold Wilson by James Callaghan. What are the consequences of thus changing the person, the party remaining constant? One part of the answer almost certainly lies in the field of foreign affairs where – especially in the age of summitry and the intercontinental telephone – much can turn on the character of the personal relations among heads of government. An important though little noticed feature of Callaghan's prime ministership was his close relationship with President Carter of the United States; Carter trusted Callaghan, and paid more attention to his advice than to that of any other western leader. Callaghan was succeeded at Number 10 by a Conservative but, even if he had not been, it is unlikely that a relationship as personal as this would have extended beyond Callaghan's departure, as an individual, from the scene. Britain's relations in the 1980s with the EEC are likewise undoubtedly coloured by the personality and negotiating style of Margaret Thatcher.

Sir Kenneth Berrill in the final chapter of this book lays emphasis on the importance of summitry in the modern world and on the importance of the prime minister's part in it but, again, this is a topic on which the textbooks are largely silent.

The main purpose of this volume is not to contradict the textbook accounts of the premiership – most, if not all, of what they say is in fact true – but to flesh them out and to indicate aspects of the subject that they tend to neglect. In these pages will be found most of the important articles and papers on the prime ministership, some of which are not otherwise easily accessible. Chapter 4, 'Margaret Thatcher: The Style of a Prime Minister', is the only one to have been specially written. Most of the materials have been reproduced uncut; it seemed better to preserve passages of marginal relevance than to remove them and risk distorting the author's meaning. Readers should bear in mind throughout that the various chapters were written at widely separated dates.

This edition of *The British Prime Minister* retains four chapters from the original 1969 edition – the two by Richard E. Neustadt (chapters 5 and 6) and the debate on prime ministerial government between Richard Crossman and G. W. Jones (chapters 7 and 8) – but is otherwise completely changed. The interviews with Harold Wilson in the first edition have been replaced by Wilson's mature reflections on the office of prime minister, written after he himself had occupied it twice. Chapter 2 by Bernard Donoughue provides a unique insight, written by someone who observed the events he describes, into two prime ministers' involvement in the substance of a specific field of policy. G. W. Jones's paper 'The Prime Minister's Aides' (chapter 3) has been brought up to date for this volume with a concluding section on the structure of Number 10 under Margaret Thatcher. Chapter 4 seeks to draw attention to a number of unusual features of Margaret Thatcher's prime ministerial style. The presence of the final two chapters – by Tony Benn and Sir Kenneth Berrill – is a reminder that the nature of the prime ministerial office has become a matter of political, not just academic, controversy. There is much talk of 'reforming' the office; some (like Tony Benn) want to weaken it, others (like Sir Kenneth Berrill) to strengthen it.

Despite all that has been said and written about the prime

ministership since 1969, this edition, like its predecessor, suffers from certain omissions. Little has been written about the selection of party leaders in Britain, with the result that not a great deal is known about the processes whereby potential prime ministers are recruited. The setting of prime ministerial goals and priorities is likewise something that outsiders know very little about. The dearth of information on the prime minister's role in selecting senior civil servants has already been referred to. Only recently has detailed information begun to become available on prime ministers' use of cabinet committees.[11] Nevertheless, this edition represents a substantial improvement on its predecessor, if only because substantially more of it is based on the direct experience of those who know Number 10, substantially less of it on the views of academics lacking such knowledge and experience. With luck, interest in the remarkable premiership of Margaret Thatcher will have the effect of further stimulating interest in the prime ministership. If it does, the third edition of *The British Prime Minister* will be able to draw on a yet wider range of materials than this one.

References

1. See, among many examples that could be given, A. H. Hanson and Malcolm Walles, *Governing Britain*, 3rd edn (London: Fontana, 1980), pp. 127–9 and Anthony H. Birch, *The British System of Government*, 4th edn (London: George Allen & Unwin, 1980), pp. 154–6.
2. For an extreme example, see R. M. Punnett, *British Government and Politics*, 4th edn (London: Heinemann, 1980), pp. 207–13.
3. Again see Punnett, *British Government and Politics*, pp. 213, 215–17, but also Hanson and Walles, *Governing Britain*, pp. 121–2.
4. Anyone wishing to undertake a sort of tour around a cliché might like to make a note of the following possible ports of call: Punnett, *British Government and Politics*, p. 222; Philip Norton, *The British Polity* (New York: Longman, 1984), p. 180; Patrick Gordon Walker, *The Cabinet*, 2nd edn (London: Jonathan Cape, 1972), p. 88; F. W. G. Benemy, *The Elected Monarch: The Development of the Power of the Prime Minister* (London: Harrap, 1965), p. 62; Humphry Berkeley, *The Power of the Prime Minister* (London: George Allen & Unwin, 1968), p. 23; Byrum E. Carter, *The Office of Prime Minister* (London: Faber & Faber, 1956), p. 193; and Philip Norton, *The Constitution in Flux* (Oxford: Martin

Robertson, 1982), p. 49. The offending phrase was originally John Morley's. To be fair to the authors cited above, many of them recognise that *primus inter pares* is indeed a cliché and many of them do not make much use of it.

5. Norton, *British Polity*, pp. 177–82.
6. Birch, *British System of Government*, pp. 150–1.
7. Norton, *British Polity*, pp. 177–8.
8. Max Beloff and Gillian Peele, *The Government of the United Kingdom* (London: Weidenfeld & Nicolson, 1980), pp. 72–7; James Barber, 'The Power of the Prime Minister', in R. L. Borthwick and J. E. Spence (eds), *British Politics in Perspective* (Leicester: Leicester University Press, 1984).
9. *Ministers of the Crown (Transfer of Functions) Act* 1946, 9 & 10 Geo. 6, Ch. 31.
10. But see the recent book by Christopher Pollitt, *Manipulating the Machine: Changing the Pattern of Ministerial Departments, 1960–83* (London: George Allen & Unwin, 1984), especially chapters 9–10.
11. See Michael Cockerell, Peter Hennessy and David Walker, *Sources Close to the Prime Minister: Inside the Hidden World of the News Manipulators* (London: Macmillan, 1984), especially chapter 5.

1

A Prime Minister at Work

HAROLD WILSON[1]

Harold Wilson, now Lord Wilson of Rievaulx, served in Number 10 for more than eight years, longer than any other prime minister in this century. Unlike most prime ministers, who are wholly preoccupied with the substance of policy and the day-to-day business of government, Wilson was also interested in the machinery of government and the prime minister's place in the constitution. He gave interviews on these subjects both before he became prime minister and during his two periods of office. In this chapter, written within months of his voluntary retirement in May 1976, Lord Wilson describes the prime minister's job as he himself experienced it.

Number 10 is best regarded as a small village. During Sir Alec Douglas-Home's premiership, I described it as a monastery and declared my intention of changing it into a power house. Whether I succeeded or not, or whether it was the right objective, historians may debate. The function of Number 10 – and clearly of the Cabinet Office – is to make cabinet government work.

Number 10 reflects the style of the prime minister of the day. The prime ministerial style of Clement Attlee was markedly different from that of Winston Churchill,[2] and that of Anthony Eden differed from both of them. Harold Macmillan gave the public impression of being something of a dilettante, fainéant and disdainful – and enjoying it immensely. Nothing could be further from the truth. Reviewing the sixth and final volume of his memoirs, I said:

> I am simply moved to confirm the provisional judgment inspired by an earlier volume I reviewed in *The Times*. Those of us were wrong who regarded him as a 'Premier Ministre Fainéant'.
>
> He was utterly hard-working, even discounting the long hours he must have spent recording the events of each day for posterity, and the time he spent on detailed and perceptive letters to Buckingham Palace.
>
> As I wrote two years ago, Mr. Macmillan's role as a poseur was itself a pose.[3]

There was a general impression that my Number 10 style was somewhat different from that of Sir Alec. In a radio interview in 1964[4] I said that, if elected, I intended to run Number 10 not only as chairman, but as a full-time managing director or chief executive for my incoming team would have almost no cabinet or administrative experience.

The style even of the same prime minister can itself change over time, as requirements change. Reference has been made to change of style of Labour premiership between the 1960s and 1974–76. At the final meeting of the shadow cabinet on 4 March 1974, as we were waiting for news that the Heath administration was finally going, I said that I would run the new government very differently from that of the 1960s. James Callaghan exchanged a knowing and disbelieving wink with Denis Healey. Within a fortnight they both agreed that the style was entirely different. At the first meeting of the parliamentary Labour party (PLP), I told them that, whereas in the 1960s I had played in every position on the field – goalkeeper, midfield, taking penalties and corners and bringing on the lemons – I was going to be an old-fashioned deep-lying centre half, lying well back, feeding the ball to those whose job it was to score goals, and moving upfield only for rare 'set-piece' occasions. A few weeks later, commenting on the metaphor, the

Liverpool Daily Post said that the analogy was rather that of the manager, sitting on the bench and encouraging his team. This was flattering, as Liverpool is Shankly country, but pursuing the theme I reminded colleagues that managers frequently sit on the substitutes' bench, pulling players off the field and replacing them at short notice.

In the two administrations, March–October 1974 and October 1974–April 1976, Number 10 and the Cabinet Office were working with me to strengthen the power and effectiveness of cabinet government, taking advantage of the successive improvements in the servicing of the cabinet as a decision making body, which had been introduced over the previous six or seven years.

Number 10 is not only a village; it is a small village. In his authoritative review of Number 10 private office, G. W. Jones records the numbers of private secretaries proper in Number 10.[5] In 1870 there were three, and the number remained constant until the 1920s; today there are five, apart from the appointments secretary. In 1951 there were 52 clerks, typists, messengers and cleaners in Number 10; by 1964 there were 59 and in 1974 98. The figures for private secretaries are, as Mr Jones points out, not strictly comparable. Nineteenth-century private secretaries had to do a great deal of copying, and until modern times the Number 10 private office was responsible for relations with the press. The creation of a separate press office, and in particular the establishment of typing pools, electronic communications and copying machines, has made the figures something less than perfectly comparable.

The Lloyd George administration provided a unique aberration, the 'garden suburb' private cabinet office and a Lloyd George-oriented private office. His successor, Bonar Law, was served by unpaid, privately recruited informal advisers, together with one Treasury appointment.

It was Ramsay MacDonald who changed the system, against the strong criticism of his party colleagues. He ended the system in which the principal private secretary, and others, were changed when the party complexion of the government changed: 'None of the private secretaries who served Liberal prime ministers from 1868 to 1921 ever served a Conservative prime minister, and none of the private secretaries who served

Conservative prime ministers from 1868 to 1905 ever served a Liberal prime minister,[6] Ramsay MacDonald took over his predecessor's secretaries: The Civil service took over the private office.[7]

Since then each incoming prime minister following a change of government has retained his predecessor's principal private secretary, with one exception: Edward Heath in 1970 got rid of a civil servant I had appointed a few weeks earlier – a career civil servant who had in fact been private secretary to Lord Hailsham during the Macmillan administration. I followed a different course. I kept on Sir Alec Douglas-Home's private secretary for nearly two years, and in 1974–75 retained Edward Heath's post-election appointee for more than a year – though he was due for a change and in fact, after nearly five years of Number 10 service, he was almost the longest-serving principal private secretary since the war.

After Robert Vansittart (later Lord Vansittart) was appointed to the private office in 1937, no appointment except from the civil service (usually from the Treasury) was made to private office, with one exception. Harold Macmillan appointed John Wyndham (whom he later created Lord Egremont) not as a political or private adviser, but in private office. As a wealthy man, he was unpaid – in fact a dollar-a-year man. Pay is not the test: here was a political appointment brought into private office itself. All other prime ministers, including Edward Heath and myself, have kept the administrative private office and the political office apart (though people associated with Mr Heath were included in the Central Policy Review Staff [CPRS], as mine were not).

As G. W. Jones, who in the essay quoted really has got the feel of what Number 10 is about, has commented, 'The Prime Minister is the one minister who stands on the peaks of both politics and administration . . . at the top politics and administration could not be kept distinct . . . at the top politics and administration are inextricably entangled'.[8]

Hence the tendency in recent years to create a political office to advise the prime minister and to provide a means of contact with the party machine, which it would be unprocedural, if not improper, to attempt through the civil service machine. To this I will return.

Number 10 is a deceptive building. From Downing Street it appears a tiny house, but in fact it is two houses linked by a passage, the larger one being built to face Horse Guards.[9]

It has, in fact, over 160 rooms, mainly offices, together with the cabinet room, reception and dining rooms, and a small flat on the second floor. To the north it links directly with the Cabinet Office; to the south there is a through passage to Number 11 and Number 12. Number 11 is the chancellor's official residence, Number 12 the office of the chief whip (his main office is at the House of Commons). Hugh Dalton used to tell me, when he was chancellor and I was a young minister, that you could always measure the situation within the cabinet by the door covering the passage between Number 10 and Number 11. If it was locked, as it had been for long periods, that augured an unhappy ministry. It was a freeway through all the years I was at Number 10; and it was used for two-way traffic.

The present Number 10 is a new building. In the 1950s its foundations began to shift, and an expensive and protracted rebuilding took place, during which time the then prime minister, Harold Macmillan, lived in Admiralty House, and made it the seat of government for meetings of the cabinet and cabinet committees. He always made clear that he preferred it to Number 10. In fact he returned to the by-then rebuilt building only in October 1963 and within days left it for hospital, where his resignation took effect.

Clem Attlee used to work from his seat at the cabinet table, and received his official visitors in the cabinet room. In 1964 I followed his example, despite the handy little study on the first floor. Three years later I took over the study and worked from there, except for formal committees, deputations and overseas visitors, as did Edward Heath, who greatly extended and refurnished it. It was there I went on the evening of 4 March 1974, to set about forming the cabinet.

Others have written about the facilities for work there – and at Chequers. The secretarial services are of the highest standard, provided by the so-called 'garden room girls' (their offices are on the sub-ground floor, level with the garden). The communications are superb. Number 10 has the best telephone switchboard in London.[10] Communications between Chequers and Downing Street are total, and secure, in contrast to the facilities in Neville Chamberlain's time, when he used to be alerted after each of Hitler's acts of weekend aggression on an ancient upright telephone, with a rotary handle, in what used to be the butler's pantry. Chequers is linked with the Downing Street communications system with secure access to hot lines, etc. to Washington (and, nowadays, Belfast).

The service the prime minister gets would soon persuade any incoming premier who had delusions about setting up the often-advocated 'prime minister's department', and I was not one of these, to think again. Everything he could expect to create is there already to hand in the Cabinet Office. Should he pursue these illusions his first visit to Washington should put paid to them. The president – who is of course head of state as well as head of government, as a result of the decision of the founding fathers two hundred years ago[11] – can hardly move for staff. (In President Lyndon Johnson's time, I was told his staff was 2,500: I understand it increased still further under President Nixon.) He is pressed on all sides for signatures, approvals, ratifications – I have seen presidents badgered to sign them in the lift, an action that must be a more or less automatic reflex. Contrast with that a *total* staff in Number 10, including private secretaries, garden room girls, the honours and church sections, telephone and communications operators, messengers and cleaners, of less than 100.

Now I turn to the pattern of a prime minister's day, with two qualifications. No two days are the same; no day ends as it began; the tidy list of six–twelve fixed engagements is not only increased; it may – and probably will – be broken into by a sudden crisis, minor or major. This could be international, parliamentary, administrative, financial or political in a party sense – not to mention a departmental problem which, on the initiative of the minister concerned, or one called in by the prime minister, becomes Number 10 business.

In 1964–70 I lived in Number 10. In 1974 I decided that I did not want to live over the shop again, and I slept each night in my home in Lord North Street, five minutes' walk from the House of Commons. Most days, after reading the morning press – two or three are delivered overnight to the prime minister's home – I would be at my desk in Downing Street at

9.30 a.m. Unless there was a ministerial committee due to meet under my chairmanship at that hour, I would have a quick check with private office to learn of any overnight developments or crises – for example, a meeting of the security council of the UN – I had not been apprised of through a late-night or early-morning telephone call or overnight overseas telegram, and would make dispositions for the work of the day.

On Thursdays, and sometimes Tuesdays – other days more rarely – there is a cabinet, usually lasting the greater part of the morning. On other days there will be cabinet committees to chair, usually two, sometimes three. There may be speeches to prepare, an ambassador or high commissioner to call or a visiting president or prime minister or colleagues to see, a meeting with the appointments secretary about a vacant bishopric, deanery or lord lieutenancy. The Leader of the House or chief whip might call to discuss overnight parliamentary developments or parliamentary prospects for the day or longer ahead. Boxes would normally have been done the previous night, however late that might be, as would parliamentary questions on Monday and Wednesday nights.

Late morning – after 1.0 p.m. if cabinet or a cabinet committee had run late – I would meet with my political office for up-to-date political issues, arrangements for political meetings in the country or messages from party headquarters. At 1.45 or later I would have a quick lunch at the House, almost always at the table where the whips and senior ministers foregather. Depending on which backbenchers were there, informal government business would continue throughout lunch and over coffee.[12] I might ask two or three backbenchers or junior ministers from other tables to join us for coffee. After that I would usually go to the tearoom for informal chats with backbenchers or ministers, and then to the afternoon's work. In all, I probably spent more time in the members' dining room and the tearoom than any of my postwar predecessors.

On question days I would return to my room at the House to prepare for the 3.15 p.m. ordeal. Usually, after that, I would return to Number 10 for a routine similar to that of the morning.

In the 1960s I extended the time for meeting backbenchers.

On Tuesdays, Wednesdays and Thursdays I was available in my room, on an open-door basis, for any members or groups of members who wanted to see me. In 1974 I tried to revive this practice. It was less successful, partly because of the immensely increased work load at Number 10, which meant that I had to be back at the ranch. Another problem was that through the open door came more clearly defined groups, not only those from the Tribune or the manifesto caucuses, but regional groups and groups concerned with individual industries, not to mention the highly articulate group concerned with members' pay, allowances and pensions.

The pattern of the day's activities could be rudely disturbed not only by a sudden crisis (including, twice in 1974–76, a hijacking), but also by overseas visits or by state visits or head of government visits from foreign or commonwealth countries. Such visits virtually took over the day. A state visit by a president or monarch involves joining the receiving line at Victoria station or Windsor, attending the formal royal banquet at the Palace, Windsor or perhaps Holyrood, giving a formal lunch at Number 10, sometimes a dinner at Guildhall, and almost invariably attending a return dinner given by the visiting head of state. In addition, where the head of state is also head of government, e.g. many of the African and Latin American presidencies, the prime minister is engaged in very full talks on all aspects of bilateral and international questions.

Though the hospitality is more restricted, a prime ministerial visit usually involves a full day's talks, perhaps more, and this means several hours of reading the very full and invaluable briefing on anything Whitehall wants raised, anything we expect the visitor to raise, and what to say, and what not to say, when he raises something we hope he will not raise ('defensive brief'). For really key discussions – also before international conferences, e.g. with commonwealth heads of government, European council (EEC summit), NATO heads of government, Helsinki – full briefing meetings are held, of ministerial colleagues and Foreign Office and other departmental officials. The briefing for conferences also inevitably includes 'bilateral briefs' for discussions which we or the other country want to seek, or which happen socially.

Very many overseas colleagues have briefing systems similar to ours, especially in commonwealth countries.[13]

The best impression of the pattern of the prime minister's day or week is to analyse his diary for a given period. An analysis of these for the last three months of 1975, 1 October–31 December, covering a period that began in the middle of the party conference and ended during a brief holiday in the South-West, leads to the following tabulation:

Audiences of the queen	8
Cabinet meetings	11
Cabinet committees	24
Other ministerial meetings	43
State visits	1
Other head of government visits	5
Other foreign VIP visits (deputy prime minister, finance, foreign ministers, etc.)	8
Visits abroad	2
Visits to Northern Ireland	1
Meetings with industry, prominent industrialists, etc.	28
Official meetings	27
Ministerial speeches	17
Political speeches	9
Visits within Britain	13
Official lunches and dinners	20
Political meetings – no speech	11
TV or radio broadcasts	8 (excluding party conference)

Christmas apart, I was not able to record a single private or social engagement.

Apart from prearranged ministerial meetings with documents circulated and written and sometimes oral briefing, each day sees a number of often unprogrammed meetings with ministers. Most days the prime minister will see the foreign and commonwealth secretary, and the chancellor. Each Friday, as already stated, I would have the informal scheduled meeting, to which reference has been made, with the Leader of the House, foreign and commonwealth secretary, chancellor and the chief whip, mainly to survey the progress of administrative business over the following two weeks, arrangements for cabinet and cabinet committee meetings. This meeting gave the opportunity for reports on the parliamentary situation and forward programme. It was not, in any sense, an 'inner cabinet'; no policy decisions were taken, it was concerned purely with business. Usually the foreign and commonwealth secretary would stay on for a discussion of problems arising in his rather extensive diocese or to discuss diplomatic appointments; when more urgent problems arose, an *ad hoc* meeting was arranged, or if we were both in the House he would come round to my room. Similar arrangements applied with the chancellor. The Lord President could even more easily drop round from the Cabinet Office whenever necessary on any parliamentary matter, including the progress of the legislative programme or the preparation of the programme for the succeeding session, as well as anything within a subject specifically remitted to him, such as arrangements for the EEC referendum and the enabling legislation, and devolution. Other ministers usually called by appointment, or one or two would stop to raise some matter after cabinet or a cabinet committee. Still more frequent – several each day – were meetings with the staff of private office and with the secretary of the cabinet.

Formal deputations would come from the principal national organisations: the Confederation of British Industry (CBI), the Trades Union Congress (TUC), the National Farmers Union and many others. The Labour government took office in March 1974 during a period of great anxiety in the medical profession and occupations ancillary to medicine about salaries following stage III of the 1972–74 pay policy and associated problems of status – these anxieties increased in the next two months; accordingly on 20 May I met a deputation consisting of the Royal Colleges of Midwives and Nursing, the Association of Nurse Administrators, the National Union of Public Employees (NUPE), the Confederation of Health Service Employees, the Health Visitors' Association, the National and Local Government Officers Association (NALGO), and the Managerial, Administrative, Technical and Supervisory Association (ASTMS).

When fresh concern arose about government legislation and action in connection with pay beds and private practice, in October and December 1975, I received two deputations of the principal professional bodies, including the Royal Colleges; the British Medical Association; the Central Committee for Hospital Medical Services; the Hospital Consultants and Specialists Association; the junior doctors and the British Dental Association. In all these meetings the prime minister is, of course, flanked by the ministers principally concerned.

In the week that ended with the announcement of the government's counter-inflation policy on 11 July 1975, I called in the TUC, the CBI and the chairmen of 31 publicly-owned industries and services. Other ministers saw the representatives of all the relevant organisations such as the local authorities and the farmers.

Sometimes the prime minister takes the initiative to invite representatives of an important profession, or group of people, to come for an informal evening meeting or dinner. In the 1960s, for example, I had two such gatherings with representatives of the Church of England; and early in 1974 with representatives of the 'charities', a convenient but inadequate description of a voluntary association of six bodies concerned with problems of poverty and deprivation, some on the domestic front (such as Help the Aged and Save the Children Fund), others with overseas countries such as War on Want and Oxfam. Their joint memorandum, based on the assertion that poverty was one single problem, home or overseas, and their determination to act on the principle of all for each and each for all, was carefully studied by departments and centrally, and our response was further discussed over a working dinner at Number 10.

Working dinners at Number 10 are of course nothing new, though the phrase came into use after 1964. (This is a phrase not to be confused with 'working funerals', invented by Robert Carvel, political editor of the *Evening Standard*, after the attendance by the world's leaders at the Requiem Mass for Dr Adenauer in 1967, and much used after the memorial service for Mr Harold Holt, the Australian prime minister who was drowned, in the same year: it is now in general journalistic – if not diplomatic – use.)

Recent working dinners at Number 10 have assembled, on separate occasions, groups of leading industrialists, merchant bankers and other city leaders, and representatives of the film industry; in addition, there was a small lunch to discuss the National Enterprise Board (NEB) and another to consider the provision of public (or private) funds for technological innovation in industry. After March 1974, a series of 'city' dinners was arranged, alternatively in Number 10 and the governor's flat in the Bank of England, with the city representatives, including some of the younger generation, chosen by the governor. Unfortunately, the sheer pressure of work with the economic crisis and other problems made it harder to set aside an evening in advance to follow up these extremely valuable occasions. The same demands, together with the need to settle the forward public expenditure programme in May–December 1975, led to repeated postponement of the follow-up (proposed for Chequers) of the work we were doing on the 'charities' front.

Different entirely from these occasions was the use of Number 10 on behalf of charitable organisations, which, in common with my predecessors, I arranged very sparingly. I recall only four in nearly eight years: one for the United Nations Association – U Thant had arranged to fly over, but was prevented at the last minute and sent his deptuy; another for the Roundhouse ('Centre 42') in Camden Town, with whose establishment I had been much involved before becoming prime minister; another for the Children's Theatre. In 1974–76 there was one only, for the Attlee Memorial Foundation, to raise money for the work done for very young deprived children in the East End, under the dedicated direction of John Profumo.

All this and speeches too. In three months from mid-September to mid-December 1975, I had 44 speeches to prepare and deliver, 18 of them major ones, involving a great deal of research, briefing and preparation. This excludes some seven or eight speeches each evening during party conference, on the nightly tours of dinners or receptions given by regional parties, associated organisations and trade unions. The heaviest concentration was the 40 days between 3 November (at the opening of the Forties Field) and 12 December when there were 15 speeches, nearly all of them major, including the Lord Mayor's Guildhall banquet, the main speech in the debate on the opening of the new session of parliament and, within 24 hours, the local government conference at Eastbourne, the London Mayors' Association dinner, two political speeches on the same day in Carlisle and Newcastle, the first Blackett Memorial Lecture, the annual conference of the National Council of Social Services and my Guildhall speech on receiving the freedom of the city of London. The only way I could keep going was to dictate the first draft of the speech on the Saturday and Sunday mornings at Chequers eight–ten days ahead of its delivery, leave it for checking and revising in Downing Street, and approve the final draft with whatever alterations I wanted the weekend, or night, before delivery.

I have always liked to prepare my own speeches. The transatlantic custom of using speech writers, recently imported into Britain for the use of certain eminent politicians and others, is only to be deplored. If you are to speak to the House of Commons, a party conference, the CBI or the TUC, an important national conference or to anyone who has issued an invitation that you have accepted, they do not want to know whether you can read – that is assumed – they want to know what you have to say in your own words, even if it rates only B-plus, B-minus or lower. For that reason, for 30 years I have prepared my own speeches, sometimes writing them by hand (taking up to 20 hours), sometimes dictating; most recently preparing a full set of notes, then dictating.

Number 10 has every facility for assisting the preparation of speeches. A draft can be prepared based on a departmental brief or a set departmental speech, some of which are very good, some of which need to be redrafted in more comprehensible language, or simply to 'make it sound like me'.

I never used any drafting, or speech contributions, until the 1974 elections, when I was faced with two or three or even five and six a day, plus a handout for each day's press conference. New material, especially for the press conference, and basic strategic speeches I dictated. Towards the end of each election when it was a question of hammering home the salient points and issues, I weakened into having these assembled from my earlier efforts and given more direct appeal and emphasis.

At Number 10 I reverted to dictating (very occasionally writing) my speeches, both political and official. On specialised subjects, e.g. those to the National Council of Social Services and the local government conference at Eastbourne, I began with a departmental brief, and suggested draft passages. Then my own draft would be dictated, followed by the processing by those concerned at Number 10, as described above. Copies were sent to the departments concerned and in all cases to the Treasury, even if it was not in the lead in the speech – or Foreign and Commonwealth Office if it had international implications – and comments, including redrafts of any sensitive passage, required by a given timetable. I would then go through the draft, approving or rejecting the suggestions. (A note to public speakers, in all walks of life: do not let them retype with their amendments, and force you to collate their redraft with yours: insist on having your own speech, with their suggested amendments written in. Theirs may be improvements, but don't risk any fast ones.)[14] Only one or two of the series of speeches in October–December 1975 started with a draft by others: one of those was the speech to US correspondents about American supplies of money and munitions to sustain the terrorist campaign in Northern Ireland, drafted in the Number 10 press office.

Political speeches, for example for party conferences, regional conferences, party and other meetings, are done by the prime minister with the help of his political office. It would be contrary to established practice to ask civil servants, whether at Number 10 or in the departments, to prepare drafts. But increasingly, and in my view rightly, it has become normal for his draft to be circulated to the relevant departments for comment and suggestion. For through every hour of his life, the prime minister is acting as administrative head and political head of Number 10 and of the entire government machine. Every word he uses can, and should, be taken, unless he is schizophrenic, as the official word of the head of government by everyone who studies his words at home or abroad. If it is true – or should be – that in all he does he himself never neglects the political implications of his actions, it is equally true that every word he utters in his political capacity is carefully construed by industrial, labour and financial circles at home as an act of government, and equally by the chancelleries of the wider world. Moreover, some speeches by their nature cannot be apolitical even though specifically directed towards a governmental objective. No speech I made in 1974–76 had, or was designed to have, a more governmental impact than one to the annual conference of the National Union of Mineworkers at Scarborough on 7 July 1975, just four days before the announcement in parliament of the counter-inflation policy for 1975–76. Every word I wrote, and rewrote, and the final passage that I added, was based on my long association with the NUM (and the predecessor organisation, the Miners Federation of Great Britain) at national and area level, and was clearly political.[15] Many observers have said that at a time when the votes seemed to be going in a way that would have made an agreed national policy an impossibility, it was a turning-point in the battle against inflation.

Standing on 'the peaks of both politics and administration', as G. W. Jones has said,[16] any modern prime minister, unless he seeks to be a political eunuch, gives primary attention, by whatever means seem appropriate, to his political advice within Number 10: this is over and above anything he receives from his own party organisation, and his parliamentary party. He must also ensure a continuing relationship with the party machine at party headquarters, and with the members of his party in the House of Commons.

All prime ministers do it, though it is a law of nature that Conservative prime ministers do not receive, or suffer, press comment on it, while Labour prime ministers can count on almost daily animadversing on the subject, even though they are adopting the practice of Conservative predecessors; and as for those they appoint to the political office, God help them.

I have recorded that Harold Macmillan was the first for 20 years to insert a political appointee into private office,[17] in the same role as the other private secretaries, all of whom, like their predecessors for a generation past, were civil servants. This was not criticised by the press of the time; it was excused by the fact that, being a dollar-a-year man, he was not in receipt of public funds. Nor have the staff of successive prime ministerial political offices, but they have not gone into private office proper. Both Edward Heath and I in the 1960s and early 1970s introduced outside economists who had worked with us in opposition; they were employed in the Cabinet Office. The system of political advisers – the Policy Unit – has now supplanted that practice. In fact, no member of my political office ever had access to classified documents. That was not the case with the appointees of Harold Macmillan or Edward Heath. Yet unremitting press comments, including unwarrantable invasions of personal and family privacy, have been addressed, uniquely, to my appointees.

The Policy Unit – and the corresponding appointments by departmental ministers – was the right solution, following the recommendations of the Fulton Report; it was based on the recruitment in specific fields of government of persons qualified and recognised in their particular disciplines, but with political affinities to the party of government – most of them were experts who advised the incoming government when the party was in opposition. But this is no substitute for the political office. Their roles are entirely different. First, the prime minister has a constituency. He must have the means of maintaining personal contact, not only with every constituent who approaches him by letter or at 'surgeries' (advice sessions), but with his agent, his local authorities, whatever their political control, and local officials, as well as local industrial, social and charitable organisations.

Second, he needs a continuing, almost daily, relationship with the backbench members of his parliamentary party – and with them one must include junior ministers, who in administrative terms have only limited access to the prime minister, since in governmental matters they normally act through their ministerial chief. But in their political capacity they have much to contribute, and the prime minister cannot afford – nor would he wish – to discount that contribution.

Third, he needs to maintain an intimate and continuing relationship with his party – the general secretary, other officials, his colleagues on the governing body of the party, and regional and constituency officials all over the country. This includes a great deal of consultation in the months preceding the annual party conference.

Fourth, there is his contact with supporters of his party all over the country, elected representatives, particularly local councillors, officers of constituency and local parties and local branches of trade unions affiliated locally and approaching him in that context. His post-box will include hundreds of letters a week from officials or members of local party organisations.

Fifth, there are individuals, many of them held in great esteem in almost every walk of life – for example the arts and entertainment – who are passionately loyal to the prime minister and his party and whose ideas and experience should be welcomed and used.

Mr Jones, in his perceptive understanding of the prime minister's dual political and administrative role – and an average prime minister's inability ever entirely to separate them – includes in his monograph on the Number 10 secretariat an interesting section headed 'The Search for Political Assistants'.[18]

After reviewing the Lloyd George 'garden suburb' and the political reactions of Stanley Baldwin and Ramsay MacDonald, he records Neville Chamberlain's reliance on Horace Wilson (as political a civil servant as one will find) and Mr Churchill's political – or at least personal – team.[19] He records the limited but clearly political advisers appointed by Clement Attlee, and Harold Macmillan's Wyndham appointment. While the Churchill and Macmillan appointees inevitably had the same access to secret and top secret documents as any civil servant appointee, which my own small separate political secretariat did not have, more thousands of acres of Swedish and British Columbian forests have been devastated to provide the newsprint for comment on my political secretariat, and everything that could be dug up about their social engagements, than was deployed on all the appointments made by every establishment prime minister, back to the Duke of Newcastle, not excluding the Rockingham Whigs.

What I had was loyalty, the political advice that every prime minister needs to counter civil service and departmental ministers' pressure, advice inspired by the closest contact with party feeling, from Transport House level right through the party in the country – with continuing parliamentary Labour party contact throughout.

Cabinet meets normally on Thursday mornings, usually at 10.0 or 10.30 (a long agenda might dictate a 9.30 start) and it lasts until around 1.0 p.m. It is not good to go on much later

than that. If business is relatively light, it can meet as late as
11.0 or 11.30, and this enables the prime minister to hold one,
or perhaps two, cabinet committees beforehand, e.g. on
economic affairs, Northern Ireland, defence or foreign policy
questions, or some *ad hoc* issue requiring collective consideration, not necessarily by the full cabinet.

When business is heavy, a supplementary cabinet can be put
in on Tuesday mornings, and meetings on Mondays, Wednesdays and Fridays are not unknown when urgent problems have
to be dealt with, or when the prime minister (and often the
foreign and commonwealth secretary with him) have to be
abroad, e.g. for an EEC summit meeting (the European
council) or for a head of government visit to a foreign capital.

I always made it a point of honour, so far as possible, to
complete the business on the day for which it was tabled. This
was not always possible: rarely it spread over into another
session. Occasionally, it was necessary to adjourn in order to
get additional information, or to consult perhaps with industry
or some overseas government, or our NATO or EEC partners
or the commission – or again, if a *prima facie* attractive
alternative solution to some difficult problem was proposed,
requiring further examination, by a cabinet committee or
cabinet itself. But in the 1960s, still more the 1970s, far fewer
cabinet decisions were deferred for further consideration than
in, for example, the time of the Attlee cabinet, particularly after
1947, when deep rifts developed between leading members of
the cabinet.

Cabinet procedure is reasonably and helpfully stereotyped:
cabinet discussion is not.

Every cabinet minister has his own regular seat. The
secretary of the cabinet sits on the prime minister's right; the
most senior ministers on his left or across the table. Thus, in
1974–76, the Lord President (Leader of the House and deputy
leader of the party) sat on my left, and across the table were the
foreign and commonwealth secretary, the home secretary and
lord chancellor. Others were seated, in some relation to
Cabinet precedence, further from the centre – the seating being
decided by the prime minister before the cabinet first meets.

It should be made clear for the benefit of cartoonists, not to
mention those responsible for television reconstructions of

cabinet meetings (e.g. Granada on Chrysler), that the prime minister does not sit at the end of the table, or with his back to the window. His seat is in the middle, in front of the Walpole portrait, facing out to Horse Guards. The table is neither oblong nor oval; it is in fact rather coffin-shaped, this design having been introduced, I understand, by Harold Macmillan, so that by leaning forward – or rocking backwards – the prime minister can see ministers far to his right or left (in geographical, not political, terms) and satisfy himself that they are paying attention to the business.

At the regular Thursday meeting two items, 'parliamentary business' and 'foreign and commonwealth affairs', head the agenda.

On 'parliamentary business' the Leader of the House outlines the course of debates for the following week, together with the proposed ministerial speakers, so that the programme can be confirmed in time for him to announce it that afternoon in reply to the leader of the opposition's routine question about the business of the House for the week ahead. The chief whip then indicates the kind of whip he will issue for each day – one-line, two-line or three. Should ministers for any reason ask for a switch of business from one day to another, or a postponement to the following week, the chief whip rushes out to confer with the opposition chief whip, who is usually helpful.

On 'foreign and commonwealth affairs', the secretary of state opens up informally, usually without circulating documents on the issues with which he is immediately concerned – it may be Cyprus, Rhodesia, Chile, the Icelandic negotiations, Anglo–US or Anglo–Soviet questions, or issues connected with forthcoming meetings of NATO or EEC ministers. More often than not he is not seeking agreement to particular lines of policy – on a major issue he would circulate a paper for decision later on the agenda – he is more concerned to keep cabinet informed on a developing situation, which might have to come up for a formal decision at a subsequent cabinet. Alternatively he may be reporting to cabinet, for information or endorsement, a decision or provisional decision taken by the relevant cabinet committee, which will have met under his own or the prime minister's chairmanship.

Mr Heath has recently made it clear[20] that under his

administration there were two further regular items on the agenda, Europe (during the EEC negotiations) and Northern Ireland, once direct rule was introduced. In 1974–76 these two subjects, in so far as they could not be adequately dealt with in the appropriate cabinet committees, would appear on the cabinet agenda not as routine items, but whenever necessary as separate items.

The agenda for cabinet and for all cabinet committees chaired by the prime minister is approved by the prime minister in consultation with the secretary of the cabinet. (The forward programme of cabinet and its committees – irrespective of who chairs them – is masterminded by an informal meeting of the prime minister, Lord President, chancellor, foreign and commonwealth secretary, chief whip and cabinet secretary each Friday morning, when the issues coming up for decision are surveyed for a period of roughly a fortnight ahead.)

It has been suggested that the prime minister is in unique control of the agenda:

> Meetings of the Cabinet are held twice a week [*sic*] during the Parliamentary session but the Prime Minister arranges the order of business and can keep any item off the agenda indefinitely. It is regarded as quite improper for a minister to raise any matter which has not previously been accepted for the agenda by the Prime Minister.[21]

In theory of course, he is in charge as chairman, but this is not how things are done.

In any case, ministers are free to raise matters under 'parliamentary affairs' or 'foreign and commonwealth affairs'. If a minister (or ministers) is worried about an issue that is disturbing MPs he can raise it under the former item, or if he is concerned over some development in, for example, Eastern Europe, or Rhodesia, he can ask about it. The appropriate minister would then explain how things stood, or he or the prime minister could say that this was coming up the following week in cabinet, or was being currently considered by the relevant committee. There is no rigidity of style in cabinet: the best style is the one that gets the boat along fast and in the right direction.

The successful working of cabinet government depends, first, on documentation. From my earliest days in the cabinet secretariat 36 years ago, through the Attlee administration and in two periods as prime minister, I have seen successive improvements in the quality and method of documentation, improvements brought about under successive governments, wartime coalition, Labour and Conservative.

The requirement is that, except in an emergency, documents relating to the main items on the agenda must be circulated a clear two days in advance, so that ministers can study them, form views on them, and be briefed both on the implications for their own departments and more generally. Only the prime minister can relax this requirement, and the minister concerned has to produce a cast-iron case to justify waiving the rule.

It has been a standing cabinet rule for a generation – my recollection is that it was begun by Clement Attlee – that ministers submitting proposals, whether for legislative or for executive action, must state what they would cost, the estimate to be confirmed by the Treasury. If the department and the Treasury cannot agree on the cost, both estimates must be quoted.

In the 1960s I gave instructions that documents must also include an initial estimate of total requirements for additional staff, agreed with the Treasury – later the Civil Service Department. In 1975, following a helpful proposal from a Conservative member of parliament, I announced that I had directed cabinet ministers to include estimates of local government staff requirements and costs for any new proposals.

Attendance at cabinet is normally strictly confined to cabinet ministers, though the attorney-general is called in for individual items where his advice is needed. Exceptionally the senior minister of state, Foreign and Commonwealth Office is called in for the 'foreign affairs' item on the Thursday agenda, and for any substantive Foreign Office subject due to come up later in the morning, if the secretary of state is abroad. Rarely, for example if another minister is ill or abroad, his deputy is called if there is a clear departmental interest in a subject under discussion. In all cases where non-cabinet ministers are invited, they wait in the ante-room until their item is reached, and leave when it is concluded. It has become the practice that, where major decisions on public expenditure are involved, and during the annual review of public expenditure,[22], the chief secretary to the treasury, who has been responsible for all the in-fighting with the departments, usually attends and sits alongside the chancellor.

The normal procedure is for the prime minister to ask the minister tabling a paper to speak to it, and to be immediately followed by any other minister who has himself submitted a paper disagreeing with, qualifying or supplementing the first.

The prime minister may then wish to indicate how the discussion should be handled and decisions taken. He may, for example, say that the question raises, say, three issues, and it might be helpful to discuss each separately, without prejudice to the decisions to be taken at the end. Or interim decisions on each of the three may be taken, and the viability of the package as a whole considered at the end, when it will be necessary to deal also with a fourth question, handling and presentation. Alternatively, particularly on a major or new issue, he might suggest that cabinet begins with a 'second reading' debate, which enables members to make their set-piece contributions, which must be short, possibly raising fundamental and long-term issues. This averts the need for wide-ranging oratory when the meeting comes to decide detailed practical questions requiring a clear decision. Again, at the first meeting on a major issue – e.g. devolution, the EEC negotiations in 1967 and 1974–75, the EEC referendum, House of Lords reform or pay policy – a wide-ranging second reading debate is virtually mandatory, and saves much time in the end. Even with such cases, a great deal of preparatory work will have been done in clearing the ground and identifying points for decision at high-level cabinet committee meetings, usually with the prime minister in the chair.

It would be usual for the prime minister to open such a discussion. On other issues, where papers had been submitted by departmental ministers, he would be unlikely to speak first, but would be ready to steer and guide the discussion to the point of taking the required decision. Very occasionally he opens the discussion, usually on a procedural point. For example, he may feel it right to remind the cabinet that they have not met to review a broad policy decision – that has been taken – but are concerned with this or that point of implementation. Alternatively, he will point out that they are not this morning taking the major decision on subject X – that will be the subject of a further meeting, separately documented – but that an interim decision on a narrower aspect must be taken now. Or if he feels, from the papers submitted and his knowledge of the strength of different ministers' feelings, that there is a danger of perhaps unnecessary polarisation, he may suggest at the outset that there is a possible third course which might be more productive, and on which agreement might be possible.

The prime minister must be ever alert to issues which raise fundamental, doctrinal or almost theological passions on the part of one or more ministers, and do all he can to avert an unnecessary clash without sacrificing principle, and without fudging an issue on which a clear decision has to be reached, binding the cabinet. Not only at that point, but by possible frequent single-sentence interventions, he has to concentrate on face-saving and binding up wounds, intervening also to soften asperities and curb the invocation of personalities. Above all, the prime minister must be ever watchful of the political implications and dangers of a given course of action, particularly when a departmental minister might be tempted to under-emphasise them, because of his immersion in administrative technicalities or his proneness to accord too much weight to outside pressure groups on his department. It is a constant vigil, requiring full concentration not only in cabinet itself, but in days and nights of studying cabinet papers, departmental minutes addressed to himself and to other relevant ministers, seeking clearance of a particular proposal.

To judge from comments by both historians and writers on current affairs, many of those concerned would, I think, be surprised at the relative informality of cabinet proceedings. As a novice cabinet minister I was myself surprised, even with Clement Attlee in the chair, running the cabinet like a nineteenth-century dominie. Every prime minister has a different style, in cabinet and outside, but the aim should be informality combined with total orderliness. A touch of humour to calm things down, or to stop excessive length and preoccupation

with technicalities, is not out of order. The purpose is to get the
business through, with full consideration, and to reach a clear
decision, with nothing fluffed or obscure – and, so far as
possible, an agreed decision, with the maximum emollient to
wounded pride. Above all, the prime minister must keep his
head when all (or some) about him are losing theirs. In this
respect as in others, Clement Attlee was a prince among prime
ministers. Professor Mackintosh has commented:

> At Cabinet, Mr. Attlee's great objective was to stop talk.
> There is evidence that two ministers rightly talked them-
> selves out of the Cabinet. Discussion was limited by the
> Premier's habit of putting his questions in the negative. A
> non-Cabinet Minister with an item on the agenda would be
> called in at the appropriate point, simply bursting to make a
> speech. Mr. Attlee would begin: 'Mr. X, your memo says all
> that could be said – I don't suppose you have anything to add
> to it?' It was hard to say anything but 'No'. Then, 'Does any
> member of the Cabinet oppose this?' Someone would
> indicate a desire to contribute, and say 'An interesting case
> occurred in 1929 which was very similar to this, and I
> remember then that we . . .'. 'Do you oppose this?' 'Er . . .
> No.' 'Very good that is settled.'[23]

I can confirm that Professor Mackintosh's description of an
Attlee Cabinet is entirely accurate, and would add only that he
was savagely cruel in rebuking, in a very few words, any
minister who didn't know the subject adequately, had not been
briefed, hadn't read the paper, particularly if it was his own.
The prime minister spared no one, except Ernest Bevin, and
reserved his most cutting quips for his most powerful colleagues. He himself, in an interview with Francis Williams,
summarised his style:

> A Prime Minister has to know when to ask for an opinion. He
> can't always stop some ministers offering theirs, you always
> have some people who'll talk on everything. But he can make
> sure to extract the opinion of those he wants when he needs
> them. The job of the Prime Minister is to get the general
> feeling – collect the voices. And then, when everything

reasonable has been said, to get on with the job and say, 'Well, I think the decision of the Cabinet is this, that or the other. Any objections?' Usually there aren't.[24]

Clement Attlee was almost certainly the coolest prime minister this century.[25] I only once saw him ruffled: he was rushing along the corridor to the House (we then sat in the Lords at the other end of the building) for a statement on Hugh Dalton's resignation after the budget incident.

It should be a matter of pride, so far as possible, to get the business through, without deferring it to another meeting. To defer a decision simply to cloak a disagreement is a defeat, above all for the prime minister. Even when there is a case for deferment, for example to consult an overseas government, a heavy cost may be involved. I have recorded the sad story of the case of the Kenya Asians, where a decision was deferred for Malcolm MacDonald to see President Kenyatta, and in the interim Richard Crossman, as Lord President, in his constant educative mission described the possible alternative courses to the parliamentary press lobby, who were less interested in erudition for its own sake than in securing an authoritative story of a split cabinet.[26]

Postponed decisions happened in the 1960s, as I have recorded, over certain issues of defence policy, principally the cancellation of certain aircraft, such as TSR-2 in the 1965 and F-111 in 1968. But it happened far less frequently in our five years and eight months of government (1964–70) than in the three years eight months I was a member of Clement Attlee's cabinet, under the clearest and most concise of prime ministers. From 1948 onwards, as a number of autobiographies have since revealed, it was a seriously divided cabinet, divided more on personalities than on doctrinal issues of left *v.* right, at least until 1950–51. In 1974–76 deferment because of an inability to agree was almost unknown.[27]

Cabinet has sometimes to take decisions, not just recorded in the conclusions, but to be announced in parliament as an oral statement, written answer or as a white or green paper. On lesser issues, the draft can be cleared by inter-departmental circulation and comment, or at most by consideration by a cabinet committee. In major cases cabinet itself has to consider a draft. It is an old canon of cabinet lore that 'cabinets can't draft'. They can go, however, and frequently must go, through a prepared draft, amending it where necessary.

With command papers, white or green, I made a rule in the 1960s – whether following precedent or not I do not know – that every such state document should be gone through by cabinet, paragraph by paragraph. In 1974–76 I started off with this procedure, but the process of Cabinet Office clearance with departments had so improved that this was rarely necessary, and at most the cabinet were taken through the document page by page. Any minister is free to raise any question of drafting – policy having always been cleared at previous substantive meetings of cabinet or the appropriate cabinet committee.

The formal taking of a decision by cabinet depends on the form of words used by the prime minister in summing up, subject to their agreement by cabinet with such drafting amendments as might be proposed.

Winston Churchill, though a great and heroic war leader and an unrivalled master of the English language, had no claims to crispness and conciseness in reaching a decision and embodying it in a summing up, certainly on non-military issues, which tended to bore him.

In my address to the British Academy, I described my own experience:

In 1940, on a famous occasion, I recorded the Cabinet minutes, at the age of 24. Sir Edward Bridges, Secretary of the Cabinet, came into my room – a gross breach of protocol: he should have sent for me – and said 'I want you to write the Cabinet Minutes. I can't make head or tail of the discussion.' I stuttered that I had not been there and did not know what they had said. He said if I had been, I would not have been any better informed than he was. I tried vainly to excuse myself, and he thrust his notes across the table and asked me to read them. I was still no better informed. In the event he ordered me to produce the minutes in one hour, saying 'This is your subject. You know what they ought to have decided, presumably. Write the Minutes on those lines, and no one will ever question it.' He was right. They didn't. That could not have happened under Attlee, whose summing

up was superb, crisp, clear – and let no one try to go against
it.

I also told them of a story I had heard at second hand from a
minister who had just come from cabinet, in the closing stages
of the war. There were six or seven subjects on the agenda. The
earlier ones were on straight war issues, relations with allies
and similar topics. At 1.0 p.m. Winston Churchill closed his
cabinet folder and lit another cigar. Sir Edward Bridges drew
his attention to the fact that there was still one remaining item.

It was town and country planning. The determination of
those days that we should not go back to the 1930s had inspired
Beveridge, the cabinet white paper on full employment, and
also the three classic reports on town and country planning by
Uthwatt, Barlow and Scott. Winston had created a minister of
town and country planning, Mr W. S. Morrison (later Lord
Dunrossil). Starting the postwar housing programme after six
years in which hardly a house had been built depended on
decisions about planning, betterment and compensation.

W. S. Morrison had assessed these reports and was present-
ing his conclusions. Winston was not amused. 'Ah, yes', said
he. 'All this stuff about planning and compensation and
betterment. Broad vistas and all that. But give to me the
eighteenth-century alley, where foot-pads lurk, and the harlot
plies her trade, and none of this newfangled planning doctrine.'

If Morrison had been wise he would have said that he fully
agreed with the prime minister, that he assumed the prime
minister was approving his paper, that he assumed the cabinet
agreed, and that in all his planning he would take care to make
full provision for narrower vistas and alleys for appropriate
activities such as those mentioned. Winston would have said,
'Quite right, my boy, you go ahead'. Instead, Morrison
stammered out, 'I take it, then, prime minister, you want me to
take it back and think again'. Winston replied, 'Quite right, my
boy'.

Morrison went back without any guidance about redrafting
and did not emerge before cabinet for some months – a vital loss
of time before Britain's postwar housing programme could
effectively begin.[28]

Cabinet colleagues of Winston Churchill have commented

on his discursive style in cabinet – not only in summing up. Lord Woolton in his memoirs, referring to the 1951–55 administration, says:

> in his earlier days in office he had never hesitated to mix freely with the people, [and] to the intense irritation of his Government officials, and in these last years of his ministerial life he distilled all this experience at Cabinet meetings for the benefit of his colleagues. It was not always for their pleasure, because not infrequently the entire time of the meeting had gone before he arrived at the first item on the agenda; he had no hesitation in keeping other ministers waiting in the corridor for an hour or more after the time when they had been called to attend the Cabinet meeting, whilst he talked to us about the things that he thought important for the country, but about which the Cabinet Secretariat had been given no notice and about which, of course, there were no papers.'[29]

Summing up is vital: it is the fine art of cabinet government. The great improvement over the past 29 years is due not only to the style of Clement Attlee: the consistent improvement in the service provided by the cabinet secretariat is itself a guarantee of clarity.

Ex-prime ministers have confirmed – as I can – that in reaching a decision cabinet does not vote, except to save time, on minor procedural matters.[30] On many issues, discussion is confined to one or two, or very few ministers; and, perhaps after suggesting a formula which appears to command assent, the prime minister asks 'cabinet agree?' – technically a voice vote, sometimes just a murmur. On a major issue it is important not only to give the main protagonists their heads, but to ensure that everyone expresses an opinion, by going round the table to collect the voices. The prime minister usually keeps a tally of those for and against, after which he records his assessment of the predominant view – or occasionally puts forward a suggestion of his own which all, or nearly all, can support. Sometimes on a minor issue where all the arguments are known – perhaps they have been discussed at an earlier cabinet – and no arguments are likely to make converts, it saves time to go quickly round the table and take the sense of cabinet.

In the very major issue of the recommendations the cabinet was to make to parliament and the country about continued membership of the EEC, following the renegotiations, the numbers for and against were reported to the press. This was inevitable, because of the unusual decision to permit an 'agreement to differ'. The House of Commons was informed of the guidelines to be followed, and parliament and the country were entitled to know which ministers had been granted a dispensation from the normal obligations demanded by collective cabinet responsibility.[31] Cabinet leaks, for example those at the time of the aircraft purchasing decisions in January 1968, sometimes purport to give the numbers on each side, as recorded by an unauthorised keeper of the tally. There have been one or two recent attempts to challenge the prime minister's weighing of the cabinet voices, by those who claimed to have counted them – a practice that I severely discouraged.

The clarity of the summing up, and the cabinet's decision, is, of course, essential to the recording of the conclusions. (The word 'conclusions', in place of 'minutes', was adopted in August 1919.)[32]

Because of recent comments by Richard Crossman and others, it must be made clear that the writing of the conclusions is the unique responsibility of the secretary of the cabinet, aided by members of his staff who have been present at the meeting, making notes, but not – this is important – a shorthand word by word record of the discussion. He may also retain the prime minister's own notes or draft of his summing up, which the cabinet will have heard verbatim and agreed in terms. The conclusions are circulated very promptly after cabinet, and up to that time no minister, certainly not the prime minister, sees them, asks to see them or conditions them in any way.

This chapter has dealt mainly with the prime minister in his official surroundings. It seems appropriate to add to what others have said about the prime requisites for a prime minister. Reference has been made to keeping in touch with party and people – what is now called two-way communication.

At home and abroad I have repeatedly been asked what are the main essentials of a successful prime minister. Over and above communication and vigilance, there are two factors I have always mentioned. They are sleep, and a sense of history. In a BBC interview with Douglas Stuart on 16 April 1975, and again in a BBC World Service interview at Chequers for my 60th birthday (less than a week before I announced my impending resignation), I was asked about these things.

Douglas Stuart quoted President Lyndon Johnson's references to the 'pressure of the telephone . . . the battery of telephones by his bed in the White House'. I described a visit there whereby, judiciously sleeping in 'British sleep-time' over the Atlantic (10.30 p.m. BST–5.30 p.m. Washington time) followed by sleeping on in Washington to 8.00 a.m. Washington time, I had $11\frac{1}{2}$ hours sleep, and found that the President had had $1\frac{1}{2}$.

I believe the biggest asset a Prime Minister can have is the ability to sleep – a good night's sleep – 8 hours' sleep when I can get it . . . you have got to be able to sleep – a statesman who can't sleep is no good. I remember there was one famous Prime Minister, Lord Rosebery, who spent two years here, couldn't sleep. So he went.[33]

In the programme in March 1976 at Chequers I answered a question about pressures:

the answer to pressure is sleep. My problem is waking up. But I have no problem sleeping. I have never had a sleeping pill in Number 10. I have never needed one. I can sleep and the other evening I was coming out to Chequers and the driver said 'You are at Chequers now' – I had slept all the way from Marble Arch in London without intending to.
[*Interviewer:*] Which is about 35 miles?
[*Answer:*] Yes, an hour, an hour's sleep. I can sleep anywhere. I can do it at command if I want to. Winston Churchill could do that.[34]

On the sense of history Douglas Stuart asked:

But here . . . in this house with its tremendous traditions in it the fact that you have to go to the House of Commons for business and things do you feel yourself hemmed in by the traditions of the past?

I replied:

I like to think I do. I think that unless you have a sense of history, and of tradition, and of the people who have been here, you can't even apply yourself to the problems of the present. That's why I think some of the greatest statesmen of all parties, in this country and abroad – one thinks of Kennedy in America for example and Roosevelt, as well as Churchill, Attlee, Harold Macmillan – irrespective of party, they had a great sense of history. Partly to put things in perspective – you know, when you read in the papers, if you have ever been politically dead by lunchtime and even worse by nightfall – well you know, others have been through it before you and you can get a sense of perspective – it doesn't mean you can't take it seriously. But a sense of history – and very often you can get analogies from history – of past wars, of past diplomatic negotiations, of past economic situations. *Without a sense of history, a Prime Minister would be blind.*[35]

References

1. Harold Wilson, *The Governance of Britain* (London: Weidenfeld & Nicolson and Michael Joseph, 1976).
2. Sir David Hunt, as Foreign Office secretary at Number 10, overlapped the Attlee Government and the early period of Winston Churchill's last administration. His comparison of the two premiers is perceptive: 'While Attlee had a great power of decision, Winston Churchill, on subjects in which he took little interest, affected horror when his advisers pressed for a decision; they were confusing him with a dictator, and he said, "This is a democratic government. These matters must be decided by the Cabinet as a whole; I cannot possibly settle them on my own authority" '. Hunt regarded this as sometimes being a way of deferring a decision: he goes on to comment: 'Many people have expressed surprise to me when I have mentioned this as a point of contrast between Attlee and Churchill. It goes completely

contrary to the popular idea of both these men. Attlee is usually thought of as good-natured, a compromiser, but not a strong character and it is always supposed that Churchill was one of those determined men who made up their minds in a flash. To assert that the opposite was true might make it seem that I was disparaging Churchill'. He goes on to develop the point, concluding that Churchill 'was a very great man, and, for all my affection for Attlee, a greater man in world history than his predecessor'. His further analysis throws an interesting and intimate light on both premiers: Sir David Hunt, *On The Spot: An Ambassador Remembers* (London: P. Davies, 1975), p. 53.

3. *The Times* (27 September 1973).
4. Harold Wilson, *Whitehall and Beyond* (London: BBC Publications, 1964), pp. 11–28; reprinted in Anthony King (ed.), *The British Prime Minister*, 1st edn (London: Macmillan, 1969), pp. 80–92.
5. G. W. Jones, 'The Prime Minister's Secretaries: Politicians or Administrators?', in J. A. G. Griffith (ed.), *From Policy to Administration: Essays in Honour of William A. Robson* (London: George Allen & Unwin, 1976), pp. 13–38. For the history of the office see pp. 14 *et seq*. Prime ministers have had private secretaries since the Duke of Newcastle (1757–62), though paid from public funds only since 1806; the secondment of a 'Treasury clerk' dates from the early nineteenth century.
6. ibid., p. 30.
7. ibid., p. 31.
8. D. Jones, op. cit., pp. 14, 35, 36.
9. For a description of the house and its history, see R. J. Minney, *No. 10 Downing Street: A House in History* (London: Cassell, 1963).
10. During the world financial crisis that followed rumours created by the German finance minister's careless reference to parties (see Harold Wilson, *The Labour Government 1964–70: A Personal Record* (London: Weidenfeld & Nicolson and Michael Joseph, 1971) pp. 506–10), all the activity centred on Washington; Number 10 was the operational headquarters in London. About 11 p.m. a senior Treasury official asked for a call to be put through to the economics minister at the British embassy in Washington, which is on the 'Hobart' exchange. He gave the number 'Hobart, etc.' and fifteen seconds later was put through to a bewildered Tasmanian doctor who was just finishing his breakfast.
11. Wilson, *Governance of Britain*, p. 171.
12. In Clement Attlee's day there was a large cabinet table, by convention used only by cabinet ministers and those who were then described as 'ministers of cabinet rank'.
13. See the account of the late Lester Pearson's amusing handling of a 'defensive brief' in Wilson, *The Labour Government 1964–70*, p. 503.
14. One day I hope to write a piece, not necessarily too serious, on the preparation of speeches: as one who for 30 years never quite knew how to begin, and who only at the end of that period began to get some glimmering about the right approach to it; it may be that others may be helped to a quicker perception.

15. 'It is now *Labour's* prime minister, your prime minister, at a critical hour in the nation's history, enjoining this community, once again, to assert loyalty *for* the nation. It is not so much a question of whether that loyalty, that response, will be forthcoming in sufficient measure to save this Labour government. The issue now is not whether this or any other democratic socialist government can survive and lead this nation to full employment and a greater measure of social justice. It is whether any government *so* constituted, *so* dedicated to the principles of consent and consensus within our democracy, can lead this nation.'
16. Jones, op. cit., p. 14.
17. Lord Wyndham.
18. Jones, op. cit., pp. 34–6.
19. Winston Churchill had been execrated in the 1930s, notably by the second-rate team of Neville Chamberlain, broadly corresponding to the then Conservative establishment; his own Number 10 team comprised a number of those who had been loyal to him in the dark years, personal, but no less political.
20. The *Listener* (22 April 1976), recording a radio discussion by Mr Heath and Lord Trend, with Robert McKenzie.
21. John P. Mackintosh 'The Position of the Prime Minister', in Anthony King (ed.), *The British Prime Minister*, 1st edn (London: Macmillan, 1969), pp. 20–1. He also mentions the frequently quoted case of Neville Chamberlain's attempt to raise House of Lords reform after the forward agenda had been settled, an attempt frustrasted by Stanley Baldwin's walking out of the room – thus ending the cabinet meeting. Too much can be made of an action taken, probably in a moment of irritation. Any prime minister I have known would presumably have suggested how the proposal might be considered, either at a subsequent cabinet or in a committee of the cabinet. Nor should much be made of another case cited in the same context, a Hore-Belisha initiative in the Chamberlain cabinet.
22. See Wilson, *Governance of Britain*, pp. 68–72.
23. Mackintosh, op. cit., p. 29. The quotation is from Francis Williams, *A Prime Minister Remembers: The War and Post War Memoirs of Earl Attlee* (London: Heinemann, 1961), p. 81.
24. Reproduced in King, op. cit., p. 71. Referring to Winston Churchill, Clement Attlee cites an occasion when Churchill as leader of the opposition complained in parliament that a particular issue had been brought up several times in the wartime cabinet. Attlee replied: 'I must remind the Right Honourable Gentleman that a monologue is not a decision'.
25. In early 1951, an extremely serious two-day debate was taking place in the House on international affairs. On the afternoon of the second day, the tickertape carried a story that President Truman had said that General MacArthur, supreme commander in Korea, had the authority to use the nuclear weapon there, without reference to the president. There was uproar in the House. Clement Attlee was to wind up. Early in the evening he called a cabinet in his room at the House. He

referred calmly to the report, and said he had concluded he must fly to Washington – then anything but a routine operation – and see the president. He would have preferred Ernest Bevin to go, but his health precluded flying, and a ship would take too long. He would try to contact the president, hoping not very confidently to get his agreement in time for an announcement in the prime minister's winding-up speech at 9.30. Telephone communication was difficult and not as secret as it is now. At 7.0 p.m. I was at the cabinet table having dinner when the prime minister came down and sat next to me. As his other neighbour was a minister of cabinet rank not in the cabinet, I could not comment on events which we were pledged to keep secret. Equally, I felt he would be too preoccupied for small talk. Suddenly he turned to me and said, 'Just been reading Guedalla. Tell me, which of the popular historians do you prefer – Guedalla or Arthur Bryant?'. I answered, 'Arthur Bryant'. 'So do I', he said and for half an hour we discussed their books. At 9.0 p.m. the president's agreement came through, and Attlee's speech steadied the entire parliamentary situation.

26. Wilson, op. cit., pp. 504–5.
27. Even in the much-publicised Chrysler case, deferment was in every case for the purpose of examining alternative proposals, e.g. the Coventry to Linwood move, or new proposals to the main Chrysler board, from the time they dropped their insistence on getting out within weeks, and their refusal to undertake to share future losses.
28. It is fair to add that, after the delivery of this address before the Academy, an historian at the Cabinet Office examined the cabinet files of the time and threw some doubts on certain details of the story I had been told. Possible cabinet meetings had been identified, but there were discrepancies with the original story. Perhaps the fitting comment, as with other Churchill stories, is that it is the legend that counts. From other sources I have received confirmation about the 'eighteenth-century alley' and all that occurred therein; the doubts surround the occasion and the general cabinet ambience.
29. Lord Woolton, *The Memoirs of the Rt. Hon. Earl of Woolton* (London: Cassell, 1959), pp. 376–7.
30. Clement Attlee, 'The Making of a Cabinet' in King, op. cit.: 'You don't take a vote. No, never. You might take it on something like whether you meet at 6.30 or 7.30, I suppose, but not on anything major'. Edward Heath, in the *Listener* (22 April 1976), p. 501: 'As a cabinet, when I was prime minister, we never voted'. He went on to say that, during his attendance at cabinet, as chief whip in 1955–59 and as a member of cabinet in 1959–63, he could not recall a vote, those years spanning the premierships of Anthony Eden, Harold Macmillan and Sir Alec Douglas-Home.
31. Wilson, *Governance of Britain*, pp. 72–6 and Appendix Note III.
32. See the history and developing practice on minutes and conclusions, together with references of the earlier practice of the prime minister's letter to the sovereign after each cabinet, in Public Record Office, *The*

Cabinet Office to 1945 (London: HMSO, 1975), paras 209–13, 411–13, 907–8 and 916.

33. BBC World Service broadcast (11 March 1976).
34. ibid.
35. Douglas Stuart, 16 April 1975.

2

The Conduct of Economic Policy 1974–79

BERNARD DONOUGHUE

*Students of politics are interested in the machinery of government.
Whether or not those who work in 10 Downing Street share that
interest, they inevitably spend most of their working time dealing with
the substance of issues in the real world. Their principal concerns are
with immediate problems of economic policy, common market policy,
foreign policy, industrial policy, and so on. They have to decide in
which policy areas to intervene, and by what means. Having decided to
intervene, they have to immerse themselves in the relevant details and the
relevant struggles for influence and power. Bernard Donoughue, a
former teacher at the London School of Economics, served as head of the
Number 10 Policy Unit under both Harold Wilson and James
Callaghan. Here he provides an unusual first-hand description, not of
the job of the prime minister, but of two prime ministers actually doing
the job. This is the prime minister 'hands on'.*

This chapter is concerned with economic policy making in
Britain during the 1970s and is based upon my experience as
Senior Policy Adviser to the prime minister and head of the
Policy Unit in Downing Street from March 1974 until May
1979.

My policy view from Downing Street was, and is, both
oblique and central. It was inevitably oblique because

economic policy in Britain has for long been the primary concern of Her Majesty's Treasury situated on the corner block of Whitehall and Great George Street. The great majority of any British government's thinking on economic policy – and virtually all the paper devoted to its economic policy – are generated along the high curving corridors of that appropriately sombre building. Internally, the Treasury is separated under deputy secretaries into divisions which conduct the various sub-strata of economic policy: domestic, overseas, financial, monetary, public sector, industrial, etc. These mini-kingdoms may rise and fall in importance, or extend or contract their subject boundaries, according to present fashion or the priorities of the elected government of the day (and the list of divisions I give is simply illustrative and not comprehensive for any point in time).

During war the Treasury's normal priorities have been temporarily subordinated to the overriding priorities of national military survival. But during the 20th century, with the increase of central government intervention in the nation's affairs, the Treasury's overall power and functions have steadily and significantly expanded – as have its numbers, though it remains small relative to the rest of Whitehall. The Treasury has been and remains today the pre-eminent domestic department. At the political/ministerial level the chancellor is in principle, and normally in practice, the most senior departmental minister within the government because he controls the resources available to other ministers – though the circumstances of personality, or of party or national influence could conceivably leave a home secretary or foreign secretary with more effective political power.

At the official level, Treasury civil servants are normally chosen from the highest calibre of applicants to the central bureaucracy. They can be criticised, with justice, for creating a departmental culture of monastic unworldliness. They may appear to spend their lives mixing only with other Treasury men. Certainly they are foolishly proud of being untainted or uncorrupted by contact with or practical knowledge of the soiled outside world into whose fiscal and monetary affairs they intervene with often devastating impact. However, their overall ability is very high and they rightly dominate central government. This intellectual dominance is assisted by a shrewd policy of territorial colonisation across Whitehall. Able Treasury Men are often placed into senior positions in other Whitehall departments (and are also despatched onto the staff of the prime minister in Downing Street and of the governor of the Bank of England in the City). Even after thus transferring, the Treasury culture continues to condition their approach to government problems and policies: once a Treasury Man always a Treasury Man. Nor is that necessarily a bad thing. As a special adviser, coming from the outside academic world into a suspicious Whitehall environment, I personally found the Treasury Men ultimately the most satisfactory and most open to deal with. Admittedly it is also true that my most brutal initial bureaucratic battles were with them. But once they are convinced that an adviser intends to be a serious player in the Whitehall game – and successfully carries some policy clout – I found that they opened up and played. They did so with little of the irritatingly snooty hostility to outside expertise which too often characterises those in the lower layers and lesser ministries of Whitehall who apparently feel most threatened by outside intruders. As often in life, it is ultimately easiest to deal with the best.

I have mentioned the Treasury first because it is the department of economic policy. However, economic policy is not conducted in isolation by the Treasury. The prime minister in Downing Street is at the heart of the central capability of British government and therefore the view from Downing Street is a central one. Indeed the prime minister is formally the First Lord of the Treasury. It will be a central theme of this analysis to describe how that often nominal and 'dignified' role of First Lord of the Treasury became increasingly an effective role during the 1970s as the prime minister became more actively engaged in policymaking.

Prime ministerial interventions to exercise influence on policy vary according to many factors, particularly (1) the temperament and career background of the prime minister of the day; (2) his or her power and standing relative to fellow cabinet ministers; (3) the advisory services available personally to the prime minister; and (4) the nature and pressure of events arising within a policy field.

Turning first to the question of prime ministerial temperament and career conditioning as a factor in the policymaking process, the political analyst is of course in danger of entering naïvely into a psychological minefield. I will try to tread lightly. Except in the exigencies of war when leaders (as Lloyd George and Churchill) emerge because of their particular temperamental suitability, British prime ministers have been selected through the party and parliamentary process for political rather than personality reasons. A wide range of personalities have therefore presided over cabinet in 10 Downing Street. The two prime ministers who I served (Harold Wilson 1974–76 and James Callaghan 1976–79) were each by then extremely experienced in politics and government. It is a feature of British government – and I believe a strength compared with, for example, the American system – that long apprenticeship is usually necessary in order to acquire high office. Wilson and Callaghan had each been in parliament since 1945. Each held office in the postwar Labour government, Wilson in the cabinet, Callaghan as a junior minister. Wilson had been prime minister for six years in the 1960s and Callaghan was almost unique in having held all three senior offices of state – Treasury, Home Office and Foreign Office – before he became prime minister. If there was an important difference of career background it was that Wilson, although long on prime ministerial experience, had run only one Whitehall department, and that a relatively junior one (Trade). This perhaps led to his being extremely reluctant to intervene in the affairs of the senior departments, especially the Treasury which he held in some awe. Callaghan on the other hand had 'seen it all before' as a minister and especially did not share Wilson's deference towards the Treasury. On the contrary he was acutely aware of the defects in Treasury advice to him when chancellor in 1964–67 and so was personally sceptical of the 'Treasury mystique'.

This difference in departmental background and departmental conditioning was reinforced by their differences of personality. Wilson was clever and subtle, but he was temperamentally soft and disliked confrontation. He also by the time I joined him in 1974 was suffering from a sense of *déjà vu*, finding the treadmill of recurring problems and stale policy solutions relating to Britain's decline boringly familiar. Both he and Callaghan were totally political animals, though the latter was more deeply rooted in the Labour movement with stronger trade union affiliations than his predecessor. There was undoubtedly significance in the fact that whereas Wilson began life as a university don and a Cabinet Office secretary, Callaghan did not go to university but began work as a trade union organiser in the Inland Revenue. This led to differences of style and of interests. Certainly Wilson absorbed figures and arguments with greater, incredible speed. But it would be a mistake to underestimate Callaghan's formidable, if unrefined, intellectual capacity (a mistake of which he was himself always guilty, but nobody who worked for him for long could be). Where Callaghan was most strikingly different was, first, in his very deep interest in the policy issues which came before him as prime minister and, secondly, in the temperament – tough, dogged and often authoritarian – which led him to face problems head on and to get personally involved in the policy solutions. He had not always appeared so tough. Earlier in his career he projected a rather rumbustious image and was accused of having more wind than marbles. And of course at the conclusion of his office in 1979, paralysed by trade union militancy in the 'winter of discontent', he seemed tired and ineffective. But for most of the time I served him he was impressively, dauntingly tough and decisive. Civil servants were actually afraid of him. As one Labour politician who had known Callaghan all his parliamentary career remarked to me in 1978: 'Jim has over the years toughened from the outside in'.

In terms of personality, therefore, Callaghan was much more than Wilson temperamentally inclined, and by ministerial experience qualified, to interfere with departmental policies and impose his will upon them. But for any prime minister to be able to do this he must have power and standing over his fellow ministers – and in particular over the chancellor in the field of economic policy. Some of this authority comes automatically with the office. Holding the prestigious position of prime minister, having the power to appoint and sack ministers, and chairing the cabinet and its senior cabinet committees, all add weight to the prime minister should he wish to exercise a policy role. But they do not guarantee a decisive influence. For instance, a prime minister who lacks an independent political power base and who clearly holds offfice only on the tolerance of his cabinet colleagues would not be in a strong position to exercise this policy role, and probably would not undertake it. In fact, both Wilson and Callaghan had the authority and prestige to influence their colleagues decisively. Each was a widely accepted and respected leader and had a strong party base (allowing for the impossibilities of any Labour leader ever attaining total acceptance across the whole breadth of ideologies which constitute Labour's coalition). Wilson probably faced more senior and imposing cabinet colleagues than his successor – Jenkins, Castle, Callaghan himself and even Ross were all of greater stature than the younger men who succeeded them at their ministries in 1976 when Wilson retired and Callaghan reshuffled the cabinet. But if Wilson was less actively interventionist it was not because he was constrained by weighty colleagues but because he chose to be so. He allocated to himself the title *primus inter pares* or, in his frequent football terminology, the role of 'defensive sweeper up' rather than as an attacking forward in the cabinet team. This was not necessary. In fact, had he chosen to be more active, he had one great advantage relative to Callaghan: he had led his party to success in four general elections, whereas his successor lost his only campaign in 1979. There is no doubt that the electorate's mandate does, for a year or so into a new parliament, convey an authority and legitimacy to a prime minister. Wilson had that electoral authority from 1974–76, even if his victories then were narrow; but he did not exploit it. Callaghan lacked it but still dominated his colleagues much more than his predecessor did (although Wilson was by repute much more aggressive in 1964–70).

As for the chancellor with whom each of my prime ministers dealt in the economic field, Denis Healey was a formidable member of cabinet. He had been a strong and successful minister of defence in the 1960s. At first as chancellor he appeared uncharacteristically reticent and uncertain. But he was a powerful personality, with remarkable intellectual and physical stamina. For any prime minister to exercise significant influence over him and the heavyweight Treasury forces backing him required considerable will and convincing arguments.

The provision of arguments to a British prime minister has been the subject of much academic debate because in Whitehall there is no separate and permanent prime minister's department. 10 Downing Street is simply a large house (technically two town houses backing on one another, joined together). It contains a large apartment for the prime minister's family (though residence is optional and Wilson did not live there in 1974–76) and various offices, reception rooms and bedrooms scattered over its five floors. There is room for only some 100 staff, including messengers, typists and policemen. Therefore the number of staff in senior advisory roles is inevitably small. These latter now break down into four main functional groups:

(1) the Private Office secretaries who are temporarily loaned to Number 10 by other Whitehall departments, and who conduct the prime minister's official relations with Whitehall, parliament and the public in his capacity as head of government;
(2) the Press Office, which handles the prime minister's relations with the media;
(3) the Political Office, which conducts the prime minister's affairs in his capacity as a member of parliament and as leader of a political party;
(4) the Policy Unit which advises the prime minister on all areas of government policy.

One of Harold Wilson's many contributions to the machinery of government in Britain was to strengthen these supportive mechanisms working for the prime minister in Downing Street. In particular, in 1974 he created the Policy Unit staffed with outside specialists and ranking as temporary civil servants. Previous prime ministers had employed individual advisers. But until then the prime minister did not have systematic policy analysis separate from the regular civil service machine and working solely for himself. This has proved a most important reform in the central machinery of

British government and it is significant that not only did Wilson's successor, Callaghan, retain the Policy Unit, but his Tory successor, Margaret Thatcher, continued and strengthened it. The particular point of importance for our argument here, however, is that by introducing a Policy Unit Wilson increased the prime minister's capacity for effective personal intervention in other ministers' policies. Previous prime ministers certainly had views, and even occasional influence on economic issues, but it is simply not possible to maintain sustained influence over economic policy without conducting a long and successful debate with the Treasury. Prime ministers do of course have ultimate power to override the chancellor and insist on particular policies; but under democratic cabinet government that arbitrary approach is not one that a prudent prime minister would for long pursue, or a self-respecting chancellor for long allow. In Britain, as in America and most accountable democracies, government is a long process of argument, at times lapsing into departmental trench warfare, and the Treasury normally carries the heaviest numerical ammunition and weapons of debate. A prime minister in debate with his chancellor needs more than his willpower and status. He needs the provision of good arguments and alternative facts and figures. That is the potential arsenal which Harold Wilson added to the British prime minister's fire power when he established the Downing Street Policy Unit. The irony is that Wilson himself did not make sufficient use of it. Probably for the reasons of temperament and career conditioning mentioned above, for long periods he preferred to stay out of Whitehall economic policymaking, leaving the Treasury to propose and his cabinet to dispose. When he did finally and decisively intervene over pay policy, as described below, he did make great use of his Policy Unit, as James Callaghan did consistently from 1976–79.

The fourth and final major factor which I initially suggested may determine the extent to which prime ministerial interventions exercise influence on economic policymaking is the nature and pressure of events arising within that field. To a considerable extent this is unquantifiable. Economic events are threatening or manageable to some extent according to how the government itself sees or assesses them. But there is an objective difference between, on the one hand, the routine management of existing policies and, on the other, a crisis threatening the whole economic strategy of a government. The former will normally be conducted by the Treasury with the chancellor only periodically reporting to cabinet and to parliament. The latter, however, requires the active involvement of cabinet. Ministers may find their departmental programmes in jeopardy. New crisis solutions will require continuing cabinet support against inevitable political unpopularity. The Treasury now has only two ministers out of nearly two dozen in cabinet – and until Joel Barnett was included in 1977 had only one. It cannot operate new policies without cabinet approval and therefore needs to gain the approval of at least a dozen non-Treasury ministers, many of whom may suffer from the impact of the proposed new policies and some of whom may even have their eyes on the chancellor's job. It is especially in this crisis situation that a prime minister has the supreme opportunity to intervene and influence. The chancellor needs the prime minister to deliver ministerial support. It is then that a prime minister – providing he has the inclination, and the will, and the authority over his colleagues, and the ideas and the economic arguments – can decisively influence economic policy. It may now be helpful to illustrate that analysis by reference to economic policymaking in Britain during the period 1974–79.

The most striking feature of the first months of Harold Wilson's third and fourth administrations in 1974–75 was the almost total absence of collective discussion of economic policy. Between the formation of the minority government in March 1974 and the second general election in October the government was primarily concerned with getting itself into a political position to win that election. Peace was made with the striking miners. A flood of 'green' discussion papers were produced indicating lines of attractive policy which a re-elected Labour government would pursue. Particular emphasis was placed on industrial policy, with proposals for extending public ownership, central planning and government financial aid, all with the purpose of regenerating British industry. Actually to a great extent this interventionist industrial policy was Labour's most visible economic policy. But in the sense of fiscal or monetary management, or direct measures to deal with the problems of burgeoning wage inflation and public expenditure, there was virtually no cabinet debate. A senior Treasury official told me in the summer of 1974 that the Treasury was holding its hand and waiting till after the second general election clarified the political situation and that then it would bring forward a crisis package of economic measures. But even after the October 1974 election (when Labour secured a small though only temporary majority) the renewed Wilson government did not grapple with the darkening economic situation. Its attention was immediately turned to foreign affairs, where the negotiations with our European partners and the preparations for the impending referendum on whether Britain should remain in the EEC dominated the cabinet's time through into the spring of 1975. The issue of the devolution of constitutional powers to Scotland and Wales also absorbed ministerial time. Prime Minister Wilson seemed to be content to be so diverted and was possibly reluctant to face up to the growing economic crisis. The Treasury was still willing to wait for that crisis to erupt, cynically convinced that ministers would deal with it realistically only when the pressure of events left no alternative.

There was anyway a major political problem concerning economic policy which faced the chancellor, the Treasury, the cabinet and the prime minister alike. The 1974 elections had been fought by Labour on party manifestos which committed the government to pursue full employment, higher economic growth, greater public expenditure, and industrial consensus through a 'social contract' with the trade unions. Incomes policy was specifically rejected. The kind of rigorous policies required to deal with a situation where inflation was rocketing towards 30 per cent and the government and trading deficits were forecast to rise beyond our capacity to finance them were bound to require breaches of all of those election promises. It is therefore not surprising that Labour cabinet ministers hesitated before confronting the economic crisis. In fact, to my recollection, there was no meaningful collective discussion of economic policy by ministers until late March 1975 when the chancellor proposed to cabinet cuts in public expenditure of £1 billion as part of his coming budget. In mid-April his budget included these cuts and some tax increases, representing a deflation of £1.75 billion, but there was still only desultory ministerial discussion – and Prime Minister Wilson appeared to hold very few, if any, private talks with his chancellor on substantive economic policy.

The economic crisis under Labour in the mid-1970s had two clear aspects: wage inflation and public expenditure inflation (there were of course other very important problems concerning competitiveness and productivity, but the government is less directly involved in these). The wages crisis erupted in the spring and summer of 1975 and this precipitated the first major intervention by Prime Minister Wilson in central economic policy and involved defeat for the Treasury in terms of policy preferences.

In June 1975 the cabinet approved a disastrous 30 per cent pay increase for railwaymen, having earlier rejected a Treasury proposal for £3 billion cuts in public expenditure. By June sterling was under considerable pressure and the prime minister told me privately that he now felt that 'something must be done about wages' and asked for suggestions. The Policy Unit in Number 10, which then contained half a dozen distinguished policy analysts quickly devised and put to the prime minister a major policy paper (to which the prime minister's very able press secretary, Joe Haines, made a major contribution). It suggested an economic package containing a voluntary pay policy based on a simple £5 norm increase for everybody and backed by a 'battery of sanctions' – tax penalties, discrimination in government contracts, a price code, etc. – which would ensure that although voluntary it was obeyed. The prime minister was immediately attracted by this approach, which enabled him (and trade union leaders) to appear not to breach his election commitments against a *statutory* pay policy while still introducing an effective incomes policy. He broadly took this position during cabinet discussions at Chequers and in Downing Street during late June. The Treasury, however, wanted a fully statutory policy backed by criminal sanctions. On 30 June, in the context of sterling collapsing and a crisis visit to Number 10 by the governor of the Bank of England, the Treasury circulated papers to cabinet proposing that on the very next day the chancellor should introduce a statutory incomes policy into parliament. However, after some midnight wavering, the prime minister decided against the Treasury, informed the chancellor of this early next morning, and then led the cabinet to reject the Treasury papers and to pursue a voluntary incomes policy approach as originally suggested by the Policy Unit. Prime Minister Wilson had finally decided to intervene in the economic crisis, had been provided with the arguments for his own policy approach, and had defeated the Treasury and imposed his own broad policy on the government.

During this crisis period not only Treasury thinking but in fact the whole Whitehall machinery for discussing and deciding economic policy was proved inadequate. This was partly because the Treasury had always actively discouraged the development of cross-departmental mechanisms for discussing major items of economic policy. As with the handling of the annual budget, it preferred to keep economic discussions tight within its corridors and then launch its conclusions onto (and through) unprepared and unbriefed ministers – a hallowed Whitehall tactic known affectionately to all insiders as 'the Treasury bounce'. Such tactics are most likely to succeed in a climate of crisis, such as a sterling collapse (real or inspired) when ministers are usually too paralysed with fear to ask searching questions. But even such economic policymaking machinery as existed was not used properly. The main economic committee of the cabinet (at the time called 'MES' for 'Ministerial Economic Strategy') met infrequently until the late spring and even then rarely discussed seriously the central problem of inflation. A separate cabinet committee considered external economic policy; and though its agenda, covering items such as oil pricing, was often strongly related to the inflationary crisis, its discussions were not treated as such. Together with the official committee on prices and incomes (PIO) these cabinet committees (on which I sat) merely watched passively the slide towards hyperinflation during the spring and early summer of 1975. Once the prime minister accepted the need for an incomes policy a further small *ad hoc* committee of ministers (Misc 91) was established to consider pay inflation. There was little coherence or co-ordination between these various economic committees. On one day in

June 1976 two separate committees met, one discussing increases in school teachers' pay and the other discussing increases in university teachers' pay, with no contact or co-ordination between the two. Economic policy items were spread over this tangle of committees in a very *ad hoc* way. Individual wage settlements were considered in various places, but never the whole inflation picture. Particular public expenditure cuts were pursued but the unemployment consequences of them were never properly presented. Indeed unemployment as such was never, I believe, discussed by cabinet until October 1975 (and then only after I had prompted a sympathetic minister to raise it). What was needed, and later emerged, was to have one senior ministerial committee actively considering economic strategy and to have, beneath that committee, ministerial and official sub-committees systematically covering all categories of micro-policy.

Such was the inadequacy of the existing economic policymaking machinery that during the spring of 1975 the Cabinet Office began to move into this policy vacuum. The able and aggressive cabinet secretary, Sir John Hunt, secured that overall consideration of public expenditure cuts should henceforward be brought from the Treasury under Cabinet Office dominion. It was also arranged that the Central Policy Review Staff (CPRS), the policy 'think tank' established in the Cabinet Office in 1971 by the Conservative Prime Minister Heath, should actively formulate and circulate economic policy papers. The Policy Unit in Downing Street also began frequently to brief the prime minister on economic policy issues – and also began discreetly to canvass and brief other cabinet ministers.

It is not surprising that, given this tangle of committees and sources of advice, the process of economic policymaking during the inflation crisis of 1975 was a little confused. At the end of June and the beginning of July the Treasury was circulating papers to ministers in the cabinet economic strategy committee (MES) and in the special pay committee (Misc 91) on the firm assumption that, despite the prime minister's initial reaction, the government was in fact moving towards a full statutory incomes policy. The Policy Unit, however, was advising the prime minister on having a voluntary policy backed by sanctions and the official committee on prices and incomes (PIO) was scrutinising the particular policy implications of that voluntary policy on the assumption that it was the government's policy. Meanwhile certain senior cabinet ministers (especially Michael Foot at Employment) were separately pursuing advanced negotiations with the trade union movement for a completely voluntary incomes policy conducted by the TUC itself. This anarchy seemed concluded when the prime minister issued a firm prime ministerial directive supporting our voluntary policy backed by sanctions. But even then, when the Treasury produced the draft white paper for this policy, its lack of enthusiasm was so transparent that the draft was rejected by the prime minister and the Policy Unit had to write a new draft white paper within 24 hours.

These policy battles inevitably had consequences for those involved. The chancellor, Denis Healey, was bruised, if only temporarily (his recuperative powers were astonishing). Prime Minister Wilson re-emerged into the forefront of economic policymaking and personally unveiled the new policy to wide approval on 11 July 1975. Actually he remained active and more prominent in this field until his long-planned retirement in April 1976 working skilfully to unite ministers and trade union leaders behind the new pay policy as it was hammered out and modified over the months ahead (eventually the pay norm was raised to £6 and most of the 'battery of sanctions' were kept as reserve powers). The Cabinet Office and the Number 10 Policy Unit had each made a big impact in the economic policy field and were henceforward to remain active and influential through their different channels and in their different styles. The cabinet secretary's appetite for policy influence was certainly further encouraged by his victorious battles with the Treasury at this time. The Treasury by contrast had lost its monopoly grip on economic policymaking. It was for a time clearly diminished in the Whitehall power game and showed its resentments. When I met the head of the Treasury at the Reform Club in late July to make peace, he was still very touchy and quite adamant that my Policy Unit would not be incorporated in the formal economic policymaking process (although the Bank of England, the CPRS and even the marginal Central Office of Information were included on the Treasury's key Short-Term Economic Policy Committee). Number 10 was apparently still to be shut out. But in practice from this time onward the active relations between myself and other Policy Unit members and the Treasury grew closer at all working levels. Now that the prime minister had shown himself active in economic policy, and the Policy Unit had demonstrated that it had a significant influence on the prime minister, the realities of the Whitehall policy process had their logical consequence. The prime minister and the Policy Unit (and the Cabinet Office) were now clearly in the economic policy game, and so most Treasury Men henceforward treated Number 10 staff as serious players.

The second strand of Britain's economic crisis in the mid-1970s concerned the dramatically increasing public sector and external financing deficits. This problem came to a head under Prime Minister Callaghan and gave him a major opportunity to impose his authority over the Treasury and to conduct economic policy from Downing Street. But the critical situation was in fact already manifest under Harold Wilson. In October 1975 he had called together the same secret inner group of ministers who had earlier considered pay policy to discuss what to do about the latest Treasury forecasts showing that the PSBR in 1975–76 would increase to £12 billion instead of the target £9 billion, and an external deficit of £1 billion and rising. The chancellor presented to them three policy options: import controls, or a 7 per cent devaluation, or an approach to the IMF for a large loan. They decided to approach the IMF. Significantly, James Callaghan, then foreign secretary, pressed the committee to 'do the tough things now'. During the following weeks the cabinet did indeed repeatedly discuss tough things – the chancellor's proposals for public expenditure cuts of £3.75 billion in 1976–79. Anthony Crosland, the economically erudite secretary of state for the environment, led prolonged cabinet resistance to the Treasury, arguing convincingly that there was no case on resource grounds for any cuts at all. But the 'confidence' arguments finally won the day and by the final cabinet discussion in mid-January 1976 Denis Healey had secured a cuts package of £3½ billion for 1976–79. It was a personal triumph for the chancellor, who had personally taken on his cabinet colleagues and slowly ground them down by the sheer weight of his argument and determination.

For the first time since 1974 the chancellor seemed fully in the saddle. But this re-assertion of Treasury authority in early 1976 was quickly subject to external pressures and afflicted by management failures. The Treasury decided in February 1976 that it wanted a lower value for sterling to maintain the 'competitiveness' of British industry. The Bank of England mishandled this policy and what started as a manoeuvre to edge the currency down developed quickly into a flight from sterling which fell below the psychological level of $2 in early March. Substantial reserves had to be spent supporting the currency and Prime Minister Wilson – who was secretly intending to resign within a few weeks – gave the chancellor a stern reprimand.

This was the serious situation which James Callaghan inherited in April 1976. Incomes policy had already been sorted out satisfactorily, though each year required a new round of intense discussion with the TUC over the new pay norm. Reductions in future public expenditure plans had been approved, but the political consequences in terms of lost programmes and jobs had still to be faced. Nor was it anyway clear that enough had yet been done to restore confidence in the currency; for the whole of the 1976–77 public expenditure contingency reserves had been allocated in the first month of the financial year, and sterling remained weak.

In fact, the technical management of the currency at this time was seriously open to question – and was questioned from Number 10. It was widely accepted that further devaluation was required to maintain competitiveness, but the approach of the banking authorities was to try to secure a 'smooth' downward adjustment – a cosmetic approach which cost one-third of Britain's reserves during March and April 1976 simply trying to smooth out the fall. It seemed to us in the Policy Unit more sensible to effect a swift 'step' devaluation to a desired level (e.g. $1.80), and then to use the reserves to defend that rate.

In June 1976 sterling again came under serious pressure. The Treasury and the governor of the Bank of England communicated to Number 10 that it would not be possible to hold the currency without a further package of public expenditure cuts. The prime minister resisted them at first, insisting that they go to the IMF for a six months' swap facility to boost Britain's reserves. But he privately told me afterwards that there was no way of avoiding further cuts. Deep down he believed that this was right, that public expenditure was still out of control, and that if tough action had to be taken he would prefer it to be done early in his administration.

From this point in June 1976 Callaghan progressively increased his influence on economic policymaking. He brought his own style to the conduct of government, insisting that economic questions be fully and openly discussed in cabinet. The 'Treasury bounce' was banished. Callaghan openly in cabinet authorised the chancellor to introduce his emergency package of cuts and said that it was most important that the cabinet choose its own priorities for cuts and not have the IMF do it for them. He held a private meeting with the Treasury and his own staff at Chequers at the end of June and personally supported the chancellor's arguments for £1 billion of cuts, even questioning whether this was enough. When he subsequently saw the governor of the Bank of England he again questioned whether £1 billion would be enough to restore confidence – and was assured it would be.

Prime Minister Callaghan was already edging into the lead hardline position on sorting out the government's public expenditure problems. He also brought his cabinet colleagues actively into the economic discussions during a succession of seven cabinet meetings during July. The objective was to cut £1 billion from the already agreed total of the existing public expenditure plan (PESC). But since there had already been an overspend of a £1 billion above that total, they in practice needed cuts of some £2 billion (or an increase in taxation equivalent to that). The cabinet was broadly divided into four camps on this issue: those supporting the Treasury line from conviction (Healey, Dell, Prentice, the prime minister and Chief Secretary Barnett who attended these discussions by special invitation); the 'Keynesian dissenters' led by Crosland and Lever who argued that during a recession it was wrong on resource grounds to make further deflationary cuts in expenditure; the left wing led by Benn and Foot (here also supported by the idiosyncratic Shore) who wanted an 'alternative strategy' based on import controls and increased public expenditure; and a rump, or 'king's party', who gave their ultimate support to the prime minister, though hoping to minimise the particular cuts to their own departmental budgets along the way.

The traditional 'Treasury bounce' approach would have been to try to railroad the cuts quickly through cabinet on the back of a currency crisis, real or inspired. Ministers would have had little chance to argue the strategic and philosophical implications. James Callaghan improved radically upon this. He allowed the issues to be put openly and the arguments to develop. Crosland and Healey argued their corners with an intellectual force and clarity to which few British academics aspire. During this debate the Treasury was forced by Crosland to refine its arguments and base its case almost entirely on 'confidence' in the currency. Crosland supported an immediate approach to the IMF in order to minimise the amount of cuts which would be required later if nothing was done now. The left wing opposition were always numerically in a cabinet minority, but Callaghan allowed them every opportunity to put their case and deliberately did not bring the individual cabinet meetings to a conclusion so that every member could feel still involved in the debate. He once said to me 'they discuss the cuts so often they come to think they have agreed them'. He also frequently met Healey, Foot and Crosland privately between cabinets to discuss economic questions in general and public expenditure in particular. He nurtured his colleagues towards the desired conclusion and, unlike Wilson, was not averse to having face-to-face disagreement with them. The main conclusion was reached on 21 July when at the seventh cabinet in the series (and the second that day) the cuts figure of £1 billion was achieved with the aid of some massaging of debt interest figures – and the chancellor immediately 'doubled up' by revealing his previously hidden intention to raise another £1 billion of tax revenues through extra national insurance contributions. Callaghan then set about selling the new policies to a wider audience, meeting with all his junior ministers to explain them, and also personally telephoning President Ford, Chancellor Schmidt and President Giscard. His only cabinet problem was inevitably with Tony Benn, who telephoned him to say that he would be taking the advice of his local party activists on whether to resign over the cuts and that anyway he would continue to campaign publicly against the measures. The prime minister advised Benn to make up his own mind whether to resign – and added that if he did campaign publicly against the cabinet of which he was a member he would be sacked on the spot. That was the end of that.

However, the wider constituency which remained unconvinced was the international financial community who saw a yawning balance of payments deficit ahead. By late September sterling had fallen towards $1.70 and Britain's reserves were disappearing fast. Healey revealed to the cabinet committee on economic strategy that he proposed to approach the IMF for another loan and that he had a scheme to introduce import deposits at seven-day readiness. But he still resisted pressures from within the cabinet to go the whole hog for import controls. When the prime minister addressed his party conference at Blackpool a week later he made a remarkably tough and realistic speech to the uncomprehending party faithful. It included sentences about the impossibility of reflating back to full employment which seemed to economic cognoscenti to reflect a conversion to many of the basic tenets of the monetarist faith. This actually exaggerated his stance, since he was not by temperament a theologian. But, always conservative in economic affairs, he had come to accept that certain monetary disciplines were essential to good economic management and conversely that monetary laxity would certainly undermine the foundations of sustained economic growth. Within those limited definitions, and also without the monetarist theology, it was a view which I shared and reflected in my advice from the Policy Unit.

For the last three months of 1976 Callaghan's Labour government was engaged in a massive economic crisis which threatened to tear it apart politically. At times there were major disagreements between the prime minister and his chancellor, between Number 10 officials and the Treasury and between ministers within cabinet. But that was an inevitable part of the democratic process. Overall, my main impression was of the skilful leadership of Callaghan and the incredible resilience of his chancellor. Neither could have succeeded without the other. But Callaghan emerged as the dominant figure, with unquestioned authority over his cabinet and, when henceforward he chose to exercise it, over Treasury economic policy.

The basic problems in the autumn of 1976 were that, domestically, we were running well above the (unpublished) 12 per cent money growth target and, externally, we could not finance the widening trade deficit. In this situation the City would not buy more gilts without evidence of a further squeeze on public expenditure and equally the IMF was refusing to make more loans without such a squeeze. The Treasury and the Bank of England shared these views. It was therefore highly likely that sterling would again collapse.

To some extent the problem was one of timing. The government's existing policies of devaluation, plus an incomes policy, plus the expenditure cuts already initiated, were already squeezing real incomes and improving Britain's relative competitiveness. Given time, that policy might have proved sufficient. But the immediate pressures meant that time would not be given. Something had to be done in the short run. Furthermore, certain people in the Treasury, and especially at the top of the Bank of England, saw this short-term crisis as an opportunity to make a major alteration in Britain's long-term economic posture – primarily through a massive switch of resources from the public to the private sector. The strategy later expounded and partly implemented by Mrs Thatcher was first prepared and launched – under the auspices of the IMF and of Mr Ed Yoder of the US Treasury and backed by the Bank of England and some of the UK Treasury – under James Callaghan's Labour government in 1976. That set the political climate within which the great arguments took place. It was not a question of whether to implement further public expenditure cuts: except for the left wing minority, most people in government accepted that need and the prime minister and his staff in Number 10 were most active in exploring the possibilities of cuts. It was mainly a question of the scale of the deflation to be imposed and the amount of resources to be transferred out of the public sector. The IMF, the Bank and officials in the Treasury proposed cuts of an order which would have produced a major slump and would probably have destroyed the political base of the Labour cabinet. The prime minister's great contribution was to resist these more extreme proposals and to argue with the Treasury and the IMF in great detail for a more modest package, one sufficient to restore confidence in sterling but not so great as to destroy his government's *raison d'être*. In doing so, he was assisted by the financial creativity of his colleague Harold Lever, who always argued that loans could be raised without spilling the last drop of Labour blood, and of Tony Crosland and other Keynesian moderates, who exposed the Treasury proposals to proper scrutiny and then finally fell loyally into line behind the prime minister's compromise package. For all involved it was an exhilarating and exhausting three months of economic policymaking. It also demonstrated the pluralism of economic decision making in Britain, with the Treasury, the Foreign Office, the Number 10 Policy Unit, the Bank of England and the IMF all deeply involved as institutions (curiously the CPRS made very little contribution), as well as the central concern of the cabinet, its committees and its ministerial members.

The Treasury's initial package in early October contained a minimum lending rate (MLR) of 15 per cent and special deposits on imports. But sterling continued to fall – assisted by a leak from the Treasury to the *Sunday Times* that the IMF would require sterling down to $1.50 (which in those pre-Thatcher days seemed immorally low). At the beginning of November the Treasury asked for a further £1 billion off the PSBR in 1977–78 through taxes or public expenditure cuts, but by the end of the month the IMF delegation was in London negotiating with the Treasury and were demanding much greater reductions: of £3 billion in the 1977–78 PSBR, bringing it down to below £7 billion, and £2 billion off the following year. The implied cuts were so savage that the cabinet strongly resisted and the chancellor and the Treasury (which was internally divided) retreated defeated. At this point, the prime minister moved in to take a more active direction of the negotiations. He had a private meeting with Witteveen and Whittom from the IMF at the beginning of December and pressed them hard on their minimum position. Afterwards he told me that we would not get away with less than £2 billion off the 1977 PSBR, and the Policy Unit began working on detailed ways of achieving that with the minimum of inevitable recessionary impact.

The prime minister also continued to give free rein in cabinet to his left wing colleagues who submitted papers on an 'alternative strategy' based on import controls and effectively creating a 'socialist fortress Britain'. But the most worrying criticisms again came from the Crosland–Lever camp, supported by Roy Hattersley and Shirley Williams. Significantly, all of these dissenting ministers employed special economic advisers, the new breed of outside advisers introduced by Harold Wilson to strengthen ministers against the conventional wisdom of the Whitehall machine. Tony Benn and Peter Shore were also similarly supported, and the resulting quality of individual ministerial contributions to the economic debate was repeatedly commented on approvingly by the Number 10 civil servants. Nearly all the rising young Turks in the cabinet had special advisers. Only the old stagers, such as Fred Peart, Elwyn Jones and Roy Mason, did without and they rarely intervened in the economic discussions. There is no doubt that the introduction of the special adviser system has significantly improved the quality of economic discussion and therefore of the economic policymaking process in Britain – and that it has seriously undermined the traditional hegemony of the Treasury. Denis Healey was the first chancellor to face a cabinet composed of colleagues fully and independently briefed on his policies. Fortunately he was one of the best qualified, in brains and muscle, to confront that exhausting prospect.

After meeting Witteveen and Whittom the prime minister decided it was time to bring his cabinet into line. He saw Crosland and Lever privately and their rebellion then collapsed. He secured their support for cuts of £1 billion for 1977–78 and then influenced the chancellor to go for that kind of figure instead of the new IMF's targets – which in early December were still to get a total of £5 billion of cuts in 1977–79. Discussion then moved to the 1978–79 PSBR where cuts of £1–2 billion were also being sought (if Britain's growth rate proved higher than expected). At two crucial cabinets in the morning and evening of 7 December the detailed expenditure cuts were approved, without ministerial resignations. It was a triumph for the prime minister. Politically he had retained the unity of his cabinet while agreeing some rigorous and painful measures. He had delivered the ministerial support to the Treasury. Equally he had personally conducted detailed arguments with the Treasury and the IMF and had forced them to modify their excessive proposals. He was particularly involved with the precise commitments contained in the Letter of Intent to the IMF, insisting that various monetary targets be loosened. He also continued to negotiate personally with Chancellor Schmidt and President Ford to arrange a 'safety net' for the sterling balances. Although many had contributed to the debate and the final policies agreed in 1976, there is no doubt that the biggest single influence on the final shape of the IMF economic package was that of the First Lord of the Treasury, James Callaghan.

One consequence of the IMF negotiations was to entrench monetarism, or some aspects of monetarism, publicly in the Labour government's policymaking. A range of monetary targets had been accepted and would be published. Yet, interestingly, the machinery of government was not organised for the transition from Keynes to Friedman. The Treasury was still primarily concerned with macroeconomic management; domestic monetary questions were basically left to the Bank of England; and the Treasury division which liaised with the Bank was of low seniority. Indeed, there was *no* cabinet committee which considered monetary matters. Questions concerning interest rates and exchange rates were not hitherto considered appropriate for ministers, and questions of money supply measurement had barely arisen anywhere at all in central government until recently. It is therefore of considerable interest and significance that following the IMF experience Prime Minister Callaghan introduced a new piece of central government machinery to reflect and process the monetarist advance. He established a small secret committee to meet regularly to consider monetary questions. It met in Number 10 under the prime minister's chairmanship, reflecting his pre-eminence in the economic policy field. Others in regular attendance were the governor and deputy governor of the Bank of England; the chancellor of the exchequer, his Treasury permanent secretary and sometimes his second permanent secretary responsible for external finance; the

Chancellor of the Duchy of Lancaster, Harold Lever; the cabinet secretary; a private secretary from Downing Street; and the author as head of the Downing Street Policy Unit. Because of the sensitivity of the issues of exchange rates and interest rates frequently under discussion, this gathering was kept secret from ministers and was not designated as a cabinet committee but was described as 'the seminar'. It met regularly throughout the rest of Callaghan's premiership (and was continued, less systematically, I believe, by his successor). It was effectively a policymaking committee. It had an agenda and the chancellor and the governor would reveal their intentions for interest rate and exchange rate policy. The prime minister, who was heavily briefed by the Policy Unit, but was anyway more than competent as an ex-chancellor to perform in these areas, would scrutinise them closely and indicate his policy preferences. It was an interesting example of the machinery of government adjusting to changes in prevailing economic theory and to the greater policy role played by the prime minister.

The years 1977–78 following the IMF agreement were a time of relative success for the Labour government. The incomes policy and the new monetarist regime combined to bring inflation down, finally and briefly, into single figures. The prime minister continued to dominate his colleagues in cabinet, though in the routine economic field, without major crises, Denis Healey and the Treasury were able to refurbish their reputations and morale. Relations between Number 10 and the Treasury were very harmonious. With the economic strategy clearly established, the Treasury re-emerged as the dominant ministry conducting the routine management of that strategy. But there was no doubt that in a crisis it would be the prime minister who would pre-eminently be in the front line. That is indeed what happened in the 'winter of discontent' in 1978–79. Then the incomes policy so cleverly put together by Harold Wilson in 1975 collapsed under the assault of several militant trade unions, mainly from the public sector which the Labour government had done so much to protect. It was James Callaghan who took the brunt of that attack and who was again expected to deliver his government from crisis. He failed. Having built his political career in alliance with the trade union movement he was psychologically unable to break the link and lead the government and the country against his old trade union allies. He stood paralysed while his counter-inflation policies collapsed. Without him, the Treasury was able to do little. The government's economic policies fell apart, and it slipped inevitably towards electoral defeat in 1979.

The above survey of economic policymaking under the Labour governments led by Harold Wilson and James Callaghan during 1974–79 is undoubtedly selective. It represents a particular view from 10 Downing Street. It concentrates on the two major issues of the construction of the incomes policy in 1975 and the IMF crisis in 1976. It certainly does injustice to the contributions of other ministers and departments. It especially does not do justice to the Treasury, which during those five years bore the brunt of the day-to-day management of a sickly economy, under a government with ambitious electoral commitments, and as yet without the massive oil revenues which subsequently made life so much easier (for the government, if not for the unemployed) under Margaret Thatcher. But it is a legitimate view from Downing Street, the political centre of British government. It does demonstrate the considerable potential power of a British prime minister in economic policymaking, and illustrates how that potential became reality. As was suggested at the beginning, given the will and the inclination and the advice and the opportunity of events, a British prime minister may operate indeed as the First Lord of the Treasury.

Reference

1. This chapter is based on a paper delivered at the British–American Festival, Duke University, Durham, North Carolina, on 13 June 1984. Dr Donoughue's paper, together with the others delivered on the same occasion, will be published in Richard Hodder-Williams and James Ceaser (eds), *Politics in Britain and the United States: Comparative Perspectives on Institutions and Political Culture* (Durham, NC: Duke University Press, 1985).

3

The Prime Minister's Aides

G. W. JONES[1]

As Lord Wilson points out at the beginning of Chapter 1, 10 Downing Street is best regarded as 'a small village'. Precisely because the Downing Street village is so small, it is important to know as much as possible about those who inhabit it. What sorts of people are they? What do they do? What roles do they see themselves playing? G. W. Jones was a colleague of Bernard Donoughue at the London School of Economics; they jointly wrote the standard life of Herbert Morrison. In this chapter, originally written in 1979, Professor Jones describes the Number 10 operation in James Callaghan's time. He has added a section on Margaret Thatcher. Professor Jones maintains that the staffing of Number 10 is more than adequate and that there is no need for a 'prime minister's department'. As Chapter 10 by Sir Kenneth Berrill shows, this view is not shared universally.

The British system of government cannot really be called prime ministerial government, nor can it be called cabinet government. The right term is ministerial government, because *legally* powers are given in Acts of parliament to ministers. No powers are given to the prime minister or cabinet: they do not exist legally; they are conventions. And *administratively* ministers have to support and sustain them in the carrying out of their tasks large executive bureaucracies, and these bureaucracies are very much concerned with particular functions and services. The bureaucracies are functionally oriented, and clustering around them, further strengthening centrifugal tendencies, are pressure groups, concerned again with particular services and functions. *Politically* ministers themselves have made their own reputations in parliament. They are ministers because of their own work in winning political credit. They are not there simply because the prime minister appointed them, or because he did not dismiss them. Most are ministers because they have made themselves indispensable to the prime minister so that he cannot help but appoint them and dare not sack them.

The prime minister is thus faced with the major task of how to keep this very fragmented system together. He has to engineer a consensus amongst this disparate group and to steer it in a consistent direction.

In the resources available to the prime minister to do this work, Britain is quite different from most other countries: it has no prime ministerial department. Other governmental systems based on the British, like Australia and Canada (not presidential but parliamentary with prime ministers like ours) have developed prime ministerial departments, in which certain functions crop up again and again. There are three central functions that prime ministerial departments, and presidential and chancellors' departments, often perform: first, control over the machinery of government, the allocation of functions, the organisation of the machine and the civil service; second, the role of co-ordinating policy, its formulation and implementation; and third, controlling and allocating resources. In Britain these functions are performed, but not by a prime minister's department. They are scattered among a number of departments. Control over the machinery of government and the civil service is given to the Civil Service Department, established in 1968; policy co-ordination is performed by the Cabinet Office, set up in 1916; and resource allocation by the Treasury. Three separate departments perform these key functions.

The ultimate political responsibility for each is in fact the prime minister's, because the prime minister is the minister for the civil service, the political head of the Civil Service

Department, although he leaves the day-to-day ministerial running of that department to the Lord Privy Seal. The prime minister is the first minister in the cabinet. He is its chairman, so he is the political head of the Cabinet Office. He is also the First Lord of the Treasury, his official title on the nameplate at 10 Downing Street. He is in fact the political boss of the three central departments, and he has reporting to him the three most important civil servants in Britain – (1) the permanent under-secretary of the Civil Service Department, Sir Ian Bancroft, the official head of the Home Civil Service, reports to the prime minister in the prime minister's capacity as minister for the civil service; (2) the official head of the Cabinet Office is the secretary to the cabinet, Sir John Hunt, who again reports directly to the prime minister; (3) the permanent under-secretary of the Treasury, Sir Douglas Wass, can report directly to the prime minister. They constitute a troika; they are the most highly paid civil servants, receiving more than other permanent secretaries. These are the 'top hamper' of the civil service. There is a fourth in this category: the permanent under-secretary of the Foreign and Commonwealth Office, Sir Michael Palliser, the head of the Diplomatic Service. These are Britain's top mandarins, the permanent governors of this country.

Of these four, two have the most regular and the closest contact with the prime minister: the cabinet secretary and the official head of the Home Civil Service. The relationship between the prime minister and these two, and indeed these four, will fluctuate depending on their personal relationships, how they are getting on with each other, as well as on the issues uppermost at the time. So the prime minister has direct, close contacts with Sir Ian Bancroft and Sir John Hunt, and perhaps less contact with Sir Michael Palliser and Sir Douglas Wass. He also has reporting to him the head of the Central Policy Review Staff (CPRS) the central 'think tank' which is located within the Cabinet Office. Sir Kenneth Berrill, the head of the CPRS, has direct access to the prime minister. The prime minister, if he wants, can also call in for help the permanent secretaries of other departments, when he is concerned with a problem that falls within the responsibility of a particular department. He has access not only to generalist administrators but also top specialists in Whitehall, scientific, military or other professionals located in different departments, and is in close contact with the security services.

When one surveys this network one can conclude that, although the levers of control may not all be gathered together into one prime ministerial department, the prime minister can touch these levers if he wants to engage them, and the prime minister can also draw on contacts with his ministerial colleagues. They meet formally in cabinet and cabinet committees and also informally. Each day the chief whip moves through the corridor from Number 12 to Number 11 into 10 Downing Street. The doors between 10, 11 and 12 are open, with constant interchange. The prime minister is not locked into monastic seclusion. He goes regularly to the House of Commons; he has a room in the House of Commons; he walks in the corridors where he can be lobbied and contacted by members of parliament. He does a considerable amount of travelling around the country, and there are deputations to him.

There are thus numerous people coming into contact with him whose services he can draw on, but the individuals mentioned so far do not have a primary loyalty to him. They are not his own aides. They have their own main functions to perform and their own careers and ambitions to pursue independently of the prime minister. The people who serve only the prime minister make up what is now officially called 'the prime minister's office'. The first time this phrase was used officially in government publications was in 1976. This staff totals about 80, and can be divided into four main groups. Each of these groups has its own chief responsibility, although the work of one group impinges very closely on the work of another.

The first group, the core of 10 Downing Street, is the private office, consisting of six civil servants. They inhabit two rooms adjacent to the cabinet – two rooms between which the interconnecting door is always open. In the first room, the one next to the cabinet room, is the head of the private office, the prime minister's principal private secretary, Mr Kenneth Stowe. He has been in this position since 1975, rather longer than usual. Principal private secretaries normally stay for about three years, but for a variety of reasons Mr Stowe has been asked to remain. He can be regarded as the prime minister's chief of staff. His rank is of deputy secretary, and his role is to oversee Number 10 as a whole. He co-ordinates the submissions that go to the prime minister. The principal private secretary is in charge of the box which contains all papers for the prime minister. He sees it last before it goes to the prime minister; he controls it. He is always involved in the most important items that interest the prime minister. Whatever is uppermost in the prime minister's mind Mr Stowe will be handling, and as the head of Number 10 he keeps in close touch with Sir Ian Bancroft, the head of the Home Civil Service, and with Sir John Hunt, the cabinet secretary, and although a deputy secretary he can ring up quite freely any permanent secretary. He is responsible for linking the prime minister with Buckingham Palace; he handles business with the Queen's private secretary, preparing the weekly audience between monarch and her chief minister. He takes a particular interest in the machinery of government, in the appointments that the prime minister makes, and in honours.

Principal private secretaries can be ranged along a continuum. At one extreme are the 'smoothers', who regard their role as to pour oil on the system, to facilitate and expedite the flow of business. At the other extreme are those who see their role as being not just to smooth the passage of business for others, but to make their own contribution, injecting their own observations into the flow of business.

In the same room as the principal private secretary is the private secretary who handles overseas affairs, defence matters and Northern Ireland. He invariably comes on secondment to Number 10 from the Foreign Office, and is of counsellor rank. In the second room beyond the door that is always kept open are crowded together the other private secretaries. There is an assistant secretary from one of the economic departments who handles economic affairs. There are two principals. One deals with other domestic issues, usually not of an economic nature. The other focuses on the prime minister's relations with parliament. His main job is to prepare the prime minister for his question periods that come twice a week, Tuesdays and Thursdays. He has to process the prime minister's parliamentary questions, especially to provide him with the possible answers he may need to deal with supplementary questions. The sixth person in these two rooms is a higher executive officer, who deals with the prime minister's correspondence with the public. He keeps his diary and fixes up his engagements and travel arrangements.

These six civil servants make up the private office. Each has his own main concern, but is not limited just to sticking to his range of responsibilities; each must be ready to take over the work of the others. This flexibility is encouraged by the nature of the room. The six are crammed together. They overhear conversations, they chat together about business, and they dip into each other's work trays. When work has been finished it is put in a tray, the 'dip', and each secretary can go along and 'dip' in and see what the others have been doing. In this claustrophobic setting, it is very easy to pick up what is going on and it is very important to get on well together. Secretaries frequently talk about the team spirit at Number 10, and how they have to act like a rugby pack and be ready to pick up the ball and run with it. This need to interchange with each other is reinforced by a rota system for the evenings and holidays so that one of them is always available to take over the work of the others.

Members of the private office are seconded on loan from their departments and usually serve about three years at Number 10. This temporary secondment is thought to be important, so that there is not built up a 'Number 10 view' or a prime minister's department. It is also thought to be important because three years is about all that one can stand at the top. Private secretaries in the private office are usually in their early 30s, 'high flyers', people who are going to go places. They are thought to be the most able in the civil service and are given a taste of what it is like at the top. The danger is that it can be too 'heady', too attractive, which makes it difficult for an official, if he stays too long, to go back into his department to routine, dull work. Three years is felt to be about enough to avoid that kind of 'corruption'. The other sort of 'corruption' that can take place is that private secretaries might become too attached to the prime minister, as happened with some of the private secretaries of Lloyd George and Harold Macmillan, who found it impossible to go back into their departments and so left the civil service.

Below these temporary denizens of Number 10 and supporting them are the more permanent staff. There are four assistant private secretaries, all ladies, who provide what continuity there is at Number 10. They are the repositories of very long experience about practice and procedure. The ones who are there go back in their experience to the 1940s, and when they first came they were working with colleagues who were at Number 10 in the 1920s. The continuity of the Number 10 assistant private secretaries can be traced back to 1916. These redoubtable ladies, 'Queen Bees', head sections on honours, on confidential filing, on records and on correspondence. Underneath them in the hierarchy are the garden room girls who inhabit a room that looks out onto the garden of Number 10. They are shorthand typists who serve the prime minister and private secretaries. They constitute a pool. The prime minister does not have his own typist; there is a pool of girls constantly interchangeable. Also making up this official element at Number 10 are the duty clerks, executive officers who are there 24 hours a day, a backup staff performing a range of supporting tasks.

The private office never sleeps. A private secretary, one of the six, is always on call, and the office is always manned at least by an executive officer. The phone switchboard is there to respond throughout the 24 hours. The private office is the operations room of Number 10. Everything going into and out of Number 10 goes through it. The private secretaries see their role as being to ease the burden on the prime minister, to help the prime minister think and act, and to ensure that he has all the necessary advice and information he requires for his decisions. They see their job as being to smooth the prime minister's way, clearing away the trivial and routine so that he can concentrate on the essential. So they perform, at one extreme, somewhat minor functions, keeping his diary, arranging his day, seeing he gets to where he ought to be and, on the other hand, briefing him on important current issues and prospective developments. They help to draft his speeches and prepare him for meetings and engagements, and in particular they are a channel of communication with Whitehall.

The private secretaries of Whitehall constitute the 'bush telegraph' of government. There is a network of private secretaries in the other departments who are closely linked with the prime minister's private secretaries at Number 10. On this network they can signal out how the prime minister is thinking, what he is intending to do, what he has done; and they can collect in from the departments what the other ministers are doing, how departments are reacting, and ferry this information to the prime minister. Number 10 is at the centre of this Whitehall 'bush telegraph' of private secretaries. They think of their job as being to ensure that the prime minister has before him full information so that he can take his decisions; and once his decisions are taken, they then convey his views back to the departments. They act also as a filter, a gatekeeper, because in their role of selecting what goes to the prime minister, they can exclude what they think is inappropriate. They choose the papers and people that go to the prime minister. Most do not see themselves simply as a postbag for others. Before they send an item to the prime minister they will scribble a few words or lines on it, pointing out its significance and perhaps commenting where they think a submission is deficient or when something new has taken place. From their central vantage point, they might spot something – a consequence or an implication – neglected by departments that might be somewhat blinkered. They say that they put more comments on the papers that come directly from ministers and departments than on papers that come from the Cabinet Office. There are basically two streams of paper to the prime minister, those from ministers' departments directly and those channelled through the Cabinet Office. The Cabinet Office itself is also performing a filtering, commenting, co-ordinating role, and the private office feels less need, normally, to comment on their submissions.

The private office is much concerned with parliament. Parliament looms very large in the eyes of civil servants. Much of their time is spent on preparing the prime minister for his parliamentary activities. One private secretary spends virtually the whole of his time planning for the parliamentary question period, and a great deal of attention is given to speeches and statements that the prime minister has to deliver in the Commons, above all alerting him to pitfalls that may lie ahead.

The private office handles all the prime minister's correspondence that flows in and out, and private secretaries try to be near him at all times and at all meetings. He is the only minister who has his own staff in the cabinet when the meeting is taking place: when the cabinet is in session there is one member of the prime minister's private office in attendance, either the principal private secretary or the private secretary who is handling the business that is being discussed at that point on the agenda. So they know what has happened in cabinet. Having the private secretaries in the cabinet room was an innovation of Harold Macmillan's. He argued it saved time; he would not have to tell them later what happened; they would know at first hand and if necessary go out of the cabinet room and immediately ring up the other departments to tell the departmental private secretaries what went on, so that when the minister arrived back he would not have to tell his own department what he thought had occurred – or if he did the department had a check on the minister's version.

The private office shadows the prime minister, taking notes of all important conversations that the prime minister has, with ministers for example. They listen in on his phone calls, unless he expressly asks them not to. This eavesdropping is essential to record the prime minister's decisions, what was discussed, and ensure they can be followed up. When David Steel wrote in the *Observer*[2] about the Lib–Lab pact, he noted that, when he had conversations with the prime minister, Mr Stowe was present taking notes. Private secretaries in the past have called this work 'watching the body', or acting as 'groom-in-waiting'. Lady Falkender was annoyed that she was at a disadvantage in this task compared with the private secretaries: she could not follow them with the prime minister into the toilet. The essence of a good private secretary is 'never to be out of the way, but never in the way'. The private secretaries carry out a variety of tasks. Their major objectives are to help the prime minister conduct his business efficiently, to do what the prime minister would do if he had the time and energy to do it himself, to provide extra hands, eyes, legs, mouths and arms for the prime minister. That is the private office, the core, the first of the four elements at Number 10.

While the private office links the prime minister mainly to the world of officials in Whitehall, the prime minister needs also to be linked to the world of politics. Before the 1920s, the private office linked the prime minister to the worlds of politics and administration, because the people in charge of the private office were themselves political appointees chosen by the prime minister from his political entourage; they were his personal appointees. The principal private secretary was a political appointee before the 1920s, but in the 1920s, under the aegis of Warren Fisher, the civil service seized the private office and have never let go of it. The prime minister from the 1920s kept close to politics through his ministers, especially the chief whip, and leading figures from party headquarters. A political element returned to the private office in the late 1950s when Mr Macmillan put into the private office his close personal friend, John Wyndham, who sat at one of the desks in the room with the private secretaries. Harold Wilson brought in as his political secretary, Lady Falkender, and Mr Heath appointed Douglas Hurd as his political secretary. Both Lady Falkender and Douglas Hurd sat in the room on the other side of the cabinet room from the private secretaries' rooms. The cabinet is therefore flanked on one side by the private secretaries linking the prime minister to the world of administration and on the other by the political secretary who links the prime minister to the world of politics.

Mr Callaghan appointed not a political secretary but a political adviser, Tom McNally, a former research official at Transport House on the international relations side, who first came to know the prime minister in the years of opposition from 1970. Mr Callaghan took Mr McNally, when Labour became the government in 1974, to the Foreign Office as his political adviser, and from the Foreign Office the prime minister transferred him to Number 10. Mr McNally is a temporary civil servant, paid from public funds, but he has a staff of four who are paid from a political fund financed by the Labour party, the trades unions and the co-operative society. With Harold Wilson a similar fund was supported by various businessmen, who provided money in a mysterious way. But Mr Callaghan arranged the financing on a more open, accountable footing, with funds contributed from the various elements of the Labour movement. The people under Mr McNally constitute the political office. Mr McNally's role is to deal with primarily party political matters, to liaise with party headquarters, the officials and the proliferation of committees at Transport House. He handles the correspondence with the party, from Labour supporters and MPs. He acts as a politically reliable channel to and from the prime minister. If one wants to contact the prime minister and does not want the civil service to know, one goes through the political secretary. He comments on papers circulating around Number 10, adds notes to the briefs and on the papers that come in from different departments and ministers. He sits in on committees of ministers and civil servants if the prime minister so desires. He helps the prime minister with his speeches, building up and drafting them. He checks over speeches written by other members of the Number 10 outfit. His concern is with their party political dimension, but he is generally available to the prime minister for political advice.

The third element at Number 10 is the Policy Unit, created in 1974 by Harold Wilson and taken over by James Callaghan. Mr Wilson's head of the Policy Unit was Dr Bernard Donoughue, his Senior Policy Adviser, and Mr Callaghan continued with him. Dr Donoughue, former journalist, political historian and lecturer at the London School of Economics, is a temporary civil servant, paid from public funds. He has a team of about seven and can also call in other people as consultants on a part-time basis. His team are specialists. He selected them because they specialised in a policy area and are therefore unlike the generalists in the private office. They are also Labour supporters, whereas the civil servants in the private office have no party affiliation. Dr Donoughue also sought people with some experience of government, perhaps as consultants or advisers earlier on. The role of this unit is forward policy analysis, medium and long term, on domestic and overseas policy. They can act on their own initiative if they think that there is a policy area that requires their contribution.

They also act in response to prime ministerial requests. Their link to the prime minister is through Dr Donoughue, who from time to time puts to the prime minister papers of about two or three pages on an issue, or else he talks to the prime minister. The Policy Unit gives the prime minister a view that is different from that of the official machine and from that coming into him from separate departments. They comment on and probe the advice coming in from the departments and the machine.

Dr Donoughue attends ministerial meetings when the prime minister asks him to and sits in on a number of official committees, including one of the most important committees in British government, the committee of deputy secretaries of the Cabinet Office, chaired by the secretary of the cabinet, who meet every week to plan cabinet business for the weeks ahead. By 'cabinet business' is meant not just meetings of the cabinet but also of the many cabinet committees. The deputy secretaries arrange what cabinet committees are to be set up, who is to sit upon them, and the timetabling of the business. They plan the cabinet's programme of work, 'the fixture list for the cabinet policy season'. Both Dr Donoughue and Mr Stowe go along to this committee, so that the Prime Minister has two people offering an input into the agenda-setting function.

Dr Donoughue maintains contact himself and through his team with the specialist advisers in the departments. One of the features of the 1970s has been the emergence of these special advisers, both the political advisers and the more expert advisers appointed by a number of ministers. They total about 25. They have built up their own informal network of regular contacts, through which Number 10 can learn what is going on inside the departments and the problems that are arising. Although the Policy Unit deals with policy in the middle and long term, Dr Donoughue is also called upon to help in immediate crises, drafting white papers, government announcements and prime ministerial speeches. The Policy Unit provides for the prime minister a source of policy analysis, loyal to him. Although the private office say they are loyal to him, he probably feels that they have to have regard to their careers and to the people who will be promoting them in the future. They might appear loyal primarily to the official machine and be reticent on certain issues, while the Policy Unit with its political composition can say the sorts of things that officials cannot (and would not want to).

There are precedents for this Policy Unit. In the First World War, Lloyd George had a private secretariat that he set up in the garden of Number 10 Downing Street in some temporary buildings, the famous 'garden suburb' headed by an Oxford academic, Professor Adams. In the Second World War, Winston Churchill had a similar sort of 'think tank' headed by Lord Cherwell, the statistical section, which Mr Churchill again tried to revive when he came back to office in the 1950s. Clement Attlee, when prime minister, had Douglas Jay (1945–46) as a one-man policy section, and Harold Wilson in the 1960s used Thomas Balogh who brought in a team of academics to act as an embryonic policy unit.

The fourth element at Number 10 is the press and information office, headed by the press secretary, Tom McCaffrey, with a staff of about ten. The first press office at Number 10 was set up in 1931 to deal with press questions about the economic crisis. Before then, liaising with the press had been carried out by the prime minister himself or by one of his private secretaries. From time to time the prime minister and the private office still handle press relations, but from the 1940s the work of linking the prime minister with the media has been put into the hands of the press office. Since the 1940s two types of press secretary have emerged, either the journalist brought into Number 10 because he is politically sympathetic to the prime minister, like Mr Attlee's Francis Williams or Harold Wilson's Joe Haines, or else the civil servant who specialises in information work. Tom McCaffrey comes into this latter category. He first worked for Mr Callaghan when he was home secretary in the 1960s. When Mr Callaghan became foreign secretary in 1974 he asked Mr McCaffrey to be his press officer at the Foreign Office, and he took him with him into 10 Downing Street. A similar figure was Harold Macmillan's press officer, Harold Evans, and Edward Heath used specialist information officers whom he had met when he had been at the Foreign Office as Lord Privy Seal. Prime ministers are better advised to reply on specialist information officers, not on politically sympathetic journalists;

the specialist information officers seem to enjoy better relations with the press than do former journalists.

The role of the press office is to link the prime minister to the press and broadcasting organisations. The press office and the press secretary handle the lobby correspondents; they give briefings each day about what is going on at Number 10 and generally in government. They plan the prime minister's broadcasts. They are the main source of advice to him about how to present his image and the whole range of government policy. They act as general public relations advisers.

At Number 10 there are also messengers, security staff, the domestic staff, the cleaning staff, and there are three other elements that are somewhat 'hived-off' in their work. There is the secretary for appointments, Mr C. V. Peterson, who occupies the best staff room at Number 10. He is a civil servant who handles the ecclesiastical and other crown appointments, acting as 'heaven's talent scout'. He is involved very much with the many appointments to various bishoprics and deaneries. He also operates a number of charities for forgotten actors, sculptors and poets who have fallen on hard times. He acts as the personnel manager for the junior staff at Number 10, and looks after the fabric of Number 10 and Chequers. These functions were once performed by one of the private secretaries, but in the Second World War they were given to an eccentric private secretary called Sir Anthony Bevir, a figure from Trollope, who left a trail of snuff and a whiff of claret behind him. He ended up with the title of KCVO; when it was announced, he went out to celebrate and lost the keys of Number 10, of which he was the guardian, and all the locks had to be changed, costing a considerable sum of money which gave rise to a new meaning for KCVO – Keys Can Vanish Overnight! The secretary for appointments serves much longer at Number 10 than the other private secretaries since he has to concentrate for some time on this sort of work, getting to know the deans, the bishops and the church. Continuity is needed.

There is also the parliamentary private secretary to the prime minister, the PPS, Roger Stott, who is a backbench MP, unpaid. He has a desk in Mr McNally's office but works mainly from the prime minister's room at the House of Commons. His job is to link the prime minister to the backbenchers in the Commons and keep him in touch with all the comings and goings in Westminster, and the gossip. The prime minister, if he wants, can use him on special tasks. There is also the prime minister's constituency and personal secretary Ms Ruth Sharp, a lady paid by Mr Callaghan personally, who has been with him for years, from when he was a backbench MP. She handles his more private correspondence, his relationships with his constituency agent and his personal and family matters.

The four main elements in Number 10 are thus the private office, the political office, the Policy Unit and press office. The heads of each have direct personal access to the prime minister and are in daily contact with him. Each one has a main responsibility, but there is no rigid demarcation of duties at Number 10. At the top in politics, sharp distinctions do not count. All is ambiguity and shading. The private office, for instance, needs to be very much attuned to political factors; it has much political business to handle, witness for instance the fact that Mr Stowe took notes of the prime minister's conversation with David Steel when the Lib–Lab pact was formed. The private office is not limited simply to handling official business. The political office is also often concerned with issues of future policy and with handling the press. The press office advises the prime minister on his speeches and on policy matters, and the prime minister depends very heavily on and listens a great deal to the influential Mr McCaffrey. The Policy Unit does not have its gaze fixed only on the future or medium term. Dr Donoughue's unit is frequently engaged in quite short-term problems – drafting a white paper, handling difficult politicians and awkward trades unionists. At Number 10 politics and administration interpenetrate.

The prime minister is at the peaks of both the political pillar and the administrative pillar, and his aides, both his political aides and his official aides, need to be aware of both aspects and to work together very closely, which is why personal relationships are so important. How people get on with each other is crucial. This aspect explains why personality and gossip are the stuff of business at the very top. At the end of the corridors of power, all is personality. At Number 10 temperaments, personal drives, neuroses, are the crucial elements. The squabbles between Lady Falkender and Joe Haines show how important personal relations are. They determine whether Number 10 is a cockpit or a commune. Normally relations are close and harmonious, and this good spirit is aided by the fact that Number 10 is such an admirable setting for intimate interactions. Number 10 is not a department. It exudes the atmosphere of a house; in fact it is two houses joined together. It does not have the feeling or look of a department. Doors are open, people pop in and out, and they chat and look through each other's trays. It is a very informal, not bureaucratic, atmosphere. When people are so very close, those who are at the top of the various units play a very personal role to the prime minister. A court jester is extremely significant at the top. The prime minister needs people he can relax with, let his hair down with, try out ideas in confidence with, and gossip with, without any fear of being betrayed. He can do this because he has around him a group of people who are not carving out their own careers as his rivals. He never lets his hair down with ministers; they are rivals. Nor can he feel wholly relaxed with the civil service, because their basic loyalty appears to be to the machine, not to him. That is why the prime minister needs aides like Dr Donoughue and Mr McNally around him; they are 'trusties'. At Number 10 distinctions are blurred. It is hard to sustain sharp divisions between official, political and personal roles.

Britain has no prime minister's department. Some people argue that we need a proper prime minister's department to enable the prime minister to keep on top of government, to initiate his own policy and to assess and challenge the policies of others. However, such a department might weaken the prime minister because what the prime minister needs are flexible arrangements, which can adapt easily to each prime minister's needs. Prime ministers have different needs, different temperaments, different styles of working, and over the years the basic structure at Number 10 has adapted easily to what the various prime ministers have required. This flexible system is responsive to his political control and direction. If it became a bureaucratic structure, it would develop a momentum of its own, have a view of its own and put up to the prime minister a certain line, whereas the advantage of the present flexible set-up is that he can pick and choose whose advice he wants – which he would be less able to do in a more structured hierarchy in which there would be demarcations. It would lose the informality and lack of protocol that is at present a dominant characteristic of Number 10.

Further, the present system hinders the emergence of one person who has the prime minister's ear. Now there exists a group of people, probably about nine, who are in constant daily touch with the prime minister. Amongst them he can pick and choose on whom to rely, and he can counter balance one against the other. There is a danger in having a single head of Number 10. Everything might be channelled through that one person. The present system enables the prime minister to be in charge, not a single subordinate. A more structured department would generate a large amount of paper, which the prime minister might find difficult to master, whereas the present system, operating informally with a word here, a little chat there, dropping in for drinks at the end of the day, enables the prime minister to keep on top of business. And in any case a prime minister's department would be a revolution in the constitution, a move from a ministerial and cabinet system to prime ministerial government. Other ministers would resist this development, and departmental civil servants too. The present system is flexible, and easily adaptable to prime ministers' needs. A prime minister's department is not required.

The Prime Minister's Office under Margaret Thatcher 1979–84

The structure of the prime minister's office under Margaret Thatcher remained from 1979 to 1984 very much as it had been under Mr Callaghan, and its size too remained roughly the same, around 70–80 people. Some slight modifications occurred, some titles changed, and new people appeared. As in the past, the office adapted to the needs and style of the prime minister. She resisted advice from a number of observers to set up a prime minister's department. She preferred not to restructure the administrative machine and set up a bureaucratic institution that would irritate her ministers and departmental civil servants. She felt that she could obtain the advice and assistance she needed by maintaining a loose network of varied aides located in different places. This system would give her the support she wanted without alienating her political and official colleagues.

She did, however, undertake two major administrative changes outside the prime minister's office that altered the arrangements for providing advice to the very centre of government. In 1981 she abolished the Civil Service Department and retired prematurely its permanent under-secretary, Sir Ian Bancroft, who was the official head of the Home Civil Service. Its functions were distributed to the Treasury and the Cabinet Office, in which was established the management and personnel office responsible to the prime minister for running the civil service. From 1981–83 there were two joint official heads of the Home Civil Service, Sir Douglas Wass, permanent under-secretary at the Treasury, and Sir Robert Armstrong, the cabinet secretary, who had replaced Sir John Hunt in 1979. On the retirement of Sir Douglas in 1983, Sir Robert became the sole official head of the Home Civil Service. Sir Robert was no stranger to the centre of government. He had been the principal private secretary at Number 10 to both Edward Heath and Harold Wilson. He is the first former principal private secretary there to go on to be secretary of the cabinet and the first cabinet secretary to have served as a permanent under-secretary elsewhere (Home Office) before going to the Cabinet Office. His influence was further enhanced following the Franks report on the Falklands affair, when the Cabinet Office was given an increased role in co-ordinating intelligence.

Margaret Thatcher's second major administrative change was to abolish the CPRS in 1983. On the retirement of its head, Sir Kenneth Berrill, in 1980, Robin Ibbs (a top executive at ICI) took over. He was in turn replaced in 1982 by a merchant banker, John Sparrow. The prime minister, however, was finding that the CPRS was not useful for her purposes. She was relying for policy advice more on her aides at Number 10, and she felt that the CPRS was a leaky vessel. It was wound up after the election of 1983.

Within the Cabinet Office, the prime minister created a new post, the prime minister's adviser on efficiency. Its first holder was the joint managing director of Marks and Spencer, Sir Derek (later Lord) Rayner, who on a part-time basis conducted reviews of the performance of selected parts of the civil service. The second holder was Sir Robin Ibbs, who in 1983 returned to serve Mrs Thatcher.

At Number 10 itself, the official side remained much as before in structure and functions. The principal private secretary, Mr Stowe, was succeeded in 1979 by Clive Whitmore, who had served previously in the War Office, Department of Defence and the Cabinet Office. In 1983, he was promoted to be the permanent under-secretary at the Department of Defence, and was followed as principal private secretary to the prime minister by Robin Butler from the Treasury. Mr Butler had been a private secretary at Number 10 when Sir Robert Armstrong had been the principal there and subsequently under Mr Stowe. Thus from 1983 the two top officials advising the prime minister were former colleagues who had served together at Downing Street when Mr Heath and Mr Wilson had been prime ministers, and both were civil servants from the Treasury.

Four private secretaries covered overseas affairs, economic affairs, parliamentary affairs, and home affairs and the diary. In the 1970s the member of the private office who handled parliamentary affairs moved on to home affairs, but under Margaret Thatcher the one responsible for home affairs graduated to parliamentary affairs. Margaret Thatcher was also eager to ensure that one of the private secretaries had a scientific background. A sixth member of the private office, Miss Caroline Stephens, was personal assistant to the prime minister. Whereas the others stayed for the usual three or so years at Number 10, Miss Stephens has been there since 1979. She looks after the personal requirements of Margaret Thatcher – for instance, ensuring the right clothes are packed; she does not handle policy. She keeps the diary of engagements under the supervision of the home affairs private secretary. The secretary for appointments, Mr C. V. Peterson, was succeeded in 1982 by Mr J. R. Catford, who continues the role of preparing the background material for appointments on which the prime minister is the critical decider, such as with bishops, regius professorships, the Poet Laureate and the master of

Trinity College, Cambridge. The chief press secretary since 1979 is Bernard Ingham, a former journalist who moved into the civil service as a chief information officer at the Department of Employment and Productivity, and was later at Energy in charge of the conservation division. He is a vigorous exponent of the prime minister's views with the media.

Within the political side of Number 10 there have been more significant changes. Indeed for the first time in the 1983 edition of the *Civil Service Yearbook* a distinct part of the prime minister's office was recognised as the 'political office'. One of Margaret Thatcher's innovations in 1979 was to appoint a political 'chief of staff'. He is David Wolfson, a former businessman from Great Universal Stores, and secretary to the Conservative shadow cabinet. He acts as a general-purpose political adviser, an emissary and a discreet aide with whom the prime minister can have a relaxed conversation. As political secretaries she first had Richard Ryder, a former journalist on the *Daily Telegraph*, who had worked in her private office during her years of opposition. He is married to her personal assistant Miss Stephens and left Number 10 to pursue his own political career in 1981, becoming an MP in 1983. He was succeeded by Derek Howe, a Conservative party press official, and then in 1983 by the current political secretary Stephen Sherbourne, from the Conservative Research Department. The main tasks of the secretary are to link Downing Street to the Conservative party and to watch over the political aspects of the prime minister's activities.

On taking office in 1979, Margaret Thatcher retained the Policy Unit but slimmed down its size. From 1979–82 it was headed by the special adviser John Hoskyns, a former army officer, a businessman who had built up his own computer firm, and an adviser to Conservative Central Office. Up to 1981 he was helped by another special adviser, Norman Strauss, a systems specialist from Unilever, and by one or two civil servants on secondment from their departments. They concentrated on economic, industrial, employment and trade union policies. From time to time they called for advice from individuals outside government, such as academics and businessmen. The placing of civil servants in the Policy Unit was something of an innovation and represents Margaret

Thatcher's greater concern to have the right people near her than for the niceties of administrative protocol. It matched her placing of Miss Stephens in the private office although she was for a time paid by the Conservative party. Rigid barriers crumble at Number 10. It is a place of distinct entities but not rigid demarcations.

As head of the Policy Unit, John Hoskyns was succeeded by Ferdinand Mount, who had been at the Conservative Research Department and was a journalist, working on the *Daily Mail* and as political editor of the *Spectator*. His appointment was thought to signify that Margaret Thatcher wanted advice specifically about the presentation of policy for the coming general election and especially on policy towards the family on which Mr Mount had written a book. Under Mr Mount the Policy Unit expanded in size and scope, for instance acquiring the services of Christopher Monckton from the Conservative 'think tank', the Centre for Policy Studies, and Peter Shipley, from the Conservative Research Department. A more obvious partisan element was implanted in the unit.

In 1980 Margaret Thatcher felt the need to have at Number 10 an adviser to focus on economic issues, to explain to her from an independent and economically impeccable standpoint what was significant, and either to reassure her that the departments were on the right lines or to mount a critique. She appointed Professor Alan Walters, a leading monetarist economist, from Johns Hopkins University in the United States. He was not located in the Policy Unit, because of his seniority and to symbolise his independent status; he was called economic adviser. So successful did this appointment seem to the prime minister that she established two similar positions in different fields where she felt she needed her own advisers. After the Falklands crisis in 1982 she brought to Number 10 as her foreign affairs adviser Sir Anthony Parsons, a former diplomat who had been Britain's representative at the UN during the Falklands war, and as defence affairs adviser she selected Roger Jackling, a civil servant from the Defence Department.

These appointments, and the expansion of the Policy Unit, reflected the more directive and interventionist style of the prime minister. She felt a personal responsibility for the policy of the government. To watch over the work of the separate departments and to monitor issues that crossed departmental boundaries she sought aides working directly to her. The growth of her assistance at Number 10 counterbalanced her elimination of the CPRS which had provided policy advice for the cabinet as a whole, and it may also have been her way of responding to calls that she set up a prime minister's department. She could achieve the substance without the troublesome form.

In 1983 there were further significant changes on the policy advisory side of the prime minister's office. In January Professor Walters returned to the USA, but was retained as a part-time adviser, coming to Britain each month for about a week. Sir Anthony Parsons was replaced in December 1983 as foreign affairs adviser by Sir Percy Cradock, another former diplomat, who had been the ambassador to China and was an expert on the looming problem of the future status of Hong Kong. The defence adviser returned to his department, and his position was not filled. An expansion of aides at Number 10 took place in the Policy Unit. Mr Mount increased its members to nine, including himself. They were young, mainly in their 20s or 30s, and had had experience as civil servants, or in commerce or industry, or in the Conservative Research Department or Centre for Policy Studies. Some in the unit had served in the CPRS, like David Pascall and Robert Young, and one, Oliver Letwin, was the special adviser to the secretary of state for education and science. They specialised in distinct policy areas, and provided a check on what departments were proposing, even initiating ideas themselves; for example, Mr Letwin focused on education and training and John Redwood on nationalised industries. At the end of 1983 Mr Mount left the unit and was replaced as its head by Mr Redwood. He is a fellow of All Souls, a banker, author of books on industrial policy and a defeated Conservative candidate.

When Margaret Thatcher had first taken office she was no enthusiast for special and political advisers and said that she intended to rely for political advice on her ministers, and by implication for policy advice on their departments. At Number 10 she cut down the number and seniority of her political aides and reduced the size of the Policy Unit. Over the period of her term of office, however, she revised her earlier judgement. She increased the political and policy components of her staff in the prime minister's office. Indeed, the current Policy Unit looks like a reconstituted version of that run by Dr Bernard Donoughue for Harold Wilson and James Callaghan.

Between 1979 and 1983 the prime minister's parliamentary private secretary, Ian Gow, achieved a degree of prominence unusual for holders of that position. He acted as the prime minister's eyes, ears and mouth amongst the Conservative backbenchers in the Commons. Margaret Thatcher realised it was important for her not to appear out of touch with her supporters, and although she maintained close personal contact with MPs she depended a great deal on her PPS. Perhaps because she was a woman she needed a gregarious male to consort with his colleagues in ways and places not thought appropriate for a female. More than earlier PPSs, he was active in giving the prime minister political advice at Number 10. For his services he was awarded a place in the government after the general election. His role as PPS was taken over by Michael Alison.

The prime minister also drew on the advice of people who held no position at Downing Street, for instance from Lord Hugh Thomas and Sir Alfred Sherman at the Centre for Policy Studies, who could bring to her their ideas, respond to her queries, or undertake missions on her behalf. Others might help with their particular expertise, advising for instance on her appearance or style of speaking, or assisting in the writing of speeches, such as Sir Ronald Millar, the playwright, or Gordon Reece, the PR specialist.

The way Margaret Thatcher has shaped the flexible elements that make up the prime minister's office to suit her requirements reveals the adaptability of the British system. There has been no need for her to create a prime minister's department to obtain the service she felt she needed. She is the most interventionist prime minister since Lloyd George, and has sought to mould the staff around her to enable her to find out more of what the departments are doing, to scrutinise their activities and to provide other options to their proposals. While she has been strengthening her own personal staff resources, she has weakened those at the disposal of her cabinet colleagues for the performance of their collective deliberations by abolishing the CPRS. So she has tipped the system a little away from collective to presidential government. But the tipping is only slight. The political and policy aides who serve her are few, junior, inexperienced in government and fluctuating. They do not stay for long to assist her. They are not as stable a component as the private office nor any real rival to the formidable array of bureaucratic resources available to ministers in their departments.

References

1. G. W. Jones, *The Prime Minister's Aides*, Hull Papers in Politics No. 6 (Hull: Department of Politics, University of Hull, 1980).
2. 4 April 1979.

4

Margaret Thatcher: The Style of a Prime Minister

ANTHONY KING

Much has been written about Margaret Thatcher's life, personality and policies but relatively little about her prime ministerial style, the way in which she personally does the job. This chapter, focusing on her style, was written shortly after her election victory in June 1983. It therefore deals largely with her first term. Readers may want to compare, for example, her handling of the government's dispute with the miners in 1981 (see p. 120 below) with her handling of the much more serious dispute with the miners that began in February 1984. This chapter describes a prime ministerial style that has great potential strengths but also great potential weaknesses. Part way through her second term, what does the balance appear to be between those strengths and those weaknesses?

Margaret Thatcher is a person who arouses strong feelings, within her own party and in other parties, among the general public, not least among her own cabinet colleagues. Precisely for this reason, dispassionate accounts of her premiership are rare. The desire to praise Thatcher, or to bury her, typically overwhelms the desire to understand how one person, at one time, does one job. This chapter does not seek to judge Margaret Thatcher, to say whether her influence on Britain has been for good or ill; nor does it seek, in the style of the armchair psychoanalyst, to plumb the depths of 'the Thatcher personality'. Rather, it seeks to describe Thatcher's characteristic working methods as prime minister and political leader. There are all sorts of ways of being prime minister. What is Thatcher's way? Given the goals she sets herself, how does she set about achieving them? In the final analysis, are *her* means well adapted to *her* ends?

An Unusual Prime Minister

Fully to appreciate her premiership, it is essential to recognise that Margaret Thatcher is a very unusual prime minister, in two crucial but little-noticed respects. The first is that she is, and always has been, in a minority inside her own party and her own government. The reason is simple. Thatcher holds strong views, especially on economic policy. But she was elected leader of the Conservative party in February 1975 not because she held those views, but largely despite the fact that she held them. A majority of Conservative MPs in the winter of 1974–75 were determined to unseat the then party leader, Edward Heath, and Thatcher was the only one of Heath's former cabinet colleagues with the courage and determination to stand against him. The relatively small number of Tory MPs who shared Thatcher's economic views undoubtedly voted for her, but so did a far larger number of Tory members who saw her chiefly as the instrument of Edward Heath's political destruction. She was the knife in the guillotine that cut off Heath's head; or, as a Tory backbencher put it at the time, 'She was the one who belled the cat'. Thatcher, in other words, was not elected primarily as a Thatcherite. To this day, while most Conservative MPs broadly sympathise with the prime minister's aims and are prepared to stand by her publicly, it is doubtful whether more than two or three dozen of them fully share her monetarist convictions. Most prime ministers represent a broad consensus of opinion, or at least majority opinion, within their party. Thatcher is considerably more isolated.[1]

The second way in which Thatcher is unusual is related to the first. Most British prime ministers have a few overarching policy aims, such as the maintenance of world peace or the restoration of full employment, and most of them are in sympathy with the general purposes of their party. Otherwise, the goals of most incumbents of Number 10 are much more narrowly political. They want to remain in Number 10 and/or keep their cabinet united and/or hold their party together and/or win the next election. They do not, in the majority of cases, have important policy aims peculiar to themselves. To be sure, the appeasement policy of the late 1930s was Neville Chamberlain's personal policy, and both Harold Macmillan and Edward Heath were personally committed to the Common Market; but examples like these spring to mind precisely because they are so unusual. And even commitments like Chamberlain's to appeasement and Heath's to the Common Market were in a single field of policy. They did not encompass the whole range.

Margaret Thatcher is different. She is probably unique among 20th-century British prime ministers in having a policy agenda – a set of views and a set of priorities – that is peculiarly her own and is in no way merely an emanation of her government or party. She feels strongly about the substance of policy. She has policy aims in a large number of fields – taxation public spending, privatisation, law and order, the welfare state, relations with the Soviet Union, defence, the Common Market, and so on – and, even when she does not have fully fledged aims, she certainly, much more often than not, has opinions. Moreover, these aims and opinions are *hers*. Harold Wilson, to take the extreme case, sought to be little more than the Labour party writ large; wherever was the balance of forces within the Labour party, there was Wilson. Thatcher, by contrast, is by no means just the Conservative party writ large. Victory for her party is not synonymous with victory for her; she has a clear, and personal, sense of the direction in which she wishes to lead the party. She describes herself, rightly, as a 'conviction politician', but she is also a 'substance politician', someone more concerned with arriving at the right outcome than with how that outcome is reached. If she often seeks to impose her point of view, it is because she actually has a point of view – and because her point of view matters more to her than preserving party unity or enjoying a quiet life. To repeat: this makes

Thatcher unusual, probably unique, among prime ministers of this century.

If Margaret Thatcher is unusual in being in a minority in her own party, and in the strength and range of her substantive political opinions, she resembles more closely her predecessors in Downing Street in having had a number of formative political experiences. In Harold Macmillan's case, they were the carnage of the First World War and the depression of the 1930s. In Harold Wilson's case, they were the Bevanite controversies of the 1950s and Hugh Gaitskell's aggressive style of Labour party leadership. Thatcher's formative experiences all occurred during the premiership of Edward Heath. There were three of them, and it is important to take careful note of each.

The first related to the famous U-turns in the economic policy of the Heath government that took place in 1971 and 1972.[2] The Conservatives under Heath had been returned to power pledged to roll back the economic power of the state, to give private enterprise its head, to give free rein to market forces, not to bale out private companies that got themselves into difficulties and, above all, not to try to control wages ('We utterly reject', the 1970 Conservative manifesto had declared, 'the philosophy of compulsory wage control'). But, within little more than two years of taking office, the Heath administration had effectively abandoned all of these commitments. The Rolls-Royce aeroengine company had been nationalised, the 1972 Industry Act had given the government sweeping new powers to assist private industry, and towards the end of 1972 the government, contrary to its pledges, had introduced the most draconian incomes policy in Britain's peacetime history. The economic wisdom of these changes of policy could be, and still can be, debated (though Margaret Thatcher was subsequently to form her own views); but of their political consequences there could be no doubt. By making Heath appear feeble and vacillating, and by demoralising many of his followers, they seriously weakened his position as party leader. Furthermore, they did not lead to victory at the next election. Far from it: the Conservatives not only lost the February 1974 election but suffered one of the most dramatic reversals in British electoral history. Thatcher drew the obvious inference.

Determination might not bring success; but lack of determination was almost certain to result in failure. If she ever became prime minister, there would be no U-turns (or at least no U-turns that could plausibly be described as such).

Secondly, Thatcher observed that Heath paid a heavy price for permitting himself to become isolated from his followers in the House of Commons. Heath enjoyed the company of a few close intimates, normally cabinet colleagues, with whom he discussed policy and when in power arranged cabinet agendas and conclusions; but he was otherwise an aloof man, with little small talk and, so far as anyone could tell, no interest whatever in his fellow Tory MPs, let alone their wives and families. He was the opposite of gregarious, and almost every Conservative MP still loves to tell the story of how Ted Heath snubbed him socially, or failed to remember his name, or by his mere presence caused a promising conversation to come juddering to a halt. The result was that, while Heath had a small circle of intimates, he lacked a larger circle of friendly acquaintances, politicians who might stand by him – or at least be loath to desert him – in some hour of need. More important, Heath apparently did not realise that, in addition to being friendly with his supporters, it was in his interest to listen to what they had to say. They, too, were members of parliament. They, too, had opinions. They wanted to be listened to, strongly believed that they were entitled to be listened to. Any leader who failed to listen to them ran the serious risk of forfeiting their support, as Heath ultimately did after the election defeats in 1974. Thatcher observed all this, and learned. From the moment she succeeded Heath as party leader, she operated on the principle: 'They elected you. They can un-elect you. Never lose touch with them'.

Margaret Thatcher's third formative experience arose out of the miners' strike of the winter of 1973–74.[3] Heath had taken on the miners – only one of a number of trade unions with formidable political muscle – and had lost. Not only had he lost in the sense that the miners eventually secured almost all of the pay rise that they had been demanding; not only had he lost in the sense that the miners' victory destroyed his incomes policy; but, as a direct consequence of the miners' strike and the early election that he called in an effort to counter it, he had lost the premiership itself, to be followed a year later by his loss of the party leadership. However unintentionally, however inadvertently, Heath had found himself pursuing a policy of confrontation. He had paid for this policy with his political life. Thatcher was determined not to repeat the experience. We shall describe in more detail later in the chapter the impact that the miners' strike, and other incidents like it, had on her thinking.

Margaret Thatcher had these three formative experiences – the U-turns, Heath's failure to listen, the 1973–74 miners' strike – all within a relatively short space of time, and they were all associated with the Heath government. It is, however, worth noting that the three experiences were quite separate: she could have had any one of them without either of the others. To learn to listen, to learn to avoid making U-turns, and to learn to avoid confronting powerful groups like the miners are to learn three different things. It says much for Thatcher's keenness as a student of practical politics that she should have drawn such wide-ranging lessons from a strictly limited experience, only three and a half years, of cabinet office.

Three Premierships, Not One

In the aftermath of the Falklands campaign and the Conservatives' easy victory in the June 1983 general election, it is tempting to see Margaret Thatcher's first term of office as an undifferentiated whole, with the prime minister as dominant from the beginning as she was to become later. To do so, however, would be to extrapolate her triumphant present (as it seemed in the autumn of 1983) back into her more troubled past. In fact, Thatcher's first term 1979–83 fell into three distinct phases.[4] Her leadership style proved more successful in some of them than others.

The first phase lasted from her election victory in May 1979 until roughly the autumn of 1981 and is a period of her life that the prime minister would probably prefer to forget. It was during this phase that she attracted such unflattering nicknames as 'Attila the Hen' and (worse) 'The Immaculate Misconception'. Apart from Lord Carrington's successful negotiation of a satisfactory settlement in Rhodesia, almost nothing seemed to go right for her and her administration (and even the Rhodesian settlement was condemned as a sell-out by a substantial section of Tory backbench opinion). The government had been elected to cut taxes and interest rates, to slash public expenditure, to cut government borrowing, to reduce the rate of growth of money supply and, above all, to bring down the rate of inflation. Instead, between 1979 and the late months of 1981, taxation increased both absolutely and as a proportion of gross domestic product (GDP), interest rates soared to record levels, public expenditure (like taxation) rose in both absolute and proportional terms, public sector borrowing went up instead of down, the rate of growth of money supply hugely exceeded the government's targets, and the rate of inflation, far from falling in the first instance, actually doubled in the course of Thatcher's first year in office, from 11 to 22 per cent. On top of all this, Britain's rate of economic growth fell to zero (and in some months was actually negative), bankruptcies in the private sector multiplied while the government poured huge sums of money into public sector industries such as coal, steel and cars (British Leyland); and unemployment rose seemingly inexorably, from 5 per cent of the labour force in June 1979, Thatcher's first full month in office, to 12 per cent in the period October–December 1981.[5] 'By their fruits shall ye know them': the fruits of Thatcher's first two and a half years in Downing Street tasted bitter, not least to many Conservative MPs.

Hardly surprisingly under the circumstances, the government's economic difficulties were accompanied by – some would say partly caused by – deep divisions in the cabinet. On coming to office, the new prime minister had had little choice but to appoint a cabinet in which her own staunchest supporters – those who shared both her economic views and her determination to put them into effect – were in a small minority. To have appointed a purely Thatcherite administration at the outset would have transformed many senior Conservatives, holdovers from the Heath era, from half-hearted friends into whole-hearted enemies, and would also have sown doubt and suspicion among those Tory MPs – probably a majority – who, while perfectly willing to give the Thatcher experiment a reasonable chance to succeed, were by

no means persuaded that it actually would. In any case, few
Thatcherites by 1979 had acquired the requisite experience
and authority for cabinet office.

Conscious of her minority position, the new prime minister
set about constructing her administration in an unusually
collegial manner. William Whitelaw, Lord Carrington and
Humphrey Atkins, the outgoing chief whip, were closeted with
her as names and offices were traded, and on one or two key
appointments the prime minister permitted herself to be
overruled. Certainly Whitelaw and Carrington, men of the old
regime, scarcely concealed their disapproval of the new
economic doctrines and of many of the young meritocrats who
espoused them, while Atkins played a role peculiar to the Tory
party, influencing junior appointments in a way unknown on
the Labour side. More than that, cabinet ministers were left
free to choose some of their own subordinates, with the result
that here too a number of Thatcherites were vetoed. The most
that the prime minister could do at this stage was ensure that,
in a cabinet of 22, four of her strongest supporters – Sir Geoffrey
Howe, John Biffen, Sir Keith Joseph and John Nott – were
given the four most important economic posts, chancellor of the
exchequer, chief secretary to the treasury, secretary of state for
industry and secretary of state for trade.

The upshot, in this first phase of the government, was that
the cabinet was deeply divided on almost every aspect of
economic policy and that the prime minister frequently failed
to get her way. She and her loyal group of economic ministers
succeeded in controlling financial policy in the narrow sense –
taxation and interest rates – but they were defeated again and
again over such matters as public spending cuts and state
subsidies to the nationalised industries; and the man she had
reluctantly appointed secretary of state for employment, James
Prior, thwarted her every attempt to persuade the cabinet to
introduce measures to curb trade unions tougher than those
envisaged in the party's manifesto. The avowedly Thatcherite
1981 budget was unacceptable to many ministers. When it was
revealed to the cabinet on the morning of budget day, it
provoked immediate criticism from ministers and then open
dissent in the lobbies later in the day. The 1981 revolt
continued throughout the summer, with even Lord

Thorneycroft, Thatcher's own choice as party chairman, siding with the dissidents. She removed him before the October party conference, where it was reckoned that his known scepticism would have a detrimental effect on the party's morale.

Cabinet meetings during this period were often fraught, personal relations between Thatcher and several of her senior ministers were not good, and accounts, often detailed, of the cabinet's internal dissensions appeared frequently in the press. A sample of newspaper headlines during 1980 and 1981 captures the mood of that difficult time:

> Cabinet at bay
> Why Tories must halt the charge of Margaret's Light Brigade
> Thatcher Bill blocked by minister
> Maggie loses fight on cuts
> Can the Tories hope to win again?
> Can the image-makers put her back in the running?
> Portrait of a prime minister at bay.[6]

Even without Lord Thorneycroft, the party conference of October 1981 probably marked the nadir of Thatcher's first term of office. The bars and lounges of Blackpool's hotels were full of disgruntled ministers and backbench MPs openly expressing their anger, frustration and dismay.

In fact, however, although few noticed it at the time, a second, more confident phase of Margaret Thatcher's premiership had already begun. It lasted from the autumn of 1981 until April of the following year. During this phase, although unemployment continued to rise, several other economic indicators began to look healthier. Public spending and the money supply were gradually brought under control, interest rates started to come down, and, best of all, the rate of inflation, having peaked at 22 per cent in April and May 1980, fell steadily until it reached 12 per cent in the spring of 1981. Single-figure inflation was confidently – and, as it turned out, accurately – predicted for 1982.

At the same time, the prime minister began gradually to win the economic argument inside the government. In one sense, she, Howe, Biffen and the others had never really been threatened; there was no way in which hard-pressed ministers in non-economic departments like Agriculture, Education, Defence and the Foreign Office could devise a plausible alternative economic strategy, let alone impose it on a reluctant prime minister and chancellor of the exchequer. But, in another sense, the very existence of a plausible alternative strategy, wherever it came from, would have provided the Tory dissidents with a rallying ground and might well have put the Thatcherites on the defensive, forcing them to make concessions. In the event, however, no such alternative strategy ever materialised. The 'wets', as the Thatcherites dubbed their critics, exploiting a convenient public-school term of abuse, could do little more than resist this or that spending cut *ad hoc* and go round the country making unhappy-sounding speeches. No one ever showed how higher public spending, or a more relaxed approach to the money supply, could create more jobs without at the same time sucking in large quantities of imports and refuelling inflation. The view gradually gained ground that, however unsatisfactory the government's existing policy might be, there was no real alternative to it and that, whatever else Thatcher was doing, she at least deserved credit for educating the British public into the hard facts of economic life. The longer the Thatcherites stuck to their economic guns, the harder it became to dislodge them – and the smaller the number of Tory MPs who even wanted to try.

Thatcher further strengthened her position at the beginning of phase two of the administration by promoting several of her own people within the government and by demoting or sacking several of the wets. Norman St John-Stevas, once a Thatcher loyalist, had been sacked earlier in the year, having allegedly (he denied it) been even more indiscreet than other ministers and having made too many jokes at the prime minister's expense ('The Immaculate Misconception' was naturally traced to him since he was a prominent Roman Catholic).[7] John Biffen succeeded St John-Stevas as Leader of the House of Commons, Biffen in turn being succeeded as chief secretary by another Thatcher supporter, Leon Brittan.

But the main changes came in September 1981. They brought about – as they were intended to – a major shift in the balance of power within the cabinet. The prime minister dropped three well-known wets, Sir Ian Gilmour, Lord Soames and Mark Carlisle, and brought into the cabinet three men on whom she could rely, Norman Tebbit, Nigel Lawson and Cecil Parkinson. Equally important, James Prior was shifted from a post where he could get in the prime minister's way on economic matters, Employment, to a post where he could not, Northern Ireland. Prior's eventual acceptance of Northern Ireland, although he had told everyone within earshot that he was extremely reluctant to move, substantially weakened his position. Having been one of Thatcher's more resourceful opponents, he suddenly looked like somebody who could be pushed around. Taken together, the effect of the 1981 cabinet changes was partly numerical; the Thatcherites' strength in the cabinet increased from four to seven, with all of the important economic posts in Thatcherite hands. But it was also moral; the changes signalled that the prime minister was ready to punish dissenters and that there was to be no fundamental shift in economic policy.

The departure of Lord Carrington, the foreign secretary, some months later tilted the balance in the cabinet still further in Thatcher's direction. Carrington had never openly opposed the prime minister on domestic matters, but then he had never actively supported her either. Indeed the Thatcherites from the beginning had regarded him with special suspicion. He had never knocked on doors or had to deal with constituency mail. He had held a 'coalface' cabinet appointment only once, and then very briefly at the start of 1974, when as energy secretary he had been instrumental in persuading Heath to take on the miners and to call the disastrous February 1974 general election. Moreover, in Thatcherite eyes, he did not know how the House of Commons worked – he had never been an MP – and cared even less, a point proved to their satisfaction by his inept handling of the backbench 1922 Committee following the Falklands invasion.

The position in the government in the early months of 1982 was thus one of uneasy compromise. The civil war of 1979–81 was over. The Thatcherites and the surviving wets had tacitly agreed that they could live together, and talk of replacing the prime minister before the next election, of which there had been so much only a few months earlier, largely subsided. All the same, Thatcher's own position was still in no sense command-ing. She was forced to yield to her critics' demand, following the unpopular 1981 budget, that major issues of economic policy be discussed in the full cabinet; and scepticism about both her and her policies was ready to resurface at any moment. At the end of this second phase of her administration, Margaret Thatcher, although she had made progress, was still a prime minister on trial.

Then the Falklands war – the Argentine invasion, Thatcher's resolute response, Britain's victory – changed everything. It proved what some had doubted, that she was capable of performing effectively under the most extreme pressure. It vindicated her posture as a leader who could be counted on to take hard decisions and see them through to success. It made her for the time being a national hero. The result was that she had, for the first time, an opportunity to take charge of the whole government and bend it to her will. As Simon Jenkins put it in *The Times*:

> From the moment the task force sailed, Mrs Thatcher emerged from the morass of factional government to achieve an extraordinary dominance over her colleagues and the government machine . . . She was always the central driving force: it was 'she who must be persuaded' on any course of action . . . This sense of Mrs Thatcher as a prime minister in absolute command – a command she never achieved during 1979–81 – was communicated swiftly both to those involved in the war and to the wider public.[8]

Following the Falklands, Thatcher could still on occasion be defeated in cabinet, but her position of overall dominance was never again in doubt. No one questioned her authority. She was respected as she had never been respected before. Her air was one of supreme confidence and success. This third phase of the Thatcher premiership was to last up to and beyond the 1983 election.

Popular Responses

One important element affecting any prime minister's influ-

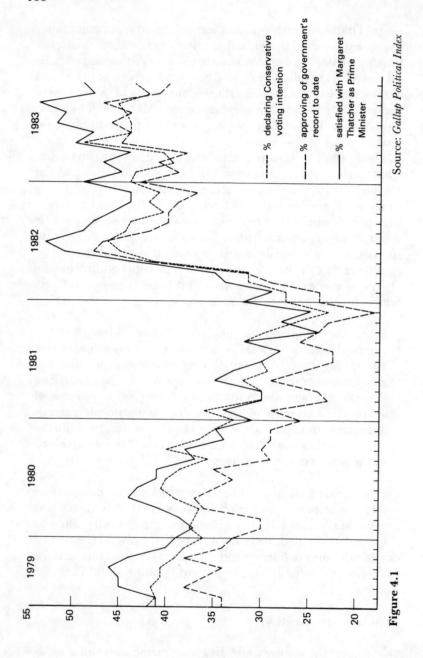

--- % declaring Conservative voting intention

-- % approving of government's record to date

— % satisfied with Margaret Thatcher as Prime Minister

Figure 4.1

Source: *Gallup Political Index*

ence is his own standing, and his government's standing, in the eyes of the general public. Other things being equal, the greater a prime minister's public prestige – or, more precisely, the greater a prime minister's public prestige is thought to be by his cabinet colleagues – the greater is likely to be his capacity to bend those colleagues to his will (always assuming that he has a will). A prime minister thought to be leading his party to electoral disaster is likely to find that his colleagues increasingly question his judgement and are reluctant to acknowledge his authority. By contrast, a prime minister believed to be an election winner will almost certainly find that outside prestige can be translated into inside influence. Every prime minister's standing with the general public is a factor operating constantly in the background, setting the tone and defining the limits of what the politicians in his immediate environment are prepared to do for him – or to him.[9]

Given the importance of public prestige, Figure 4.1 tells a fascinating story about Margaret Thatcher's first term. The three lines on the graph – all based on Gallup Poll data – plot, first, the percentage of voters saying in each month between June 1979 and November 1983 that they were satisfied with Thatcher as prime minister; second, the percentage saying that they would vote Conservative at an early general election; and third, the percentage saying that they approved of the government's record to date. Predictably, the three indicators of the prime minister's and the government's standing, although separate in theory and to some extent in fact, track broadly together. Someone satisfied with the prime minister is more likely to favour the prime minister's party; someone who approves of the government's record is more likely to be satisfied with the prime minister; and so on. Nevertheless, as can be seen, Thatcher's personal standing was somewhat higher than that of her party and government during most of her first year in Number 10 and again after Britain's victory in the Falklands.

What is significant about the figure, however, is the close correspondence between it and the three phases of the Thatcher premiership that we have just been describing. In phase one, especially from the spring of 1980 onwards, the standings of prime minister, party and government alike – none of which had ever been very high by the standards of the 1950s and early 1960s – declined steadily and at times sharply until, in the last months of 1981, they hit an all-time low. This was the period when the government was failing to achieve any of its economic objectives and when dissension in the government and the Tory party was rife. Then, in phase two, Thatcher's own standing, and those of her party and government, improved to a limited degree (though the position just before the Falklands invasion was no better than it had been a year before). Finally, in phase three, following the invasion, the war and the British victory, the standings of prime minister, Conservative party and government all but took off, soaring to heights never reached even in the aftermath of the 1979 election victory. The events in the South Atlantic, together with the government's increasing success in the battle against inflation, transformed Thatcher's and the government's standing in the eyes of the public. That fact in itself helped to consolidate Thatcher's position within her administration.

The sheer scale of the shifts in public attitudes towards Thatcher – from, as the figure shows, a satisfaction rating of 46 per cent in October 1979 to one of 24 per cent in October 1981 to one of 52 per cent only nine months later in July 1982 – is mainly the result of external events (the state of the economy, foreign affairs, etc.); but it probably owes something, too, to the unusual clarity of Thatcher's public image and to the pro-foundly divergent responses her image evokes. From time to time the Gallup Poll asks its respondents to say whether they think each of a series of short statements ('in touch with the people', 'takes moderate positions', etc.) applies to each of a number of prominent politicians. The statements take the form of paired opposites, so that 'sincere', for example, is paired with 'not sincere'. Gallup's findings for February 1983 are set out in Table 4.1, which compares Thatcher's public image at that time – about a year after the Falklands war – with those of seven Labour and Liberal/SDP Alliance politicians: Michael Foot, Tony Benn, Denis Healey, David Steel, Roy Jenkins, Shirley Williams and David Owen. (Francis Pym, Thatcher's then foreign secretary, was also included in the original Gallup data, but his image was too faint and blurred to warrant inclusion here.)

Table 4.1 testifies, if testimony were needed, to the strength of Thatcher's image. Not only did large numbers of people apply a large proportion of the statements to her, but their responses were in the great majority of cases unequivocal. When compared with the other seven politicians, she was almost invariably placed either towards the top or near the bottom of the range; she was seldom placed anywhere in the middle. Fully 67 per cent of Gallup's respondents thought she had a 'strong forceful personality'; a miniscule 2 per cent thought she was 'weak'. Far more people, 43 per cent, thought she was a 'good speaker' than thought the same of anyone else; only 6 per cent thought she was a 'poor speaker' (compared with the 43 per cent who thought the same of Michael Foot).

But, although Thatcher's image was strong, it was by no means overwhelmingly favourable. On the contrary, if she elicited an unusually large number of positive responses, she also elicited an unusually large number of negative ones. Unlike David Steel, for example, who is seen by the British public in an almost uniformly favourable light, or Tony Benn, who is seen in a uniformly unfavourable light (see Table 4.1), Thatcher's personal and political style produces sharply different reactions in different people. In the language of statistics, attitudes towards her are distributed 'bimodally' – she has both admirers and detractors in large numbers. The top half of Table 4.1 makes this clear. In 1983 more people said of Thatcher than of any other prominent politician that she 'put the country's interests ahead of politics'; but at the same time more people said of her than of any other politician that she was 'too much of a politician'. Similarly, as Table 4.1 shows, she scored high on both sincerity and lack of sincerity, on being in touch with the people and not being in touch with them, on having the qualities of a good prime minister and on not having them. People are in no doubt where they stand on Margaret Thatcher; but they do not all stand in the same place. Comparable data for all periods of her prime ministership are not available, but it seems likely that, among substantial numbers of voters, attitudes towards her are as volatile as they are strongly felt.

One further point concerning Thatcher's standing with the public should be made. It is widely believed, in other countries

TABLE 4.1 *Personality images of eight prominent politicians, February 1983 (% saying each statement applies, and rank order)*

	Thatcher %	Thatcher rank order	Foot %	Foot rank order	Benn %	Benn rank order	Healey %	Healey rank order	Steel %	Steel rank order	Jenkins %	Jenkins rank order	Williams %	Williams rank order	Owen %	Owen rank order
Puts country's interests ahead of politics	26	1	9	3	4	7	7	5	14	2	6	6	8	4=	8	4=
Too much of a politician	27	1	13	4	26	2	11	5	7	7=	15	3	8	6	7	7=
Sincere	28	1	13	5=	14	4=	14	4=	27	2	10	6	22	3	13	5=
Not sincere	25	2	22	3	29	1	13	5	9	8	15	4	10	7	12	6
In touch with the people	27	2	13	4=	9	6	15	3	29	1=	10	5	29	1=	13	4=
Not in touch with the people	39	1	30	3	38	2	20	4=	13	6=	20	4=	13	6=	15	5
Has the qualities for a good prime minister	39	1	7	6	5	7	16	3	27	2	9	5	11	4=	11	4=
Hasn't the qualities for a good prime minister	20	3=	54	1	41	2	15	4=	12	5	20	3=	20	3=	15	4=
A strong forceful personality	67	1	8	6	21	2	13	4	11	5	6	8	17	3	7	7
A weak personality	2	5	40	1	8	3=	6	4=	8	3=	13	2	6	4=	8	3=
Is a good speaker	43	1	12	7	23	3	20	5	33	2	13	6	21	4=	21	4=
Is a poor speaker	6	6	43	1	12	3	9	4	4	8	14	2	8	5	5	7
Cold and distant	33	1	11	3	21	2	8	5	6	7	10	4	4	8	7	6
Warm and friendly	7	5	6	6	4	8	12	3	22	2	5	7	26	1	10	4
Takes extreme positions	29	2	9	3	50	1	4	5	2	6=	2	6=	5	4	2	6=
Takes moderate positions	6	6	11	5	3	7	21	3	30	1	23	2=	15	4	23	2=

Source: *Gallup Political Index*, March 1983.

as well as in Britain, that Thatcher is an unusually popular prime minister and that her popularity with the public is an important source of her authority within the government. This belief is certainly correct, but only of the post-Falklands period. Before the Falklands war, Thatcher was not only unpopular in an absolute sense (see Figure 4.1), she was in fact very nearly the most unpopular prime minister in modern British history. The Gallup Poll in 1945 began to ask voters, infrequently to begin with, then every month, the standard question, 'Are you satisfied or dissatisfied with . . . as prime minister?'. Table 4.2 sets out, for each prime minister's period of office since the war, the average proportion of Gallup's respondents offering an

TABLE 4.2   *Average satisfaction ratings of postwar prime ministers*

		average satisfaction rating[a] %	*number of surveys on which rating based*
Clement Attlee	1945–51	46.8	29
Winston Churchill	1951–55	51.7	9
Sir Anthony Eden	1955–57	57.0	16
Harold Macmillan	1957–63	51.0	68
Sir Alec Douglas-Home	1963–64	44.4	12
Harold Wilson	1964–70	46.1	66
Edward Heath	1970–74	37.5	42
Harold Wilson	1974–76	45.9	24
James Callaghan	1976–79	46.4	37
Margaret Thatcher	1979–83	39.0	48
Pre-Falklands[b]		36.0	35
Post-Falklands[c]		47.2	13

[a]   The rating is arrived at by summing the percentages of respondents saying 'satisfied' in response to the question 'Are you satisfied or dissatisfied with . . . . as prime minister?', and dividing the total by the number of occasions on which the question was asked during each prime minister's term of office. The question has been asked every month only since February 1960. Between April 1955 and January 1960 it was asked in more months than not. Before April 1955 it was asked only sporadically.

[b]   June 1979–April 1982.

[c]   May 1982–June 1983.

Sources: Norman Webb and Robert Wybrow, *The Gallup Report, 1980* (London: Sphere Books, 1981); Norman Webb and Robert Wybrow, *The Gallup Report, 1981* (London: Sphere Books, 1982); *Gallup Political Index*.

affirmative, 'satisfied' response to this question. In addition, Thatcher's first term has been divided into a pre-Falklands phase (June 1979–April 1982) and a post-Falklands phase (May 1982–June 1983). The entries in Table 4.2 largely speak for themselves. Only Heath among postwar prime ministers has had a lower overall satisfaction rating than Thatcher; but Thatcher's low overall rating conceals the remarkable surge of public support for her that took place during and after the Falklands war. Before the war, the prime minister's ministerial and parliamentary colleagues saw her as someone who might well drag them down to defeat at the next election; after the war, they saw her as someone who would almost certainly lead them to victory. The gain to her authority was immense. 'Thatcher *victrix*' is a post-Falklands phenomenon.

The Prime Minister as Leader

So much for the record of Margaret Thatcher's first term. The question now arises: how has she comported herself as prime minister, both during the three phases of her first term, and in general? Is there anything distinctive about the way in which this individual does this job? It turns out that indeed there is.[10]

All British prime ministers, like all American presidents and German chancellors, are conventionally described as 'political leaders', the clear implication being that their task consists of determining the direction in which their government shall go and then of persuading their governmental colleagues to follow them. The image conjured up is of a scout master leading a troop, or a choir master leading a choir. Leaders lead. A leader who did not lead would be a contradiction in terms.

This image, however, is in fact false to the way in which most British prime ministers comport themselves most of the time. There are two reasons for this. The first has already been referred to: most British prime ministers are not in the position of having a large number of aims, personal to themselves, across a wide range of fields. Their preferences are very largely those of their party and the majority of their cabinet colleagues. Thus, Attlee did not 'lead' his government on the issue of giving independence to India: that was the direction in which the Labour party and the postwar Labour government wanted to go anyway. Likewise, the Conservatives in the 1950s were not 'led' by Churchill, Eden or Macmillan to cut taxes and relax the controls on British industry: party, government and the mood of the time were at one. Acts of genuine leadership, in which prime ministers try to steer their cabinets in directions in which they might not otherwise go, stand out precisely because of their comparative rarity. Such an act of leadership was Macmillan's over Europe in the early 1960s, when he set about persuading the Tory party and the cabinet, against all their instincts, that Britain should seek to join the EEC; another, more negative in character, was Harold Wilson's leadership of his first government in resisting, for as long as he could, the devaluation of sterling. But such episodes are not the norm. Heath's cabinet was so united that it did not require leadership in this sense. Wilson was usually content to count heads round the cabinet table. Callaghan in his cabinet took the occasional initiative – for example, over educational standards – but generally concerned himself, inside the administration, with keeping his colleagues out of trouble and refereeing intra-cabinet disputes. If prime ministers actually were 'leaders' in the popular sense of that term, there should have been more policy differences between, say, the Macmillan and Home Conservative administrations, or the Wilson and Callaghan Labour administrations. In fact, there were almost none.

The second reason why British prime ministers are leaders who so seldom lead relates to their position within their own governments. British prime ministers cannot take many decisions entirely on their own; most of the time, they have to carry their cabinets – or at least their senior colleagues – with them. Moreover, they do not enjoy security of tenure; in the back of their own minds, and everybody else's, is the thought that a prime minister who loses his party's confidence, or seems to be about to lead his party to defeat, can be got rid of (however difficult it may be to get rid of him in practice). It follows that a prime minister who takes a personal policy initiative in cabinet, and who sees that initiative rebuffed by the cabinet, suffers not one defeat but two. He *both* fails to achieve that specific policy objective *and*, simultaneously, suffers a diminution of his authority as prime minister, by however small an amount on any single occasion. Each defeat makes another defeat more likely. Each is a demonstration of the prime minister's political vulnerability. Not surprisingly, most prime ministers take few policy initiatives of this kind; and, when they do, they usually make sure in advance that they can count on their colleagues' backing.

Not so Thatcher. Indeed it would be hard to imagine a prime ministerial style more different from that of the majority of her predecessors than Margaret Thatcher's. She is in politics, as she often says, not 'to be' but 'to do', not to preside over Britain's economic decline but to try to reverse that decline. She is by temperament and political instinct an activist. However, she found herself in a minority in her own cabinet in her first two or three years in Number 10 – and was still in a minority, though a considerably larger one, even after the 1983 general election. After all, as we saw earlier, she was elected Conservative leader, not because of her economic views but, if anything, in spite of them. She therefore had no choice, given her aims and determination, but to lead in an unusually forthright, assertive manner. Partly this was a matter of her personality; she is a forthright and assertive person. But it was at least as much a matter of the objective situation in which she found herself. She was forced to behave like an outsider for the simple reason that she was one.

Her approach manifested itself most strikingly at meetings of ministers. Most prime ministers tend to play a waiting game in cabinet and cabinet committees. They encourage the minister or ministers most centrally concerned with an issue to introduce the discussion and then intervene themselves only at a fairly late stage. The aim is to see whether a consensus emerges around the table. If one does, that settles the matter unless the prime minister has some particular reason for expressing a contrary view. If no consensus emerges, even amongst the more important ministers present, then the prime minister may well come in and try to steer the final decision in one direction or another. Prime ministers may, of course, influence the discussion by the order in which they ask ministers to speak, by the tenor of the questions they ask, and so on; and they may well have nobbled one or more of their cabinet colleagues beforehand. But typically, except on a few major issues about which they feel strongly, their approach tends to be cautious and circumspect. Thatcher, by all accounts, operates in a totally different manner. She states her views at the outset, or lets them be known. Often, unusual in a prime minister, she thinks aloud. She interrupts ministers with whom she disagrees and insists on standing and fighting her corner. Unlike most prime ministers, she does not merely chair cabinet discussions; she is an active participant in them. More often than not, she dominates them.[11]

This technique must ensure that the prime minister frequently gets her way when she would otherwise not have done; other things being equal, most ministers would much rather be on the prime minister's side than anywhere else. But it also ensures that she is frequently defeated in cabinet – and is seen to be defeated. Indeed Thatcher probably finds herself on the losing side of arguments in the cabinet more often than any other prime minister in this century. In February 1980, during the national steel strike of that year, she failed in an attempt to persuade Prior to bring in a one-clause bill to ban secondary picketing. In November of the same year the cabinet forced Thatcher and Howe to raise taxes by refusing to accept public spending cuts on anything like the scale they were demanding (at one point, the social services secretary Patrick Jenkin, torpedoed a proposal to cut the real value of old age pensions by quoting to the cabinet the text of a television interview in which the prime minister had promised that she would never cut pensions).[12] In mid-1981, as we saw earlier, she was forced to yield to cabinet pressure for full-dress discussions on economic policy. In July 1982, even after the Falklands victory, the wets overcame prime ministerial objections to a £500 million package for aiding the jobless. A few weeks later, after what was said to be 'a monumental row' in the cabinet, the Central Policy Review Staff's controversial report on the national health service was shelved.[13] None of these events, however, caused the prime minister in any way to alter her style.

This unusual insistence on being the active leader of the government – on leading it, as it were, from outside rather than inside – manifests itself in another, rather curious way: in the prime minister's penchant for talking about the government as though she were not a member of it. The customary pronoun used by prime ministers when speaking about their own government is 'we'; Thatcher's pronoun is usually 'we', but often 'they'. 'They' are making life difficult for her; 'they' are having to be persuaded; 'they' are too concerned with defending the interests of their own departments. The language is not typically British. It is more like that used by American presidents when speaking about Congress. It is significant that the prime minister thinks in this way of her own cabinet as being, in effect, another branch of government. And, just as American presidents have to put up with hostility from Congress, so Thatcher has to put up with her not always amenable cabinet colleagues.

Respecting Power, Weighing It

Margaret Thatcher thus leads from the front. She stamps her foot, she raises her voice. For a British prime minister, she is extraordinarily assertive. Given this element in her style, it might be supposed that Thatcher was a rash politician, given to rushing in, acting on impulse, taking uncalculated risks. But nothing could be further from the truth. Thatcher is in fact a remarkably cautious politician. Not only is she cautious, but she respects power and has an unusually well-developed capacity for weighing it, for seeing who has it and who has not, for calculating who can damage her and who cannot. She is often described as an emotional person; in her ability to weigh power, she is more like a precision instrument.

One obvious illustration of this point is her handling of cabinet appointments. She probably hoped from the beginning to be able to reduce the proportion of non-Thatcherites in her administration. Certainly the behaviour of several of them – Sir Ian Gilmour in February 1980 delivered a scarcely-veiled public attack on the government's economic policies under the guise of a lecture on 'Conservatism' – irritated her intensely. But some of those who were wet in the political sense were not at all wet in the temperamental sense: if sacked from the government, they could, and would, mount a formidable campaign against her policies from the back benches. She was therefore careful to pick off only those whom she calculated would not make a nuisance of themselves. St John-Stevas went first. An amusing but gentle aesthete, he would shed a tear or two but would not cause real trouble. Next went Gilmour, Soames and Carlisle. Soames was safely lodged in the House of Lords, Carlisle's was a rather recessive personality. So no trouble from them. To sack Gilmour was to take a marginally greater risk, since he had something of a backbench following; still, he would probably go off and write a book. Then, following the 1983 election, she dismissed David Howell, the transport secretary, and Francis Pym, the foreign secretary. Howell was actually close to her philosophically but had a reputation for being indecisive. Pym, long regarded as a possible future Tory leader, was potentially much more dangerous, and, but for that, he probably would have been sacked at least two years earlier for resisting cuts in defence spending. The expectation in his case was that he would be disarmed by his loyalty to the party, his lack of economic knowledge and his somewhat fatalistic personality.

Thatcher thus sacked ministers, not according to how much they disagreed with her but according to how weak they were – and how strong she was.[14] There were two other men in the cabinet whom she would probably have loved to get rid of, James Prior and Peter Walker, both of whom did little to conceal their distaste for monetarist economics or their dislike of her personally; but, if either of them went, they would certainly not go quietly and would become a focus for discontent amongst Conservative MPs. So they stayed. Even so, the prime minister, carefully taking the measure of each, neutralised Prior by sending him to Northern Ireland and Walker by relegating him to relatively minor posts, first at Agriculture, then at Energy. Measuring the political power of others was important to her. As of the autumn of 1983, she had not made any mistakes.

Thatcher's careful handling of her cabinet changes is well known. Less widely apreciated is the extreme circumspection that she and her government have shown in their dealings with powerful trade unions. The lessons of Heath's confrontation with the miners in the winter of 1973–74 were not merely learnt; they were studied carefully. Before being ousted as party leader, Heath had commissioned a report from Lord Carrington concerning the ability of a Conservative government, or any government, to resist the claims of militant trade unions that were in a position to disrupt the whole of the country's economic and physical life. Heath had in mind the miners, but also such groups as the power workers, gas workers and railwaymen. Carrington's conclusions, leaked to the press in 1978, were bleak.[15] Once the miners had gone on strike, the Heath government had been defeated not because it was ill-organised or inept but quite simply because the miners had more power than the government did. A government's only recourse in such a conflict would be to the use of troops, and Britain did not have enough troops, nor did they have the requisite skills. In any case, the use of troops would do irrevocable damage to the fabric of the country's social and political life. The conclusions to be drawn were obvious (though they were not spelled out in the version of the report that appeared in the press): avoid confrontations with powerful unions at almost any cost; if a powerful union makes menacing noises, buy it off as quickly and as unobtrusively as possible. Such an approach would be dependent on the government not having an incomes policy; but the Conservatives did not want to have an incomes policy in any case, on other grounds.

The cautious thinking behind the Carrington report guided the Thatcher government in all of its dealings with the trade unions, at least during its first term. The most clear-cut case occurred in January and February 1981, when an announcement by the National Coal Board that it proposed to close 23 uneconomic pits resulted in unofficial strike action by miners in many parts of the country and the threat by the National Union of Mineworkers' executive of an all-out official strike. Ministers, caught unawares, at first insisted that there could be no retreat and that the coal industry would have to operate within the cash limits previously laid down; but then, as the scale of the potential crisis became clear, they did a complete about-face, brought forward talks with the miners' leaders and agreed to provide the industry with additional funds. The threat of pit closures was withdrawn; the strikes were called off. No one tried to deny that the government had been defeated. More to the point, it was the prime minister herself who had insisted on the government's climb-down, however embarrassing. Biffen said later that he had not gone into politics 'to be a kamikaze pilot'. Thatcher was obviously of the same view.[16]

TABLE 4.3 *Cumulative wage increases awarded to groups of public sector workers, 1981–82*

	%
Electricity supply workers	25
Water workers	22
Gas workers	20
Railwaymen	18
Miners	17
Local government manual workers	16
Teachers	14
Nurses	14
Hospital auxiliary workers	14
Non-industrial civil servants	14
Local government white collar workers	12
Doctors	12[a]
University teachers	11

[a] See the note about the doctors in the text.
Source: Reports in *The Times*, various dates.

The case of the abandoned pit closures was especially clear-cut, but it was not at all isolated. In dealing with public sector pay during its first term, the Thatcher government consistently conceded much larger increases to militant groups of workers possessing industrial muscle than to groups that were either less militant or possessed less muscle. Table 4.3 sets out the cumulative percentage increases in pay awarded to different groups of public sector workers over the two years 1981–82 (1980 having been omitted because that year's figures were distorted by the government's honouring of the Clegg 'comparability' awards inherited from the previous government). Table 4.3 could hardly provide a clearer insight into the government's thinking. It makes sense only in terms of a conscious decision by ministers to resist pressure where they could, to yield to it where they could not. Manual workers in the electricity, gas and water-supply industries did best; university teachers and local government white collar workers did worst. (The doctors would certainly have done better but for the fact that the medical profession in the previous year had received much the largest of the Clegg awards.)

Data like those in Table 4.3 refute the suggestion, alluded to in one of the newspaper headlines quoted above, that Margaret Thatcher is some sort of latter-day Lord Cardigan, eager to lead political charges of the Light Brigade. She is not. She is someone who prefers to fight another day, who is always ready to compromise (though only when she believes that there is no alternative). Those who overlook Thatcher's sensitivity to power – her respect for it, and her ability to weigh it – overlook an essential element in her prime ministerial style.

People, Not Organisations

A different element in her style, consistent with her respect for power but not in any way stemming from it, is her approach to techniques of decisionmaking. Most politicians, like most business managers, probably fall into three rough categories. The first consists of those who, confronted with a new situation or problem, instinctively think in terms of an organisational response – the setting up of a new committee, the merging of two departments, the creation of a specialist policy unit. The second consists of those who, possibly for reasons of personality or simply because they are unaccustomed to working in large organisations, are more people-centred. Their response to a new situation or problem is to think in terms of individuals: who would be good at dealing with this new situation or problem? The third category, considerably rarer than either of the others, consists of people capable of thinking both organisationally and in human terms at the same time.

Few politicians fall into this last category, but Edward Heath provided an unusually clear instance of the first. Hence his wholesale reorganisation of government departments and his creation of new institutions like the CPRS. Margaret Thatcher, by contrast, provides a striking instance of the second category. Hers is an almost exclusively people-centred style of government. Her interest in the structure of government is minimal. She is unconcerned with nuts and bolts, and organisation charts bore her. Instead, she feels at home working with, through – and, if need be, around – individual human beings. Faced with a new problem or determined to embark on a new initiative, she asks, not 'How can I organise this work so that it will be done effectively?' but rather 'Who can I get to help me?

Who would be the best person to turn to?' Weighing people, like weighing power, is central to the way she does her job.

Against this background, one of the first decisions – or, rather, non-decisions – of her administration may seem curious. On entering Downing Street in May 1979, she brought with her only a handful of her own people. She behaved as though she were perfectly content to operate for the most part through the established institutions of government – the civil service, the cabinet and cabinet committees. She appointed David Wolfson, a member of the Great Universal Stores family who had run a mail-order business, to be her personal assistant at Number 10 and John Hoskyns, the founder and former managing director of a computer company, to be the head of her Policy Unit. Neither had had much previous political experience, nor had either previously had connections with the Conservative party. Over time the number of her own people housed at Number 10 gradually increased. Her Policy Unit expanded from one to three, and she recruited Alan Walters, an early monetarist, to be her specialist economic adviser and Sir Anthony Parsons to provide her with a direct link to the Foreign Office. In due course, Hoskyns was succeeded by Ferdinand Mount, a journalist, and Richard Ryder, her original political secretary, left, to be replaced by Derek Howe. Nevertheless, at the end of her first term, fewer of Thatcher's own people, as distinct from permanent civil servants, were working at Number 10 than had worked there in the time of either Harold Wilson or James Callaghan. John Hoskyns and one of her informal advisers, Alfred Sherman, were both keen that she should expand her personal operation at Number 10 and establish a genuine 'prime minister's department'; but there is no evidence that she more than toyed with these ideas.[17]

Given her intention to be an activist prime minister, given that she found herself in a minority in her own government and given that senior officials were well known not to be enthusiastic about the main lines of her policy, Thatcher's failure to build up her own staff at Number 10 is, on the face of it, puzzling. A person in this position might have been expected to surround herself with like-minded people whom she could trust; she might have been expected to create a prime minister's department which could serve as a counterweight to all the other departmental interests in Whitehall. Paradoxically, however, it was almost certainly her very 'people-centredness' that caused her not to behave in this way. In the first place, it was not her instinct to think in terms of institutional solutions to substantive problems. In the second, and more important, all of her previous experience had taught her that, if she knew her own mind and were determined and forceful enough, she could attain her objectives through the medium of face-to-face argument and persuasion. She was easily her own best advocate and also her own chief of staff. She had no need of hordes of assistants and intermediaries. On the contrary, they might have the effect of diluting the direct force of her own strong personality and of coming between her and the substance of the arguments. In the end, she had mastered the civil servants in the Department of Education and Science in this way, and her campaign for the Tory leadership, however much help she received from supporters like Airey Neave and William Shelton, had been essentially a one-woman affair. In Downing Street, as in opposition, she wanted to ensure that *she* was in control.

This determination to be at the centre of things, to direct rather than merely supervise, has influenced her operating style in other ways. Thatcher in no sense 'abolished cabinet government', at least during her first term. As we have seen, she was frequently defeated in cabinet; and, even on the Falklands, in the words of one cabinet minister, 'She had to carry us on every major decision. That task force would never have sailed without cabinet approval'.[18] Nevertheless, like other prime ministers before her, but on a larger scale, she has often sought to get her own way by circumventing the cabinet, by bringing public pressure to bear on it from outside and even by semi-publicly opposing the policies of her own ministers. Despite the cabinet discussions of economic policy forced on her in 1981, she has largely succeeded in keeping the direction of economic policy in her own hands and those of her Treasury ministers. Likewise the full cabinet was not consulted in July 1980 about the decision to purchase the Trident missile system from the United States or in February 1981 about the climb-down over pit closures. During the summer of 1981 she made a series of speeches so totally identifying herself with the general thrust of the government's economic strategy as to make it virtually impossible for the whole cabinet to reverse the strategy without appearing to repudiate her. A year later she made no secret of her dislike of James Prior's proposals – i.e. the proposals of her own government – for the creation of a Northern Ireland assembly. Her own parliamentary private secretary, Ian Gow, went so far as to lobby backbench Conservative MPs against the proposals, albeit unsuccessfully.[19] As time went on, she chose to work more and more frequently through small groups of ministers – if need be, augmented by officials and other advisers – rather than through formal meetings of the cabinet and its committees.

Whatever the issue or forum, Thatcher is a prime minister who characteristically reaches out for decisions. She does not just wait for them to come to her. To be sure, she prefers to delegate when she can be certain that the consequences of the delegation will be to her liking; but, since delegating invariably means losing some element of control, her premiership has been marked – as was Harold Wilson's first term to a lesser extent – by a tendency for decisions on small matters as well as large to be pulled into Number 10. Ministers are reluctant to consult her too frequently because, if they do, they are liable to be accused of not being on top of their job; but, equally, they are reluctant not to consult her for fear of doing the wrong thing, incurring her wrath and possibly finding themselves countermanded. Sir Michael Edwardes, the former chairman of BL, contrasts in his memoirs the freedom of action that James Callaghan gave to his industry secretary, Eric Varley, with Margaret Thatcher's insistence that her industry secretaries, Sir Keith Joseph and Patrick Jenkin, consult her about almost every detail.[20] Her most recent biographers, Nicholas Wapshott and George Brock, similarly observe:

There are few discussions in Whitehall in which Number 10 does not make an appearance, if only to be ruled out as a factor for consideration ... The frequency with which Number 10 has to be considered is a hallmark of Thatcher government.[21]

Thatcher, unlike most prime ministers, is not seen in Whitehall as a somewhat remote figure. Her presence is all-pervasive.

Another corollary of her desire to dominate her government, and of her preference for doing so through contact with – and judgements upon – individuals, is her concern, unusual amongst prime ministers, with senior appointments in the civil service. There exists in Whitehall a Senior Appointments Selection Committee, consisting of the head of the Home Civil Service and a number of other senior permanent secretaries; and the normal practice has been for most of this committee's recommendations to be accepted by the prime minister of the day without question, or at least without much in the way of active involvement – this despite the fact that appointments at permanent secretary and deputy secretary level are among the few appointments (ministers apart) that the prime minister can make on his or her own authority, without having to consult colleagues. Thatcher, by contrast, determined from the moment she arrived in Number 10 to interest herself in the selection of top civil servants, to make her own enquiries about candidates for promotion and to be prepared to question, even on occasion to reject, the SASC's recommendations. She has shown a similar interest in appointments to the chairmanships of nationalised industries. She undoubtedly shows a marked preference for people who, temperamentally at least, are like her: hard-working, tough-minded and assertive. There is less agreement in Whitehall about how far she also leans towards officials who share her free-market, monetarist economic views.[22]

Thatcher thus reaches out for decisions; she reaches out for people. She also reaches out for ideas. Although she has chosen not to surround herself in Downing Street with a close circle of personal advisers, she partially offsets this lack in a highly personal way, one that would have been inconceivable in the time of Callaghan, Wilson, Heath, Home or even Macmillan. She encourages the existence of, and participates actively in, what amounts to a higgledy piggledy on-going academic seminar on the theory and practice of modern conservatism. The membership of the seminar is not fixed but is constantly shifting, and different members have different institutional foci. Some have academic appointments, mainly in London or

Cambridge; some are associated with the Centre for Policy Studies, set up by Thatcher, Sir Keith Joseph and Alfred Sherman in 1974; some attend the weekly lunches at the Institute of Economic Affairs; some are active in the Conservative philosophy group; a number write for the *Spectator* and the *Daily Telegraph*. The group includes at least one American, the economist Milton Friedman, one theologian, Edward Norman of Peterhouse, Cambridge, and one person who is not a member of the Conservative party, Enoch Powell. The group, moreover, cannot be said to constitute a 'staff'. A few of its members, notably Sherman, occasionally offer advice on matters currently before the government, but the great majority – Paul Johnson, Robert Conquest, Hugh Thomas, Shirley Letwin, T. E. Utley, Roger Scruton, John Casey, Maurice Cowling – simply come together to exchange ideas with her and with each other. As one of them said:

> The prime minister plays with ideas as though they were ping-pong balls. She just likes to knock them about a bit. It makes her feel relaxed.[23]

It is striking how many members of the Thatcher seminar resemble both her and a considerable proportion of her cabinet in not being members of the old Tory establishment, in being outsiders, 'marginal' people, socially or intellectually and sometimes both. Many, like her, are lower middle-class or working-class in their social origins. A considerable number are converts to the Tory party from the more or less extreme left. Sherman was a communist and fought in the International Brigade in Spain; Paul Johnson once edited the *New Statesman*; Hugh Thomas resigned from the Foreign Office over Suez, joined the Labour party and was elevated to the peerage by Harold Wilson. Most of the converts, however, although they have ceased to be socialists, have not ceased to be radicals. Typically they have exchanged one set of absolutes and certainties for another. Their sense of their own minority status, and of still being 'against the system', accords well with Thatcher's own self-image as someone who stands outside both the old economic system and the old system of ideas the better to change them both.

Presentation of Self, Uses of Self

Prime ministers vary considerably in how far they seek consciously to project an image of themselves and in how far they consciously use their own personalities as a means of achieving their political objectives. Winston Churchill and Harold Macmillan were highly self-conscious, self-projecting politicians; Clement Attlee and Sir Alec Douglas-Home in their different ways represented the other extreme of unselfconsciousness, almost insouciance. Margaret Thatcher is firmly in the Churchill–Macmillan mould. 'She is', said an official who worked under her at the DES, 'an actress . . . She is very conscious of the impression she is making'.[24] That being so, it is important to see how she uses her personality, and to what ends.

One element in her style will be evident to anyone in Britain who has ever switched on a television set: Thatcher seeks to command partly by appearing to be in command. Her hair is permed, her clothes are neat, her make-up is carefully applied; and her manner is every bit as unruffled as her appearance. She controls her gestures, regulates her smile, adjusts the timbre and pitch of her voice. She is careful to appear emotional only when she wants to appear emotional and to appear cool and collected when, far more often, that is how she wants to appear. Moreover, the same self-control and attention to detail that are lavished on her personal appearance are also lavished on her public speeches and her appearances in parliament. Hours are devoted to briefing her for prime minister's question time, and time spent under the hair-drier is typically time spent polishing each phrase and paragraph of a speech to be delivered three weeks hence. Little of this, if any, is the product of vanity. It results from the belief that, if one is to control others, one must first exercise self-control. The iron lady is, above all, iron with herself. Nor, it should be added, is Thatcher's concern with 'presentation of self' peculiarly feminine. Macmillan, to take only one example, conducted himself in almost exactly the same way (though the details of his personal style were, of course, different).

Her hair-dos and her way with television interviewers are public property. Equally important are the ways she uses herself in private. To the public at large, she often appears cold, mannered, slightly inhuman; a newspaper columnist once said that she always looked as though she were putting on a sympathetic air in order to break the news to someone that their pet cat was dead.[25] In private, however, her consciousness of others and consideration for them account in part for her political success. Shortly after the 1979 election, a private secretary who had worked for Callaghan at Number 10 and was now working for Thatcher was asked which of them he preferred as his boss. 'Thatcher', he replied, 'by a wide margin. Jim always thought you had absolutely nothing to do in life except work for him. Mrs Thatcher never forgets that you have a wife who may be expecting you home for dinner'.[26] In remembering people's names (and their spouse's and children's), in remembering what was on their mind the last time she talked to them and in being willing to take time to listen to their troubles, Thatcher is the antithesis of Heath. Her ability to relax people, to make them feel that they matter to her, not only endears her to Conservatives in the country; it also comes through in films of her visits to shopping centres and factories. She seems to care for others. Her handling of the Parkinson affair early in her second term suggests that she really does.

Thatcher has also made a point, as we remarked earlier, of being a good listener. Before campaigning for the leadership of her party, she spent little time mixing with her fellow Conservative members of parliament. Ever since then, she has gone out of her way to be accessible – in her room at the House, in the members' dining room, in the division lobby. One of her boasts is that she has never refused a private meeting with a Conservative backbencher, however trivial-seeming the purpose of the discussion. Edward du Cann, the chairman of the backbench 1922 Committee, similarly says that, ever since she became prime minister, he has been able to get through to her more or less whenever he wants, even at short notice. Since her time as prime minister is limited, her main conduit to and from the back benches, apart from the 1922 Committee, is – and has to be – her parliamentary private secretary. Ian Gow, who served during her first term, was often dismissed as being the prime minister's personal spy, a sort of political 'supergrass'. Such allegations, however, missed the point. Gow remained useful to her not only, or even mainly, because he passed on to her items of information that MPs did not want her to hear, but precisely because he kept her in touch with what they did want her to hear. If he had ever been thought to be merely a spy, his usefulness to the prime minister, even as a spy, would have ceased.

If Thatcher is a prodigious listener, she is also a prodigious worker. Probably few prime ministers have put in more hours. Her working day starts at 6.30, when she listens to the 'Today' programme on radio, and does not end until 1 or sometimes 2 o'clock the next morning. She works on holiday as well as at Number 10 or Chequers. She enjoys working and, by all accounts, is apt to become bored when not working. Nevertheless, the main purpose of her industry, as with almost everything else she does, is political. She wishes to bring about great changes in British society, changes that are often not welcome to others, including many in her own party and government. If she is to persuade others, if she is to goad them into action, if she is to catch them out doing things that she does not want them to do, then she must know their business almost as well as her own. And, since she is only one individual, whereas her cabinet contains fourteen departmental ministers, she has to work harder than any of them. She operates on the principle: 'Get on top of the facts or they will get on top of you. Get on top of your ministers' facts or your ministers will get on top of you'. Being on top of the facts means that she can deal with her ministers on equal terms, even on strictly departmental issues; it also means that her ministers are unusually attentive to the prime minister's wishes and unusually reluctant to try to put things past her.

Thatcher is, necessarily given her ambitions, a quick and eager learner. Conscious when she became leader of the opposition of her ignorance of foreign affairs (and conscious that others were conscious of it), she took the trouble to visit in the space of four years: France, West Germany, the Netherlands, Belgium, Italy, Switzerland, Finland, Rumania, Egypt, Iran, Syria, Israel, the United States, Canada, Pakistan, Singapore, New Zealand, Australia, India, China, Japan, Yugoslavia and Spain. She also visited hundreds of factories and business premises, closely questioning managers and shopfloor workers about everything from the details of production processes and stock control to how they were coping, or failing to cope, with foreign competition. By the end of these four years, Thatcher could still be accused of lacking real experience, but not of lacking knowledge. Her curiosity and her keenness as an auto-didact remain among her most conspicuous characteristics.

To those whom she likes and trusts, the prime minister is, as we have seen, considerate and solicitous. She is a loyal person and inspires great loyalty in those close to her. But to strangers, or people she has reason to dislike or distrust, she frequently shows another side of her personality. She clearly makes use of fear as a conscious weapon in her armoury of command. Carefully controlled displays of anger and disdain, together with her own superordinate position as party leader and prime minister, are used to wrong-foot ministers and civil servants, to bully them, on occasion to humiliate them. In this respect, as in no other, her leadership style is faintly reminiscent of Lyndon Johnson's. Few ministers and civil servants are prepared to admit that they are afraid of the prime minister; they prefer to describe themselves as being sometimes 'a little nervous' in her presence. But fear is the word and the concept used by most onlookers, and it is notable that her most sympathetic and admiring biographer, Patrick Cosgrave, scatters phrases and sentences like the following throughout his text:

> Her wit . . . is often cruel and she is inclined, if not exactly to be overbearing, to make some of her questioners the butts of her jokes and briskness

> Few disputed her greater knowledge or command . . . but nearly all felt she had been wantonly rude

> a frequent peremptoriness of manner

> She is given to personal remarks, even to slight acquaintances, which are often thought rude. She can be cutting with opponents, especially within her own party.[27]

She provided a good example of the 'rude remark made to a slight acquaintance' (or possibly even a complete stranger) after her eye operation in the summer of 1983. As the prime minister left the hospital, she was asked by a reporter whether she was now able to see properly. 'I can', she replied waspishly, 'see everything that's wrong with you'. Not surprisingly, responses to Thatcher among those with whom she has direct dealings are as bimodally distributed as they are among the public at large. She can inspire devotion, but she also has an unusually large number of enemies.

Her conscious use of fear as a weapon is allied – another faint echo of Lyndon Johnson – to a disposition to see the political world as being divided into friends and enemies, goodies and baddies, the baddies, in terms of her role as Conservative leader and prime minister, being almost entirely members of her own party (together with sluggish or recalcitrant civil servants). This disposition permeates the language of both her and her advisers. Her supporters are 'on my side', 'our people'; her critics are 'wet', 'unreliable', 'the enemy' or, when tempers are running especially high, 'reptiles'. That this Manichaean disposition exists is not in doubt. Whether it adversely affects her judgment is disputed.

What is not in dispute is that, Manichaeism apart, Thatcher has probably been more concerned than any other postwar prime minister with promoting her own supporters inside the government and with ensuring that the departments of government that matter to her – principally the economic departments – are manned exclusively by those who share her views. She told Kenneth Harris of the *Observer* before the 1979 election that she wanted in her cabinet 'only the people who wanted to go in the direction in which every instinct tells me we have to go'; she wanted hers to be 'a conviction government'.[28] Because of the divisions in her party, and because of the initial shortage of experienced politicians who fully shared her convictions, she was forced in 1979 to appoint a less united and less Thatcherite cabinet than she would have liked; but, precisely for that reason, she has used government appointments ever since in a peculiarly political and policy-oriented way. Supporters of hers like Nigel Lawson, Leon Brittan and Norman Tebbit might well, on the basis of their talents alone, have been appointed to the cabinet by some other Conservative prime minister in the 1980s; but Thatcher beyond any doubt has promoted them further and faster than anyone else would have done. Moreover, not only have posts in the economic departments become the exclusive preserve of Thatcherites; wets in the government, too able or too dangerous to be left outside, have increasingly been herded into ministerial ghettos. The Northern Ireland department is the extreme case. Following the 1983 election, almost all of the Northern Ireland ministers – James Prior, Nicholas Scott and Chris Patten – were wets, and Peter Walker was virtually the only outspoken wet in the government not exiled to that department. Northern Ireland is, of course, not a political base from which anybody can cause trouble on the economic front.

Previous prime ministers have used ministerial appointments to bring on talent, to broaden their basis of support in their party, to protect their political position, to strengthen their government in the eyes of the general public. Thatcher is unusual, possibly unique, in her single-minded use of appointments to promote policy ends. The Thatcher government is, by design, *her* government. Her decisions reflect equally her determination to lead and her people-centred approach to the business of government.

Means to Ends: Match or Mismatch?

Margaret Thatcher's is a formidable personality, and hers is a distinctive prime ministerial style. No one in 10 Downing Street before has been quite like her; no one has operated before in quite the way that she does. It is important therefore to emphasise that both her personality and her style are politically neutral. For a politician, Thatcher arouses unusually strong emotions, of admiration bordering on adoration on the right, of animosity sometimes approaching hatred on the left. But the real focus of contention is, or ought to be, not her person but her policies. If someone with her personality and style were the leader of a left-wing government, pursuing left-wing policies with the same single-mindedness and determination, qualities that seem in her vices would instead seem virtues, and 'iron lady' would be a term of praise rather than abuse. Not least for that reason, Margaret Thatcher deserves to be judged on professional as well as partisan grounds. Are *her* means, to repeat the question asked at the outset, well adapted to *her* ends?

One way to approach the question is to run a 'thought experiment' – to ask what the policies of a Conservative government elected in 1979 would have been like if the prime minister had not been Thatcher but one of the other leading contenders for the Tory leadership in 1975, William Whitelaw, James Prior or Sir Geoffrey Howe. Merely to ask this question, given everything that is known of these three men, is already to answer it. A Conservative government led by any of them would have been a very different government, in its policies as well as its style and rhetoric. Such a government would almost certainly have maintained a quasi-corporatist relationship with the trade unions instead of largely excluding them from economic policymaking. It would probably not have pressed nearly so hard or fast with union-curbing legislation as did the Thatcher government following the 1983 election. It might well have cut the highest marginal rates of income tax, but it would probably not have moved nearly so swiftly to shift the burden of taxation from direct (mainly income tax) to indirect (mainly VAT). A Whitelaw, Prior or Howe government would almost certainly not have built up the Thatcher government's massive programme for the privatisation of state-owned industry. It might well not have fought the Falklands war in the same way, or possibly at all. It would have been far more tempted than was the Thatcher government during the depths of the recession in 1980–81 to reflate the economy in order to reduce unemployment, even at the risk of some increase in the rate of inflation. 'The lady', said Thatcher in a famous speech, 'is not for turning'. Given their outlooks and temperaments, any of the other three probably would have been.

The Thatcher government, in short, is not just any Tory government of the 1980s; it is different. But does the fact that it is different stem from the way in which Margaret Thatcher does the job of being prime minister, from her determination to lead, her respect for power, her people-centredness, her presentation of self, her uses of self? Again, merely to ask the question is to answer it. Given Thatcher's minority position on economic and industrial issues within her own government, it is inconceivable that she could have bent the administration to her will as far as she did without leading from the front, without reaching out for decisions, without carefully calculating ministerial appointments, without bullying people, without working all hours of the day and night. Her personal style has been essential to the achievement – in so far as they have been achieved – of her personal ends. 'The Thatcher government' is not just a conventional phrase; it captures a central political reality. Whether Thatcher's policies are good or bad for Britain, whether they will actually bring about the social and economic transformation that she desires, is, of course, a different question.

All that said, there are undoubtedly dangers, from her own point of view, in the highly individual way in which Thatcher operates as prime minister. Several of them are implicit in what has been said already. Some critics continue to question the wisdom of her refusal to create a prime minister's department, or at least a strong staff of her own, at Number 10 – though it must be said, in the light of the success of her face-to-face person-centred approach, that that criticism looks less telling early in her second term than it did at the beginning of her first. More worrying from her point of view is that her understandable desire to pull decisions into 10 Downing Street – to be in charge and to be seen to be in charge – will result in dilatoriness as well as in weakening the authority of departmental ministers. Her involvement in the taking of all major decisions, and many minor ones, means that many of them do not get taken for a very long time. Delay is likely to have adverse consequences in itself; it could in time come to be portrayed, however inappropriately, as a consequence of indecision. As her tenure of Number 10 lengthens there is also the danger that, although hitherto an assiduous listener, she may stop listening; that, although previously a very careful weigher of other people's power, she may neglect to do her sums or may come up with the wrong answer; that, although in the past a cautious respecter of other people's power, she may in the future fall into the trap of exaggerating her own. *Hubris* is a danger to Thatcher no more, but no less, than to other political leaders.

Another set of risks, however, is more specific to the present prime minister. In so far as she uses rudeness as a political weapon, in so far as she governs through fear, she makes enemies; and, as Machiavelli observed long ago, fear is the most effective of all political weapons, but only for so long as it can be sustained. If for any reason people cease to be afraid, they will also cease to be obedient – and indeed are likely to turn with some ferocity upon whomever it was that once frightened them. A weapon that is highly effective in the short term could turn out in the long term to have been very costly if the prime minister, on other grounds, were ever to become politically vulnerable. By the same token, every time that Thatcher, in her natural desire to lead, is rebuffed by her own cabinet, to some small extent her authority is thereby diminished. In the post-Falklands period, rebuffs are rare, her authority as prime minister is beyond question; but, in a changed political climate, determination could be construed as pig-headedness, defeats inside the government as signs of political weakness. It is also the case that, in sacking most of her cabinet critics and in giving all of the top jobs in the government to her own supporters, however politically inexperienced, she runs the twin risks of creating a strong body of hostile Conservative opinion outside the government and of depriving herself of a wide range of competing sources of advice. All prime ministers are isolated; Thatcher is probably more isolated than most. Her future depends unusually heavily on her ability to continue to deliver political success.

Has Thatcher in her first period of office fundamentally changed the office of prime minister? Will she bequeath to her successors an office significantly different from the one that she inherited from Callaghan? Up to a point, the answer to these questions is 'no'. For the reasons given elsewhere in this volume, notably by G. W. Jones in chapter 8, the British constitution and the imperatives of party leadership in the British system mean that the office of prime minister evolves only slowly and that it is probably beyond the capacity of any one holder of the office to change it both radically and permanently. Norman Tebbit, Michael Heseltine, Neil Kinnock or David Steel as prime minister would probably resemble Edward Heath, Harold Wilson or James Callaghan far more than Margaret Thatcher. The job can be done in different ways. Thatcher has developed a new way. But the job itself has not greatly changed.

But it would be a serious mistake just to leave it at that because, whatever happens during the remainder of her time in Downing Street, Thatcher will bequeath to her successors two important legacies. The first is simply a powerful example. We now know what we did not know before: that the job of prime minister can be done in Thatcher's way. The repertory of available prime ministerial styles has been extended. Politicians of the future will read biographies of Thatcher, just as they now read biographies of Lloyd George and Winston Churchill, and they will reckon that they can learn a thing or two. Those who have observed Thatcher at first hand, her present and future cabinet colleagues, are, of course, especially likely to profit from her example. If Thatcher's prime ministership turns out to be a large success, they will probably draw one set of inferences. Should it, however, end in political disaster – especially if the disaster seemed to result directly from flaws in the Thatcher prime ministerial style – then they would be likely to draw a different set of inferences.

Thatcher's second legacy is more subtle and could easily be overlooked. The great weakness in the British prime ministerial office – as compared with, say, the American or French presidencies – is that there are so few decisions that a prime minister can take on his or her own authority; the prime minister has few statutes to administer, no department of his or her own. But one of the great strengths in the British office lies in the fact that the outer limits of its authority are so ill-defined. It is open to a determined prime minister to take more and more decisions and to defy other members of the cabinet to say that he or she has no right to take these decisions. This is precisely what Thatcher has been doing, in extending her surveillance of senior civil service appointments, in working increasingly through small groups of ministers rather than through the cabinet and cabinet committees, in making it clear to her colleagues that she expects to be consulted about virtually the whole range of ministerial activity. She has been pushing out the frontiers of her authority ever since she took office in 1979; she may well continue to do so in the future. And it would take a brave, determined, powerful and well-organised set of ministers under her to tell her to stop. Who will say that the rules have been broken when, first, there are no hard and fast rules and when, second, the alleged breaker of the rules is one's own boss on whom one's political future is likely to depend? Margaret Thatcher's example will be important in future not least because it will make it clear to her successors that the job of prime minister can be an even bigger one than had previously been supposed. It will be up to them to decide whether they want to, and are politically in a position to, follow the example that Thatcher has set.

References

1. On the circumstances of Thatcher's election as Conservative leader see Anthony King, 'Politics, Economics, and the Trade Unions, 1974–1979', in Howard R. Penniman (ed.), *Britain at the Polls, 1979: A Study of the General Election* (Washington, D.C.: American Enterprise Institute, 1981) and also the various biographies of Thatcher that have appeared so far, especially Patrick Cosgrave, *Margaret Thatcher: Prime Minister* (London: Arrow Books, 1979), chapters 1–2; Nicholas Wapshott and George Brock, *Thatcher* (London: Futura, 1983), chapter 7; Russell Lewis, *Margaret Thatcher: A Personal and Political Biography*, 2nd edn (London: Routledge & Kegan Paul, 1983), chapters 10–11; and Penny Junor, *Margaret Thatcher: Wife, Mother, Politician* (London: Sidgwick & Jackson, 1983), chapter 4. All of these biographies contain interesting material, the two most useful being Cosgrave, and Wapshott and Brock.

2. On these U-turns and their consequences, see David Butler and Dennis Kavanagh, *The British General Election of February 1974* (London: Macmillan, 1974); Howard Penniman (ed.), *Britain at the Polls: The Parliamentary Elections of 1974* (Washington, D.C.: American Enterprise Institute, 1975); and, for a view from inside the Heath administration, Douglas Hurd, *An End to Promises: Sketch of a Government 1970–74* (London: Collins, 1979). The biographies of Thatcher also report on her reactions and the reactions of her supporters to the experience of the Heath administration.

3. On the miners' strike and its aftermath see the works cited in the previous note, especially Butler and Kavanagh, *British General Election of February 1974* and Penniman (ed.), *Britain at the Polls*.

4. Accounts of Thatcher's first term can be found in Peter Riddell, *The Thatcher Government* (Oxford: Martin Robertson, 1983); William Keegan, *Mrs Thatcher's Economic Experiment* (London: Allen Lane, 1984); David Butler and Dennis Kavanagh, *The British General Election of 1983* (London: Macmillan, 1984), chapter 2; Anthony King, 'Thatcher's First Term', in Austin Ranney (ed.), *Britain at the Polls,*

1983 (Durham, N.C.: Duke University Press, 1984); and Wapshott and Brock, *Thatcher*, chapters 9–12. Riddell and Keegan are chiefly concerned with the substance of policy; the other writers are more concerned with the politics of Thatcher's administration.

5. On the Thatcher government's economic record see especially Riddell, *Thatcher Government*, chapters 3–5.

6. The headlines are, in order, from *Sunday Times*, 10 February 1980, p. 17; *Observer*, 17 February 1980, p. 6; *The Times*, 22 February 1980, p. 1; *Observer*, 16 November 1980, p. 1; *The Times*, 19 June 1981, p. 12; *The Times*, 9 October 1981, p. 11; and *The Economist*, 10 October 1981, p. 21.

7. For St John-Stevas's own reflections on these events see Norman St John-Stevas, *The Two Cities* (London: Faber & Faber, 1984), chapter 1.

8. Simon Jenkins, 'The birth of the Thatcher factor', *The Times*, 31 March 1983, p. 14.

9. The sentence in the text is based directly on the analysis of public prestige in the context of the American presidency, in Richard E. Neustadt, *Presidential Power: The Politics of Leadership from FDR to Carter* (New York: John Wiley, 1980), pp. 64–5.

10. In addition to the present chapter, see Martin Burch, 'Mrs Thatcher's Approach to Leadership: 1979–June 1983', *Parliamentary Affairs*, 36 (Autumn 1983), pp. 399–416.

11. On Thatcher's style in cabinet see Wapshott and Brock, *Thatcher*, pp. 192–3, 204–5 and 207.

12. Wapshott and Brock, *Thatcher*, p. 196.

13. A detailed and vivid account of the row can be found in Michael Cockerell, Peter Hennessy and David Walker, *Sources Close to the Prime Minister: Inside the Hidden World of the News Manipulators* (London: Macmillan, 1984), pp. 130–4.

14. As Wapshott and Brock (*Thatcher*, p. 206) remark in connection with the September 1981 sackings, 'She had picked off the weaker parts of the Cabinet opposition, knowing that none of them, either individually or united, would be able to cause very much dissent among backbench MPs'.

15. See the report in *The Times*, 18 April 1978, p. 1.

16. John Biffen made the 'kamikaze pilot' remark on BBC Radio 4's 'The World this Weekend' programme: *The Times*, 23 February 1981, p. 1. For a detailed account of the 1981 miners' dispute and the prime minister's role in it, see John Fryer and Michael Jones, 'What really made the lady turn', *Sunday Times*, 22 February 1981, p. 17.

17. A brief outline of Hoskyns's and Sherman's ideas can be found in J. R. Greenaway, 'Bureaucrats under Pressure: The Thatcher Government and the Mandarin Elite' in Lynton Robins (ed.), *Updating British Politics* (London: Politics Association, 1984).

18. Quoted in Peter Hennessy, 'Shades of a Home Counties Boudicea', *The Times*, 17 May 1983, p. 4.

19. See, for example, Wapshott and Brock, *Thatcher*, p. 229.

20. Michael Edwardes, *Back from the Brink: An Apocalyptic Experience* (London: Collins, 1983), chapter 11 (entitled 'The Iron Lady').

21. Wapshott and Brock, *Thatcher*, p. 228. Francis Pym has since put the same point with considerably greater acerbity: 'My final criticism of the Government . . . is that its style of operation has steadily become less flexible and more centralised. This process stems from the Prime Minister's tendency to think that she is always right. In turn, this leads her to believe that she can always do things better than other people, which then encourages her to try to do everything herself. The two consequences of this are, first, that central government now exercises direct control over more and more aspects of our lives and, second, that within the Government the Prime Minister exercises direct control over more and more Departments'. See Francis Pym, *The Politics of Consent* (London: Hamish Hamilton, 1984), pp. 16–17.

22. On Thatcher's role in civil service appointments, see Greenaway, 'Bureaucrats under Pressure'; David Blake and Peter Hennessy, 'Mrs Thatcher keeps close eye on top Civil Service postings', *The Times*, 14 February 1980, p. 5; and Richard Norton Taylor, 'When Thatcher lifts the knife mandarins fear for their skins', *Guardian*, 1 July 1983, p. 3.

23. Quoted in Peter Stothard, 'Who thinks for Mrs Thatcher?', *The Times*, 31 January 1983, p. 10. The most complete description of the Thatcher seminar is to be found in Godfrey Hodgson, 'Now is the time for all Right-thinking men . . .', *Sunday Times Magazine*, 4 March 1984, pp. 44–52.

24. Quoted in Wapshott and Brock, *Thatcher*, p. 95.

25. Keith Waterhouse of the *Daily Mirror* quoted in Junor, *Margaret Thatcher*, p. 200.

26. Private information.

27. Cosgrave, *Margaret Thatcher*, pp. 16, 17 and 28. Hugh Stephenson has similarly written: 'She has . . . a capacity for being extremely and gratuitously offensive to people in circumstances where they might otherwise be open to persuasion'. See Hugh Stephenson, *Mrs Thatcher's First Year* (London: Jill Norman, 1980).

28. *Observer*, 29 February 1979.

5

10 Downing Street

**RICHARD E. NEUSTADT, INTERVIEWED BY
HENRY BRANDON[1]**

*In Chapter 3, G. W. Jones described the people who work for the prime
minister in 10 Downing Street. But the phrase 'work for' turns out to be
ambiguous. A civil servant serving in the private office may work for
the prime minister in the sense that his job is to attend to whatever
business the prime minister wants attended to; but that same civil
servant will work in Number 10 for only a relatively brief period and
his or her long-term career prospects depend less on the incumbent prime
minister than on the judgements of higher-ups elsewhere in the
permanent civil service machine. In this chapter, dating from the
mid-1960s, Professor Neustadt, a long-standing member of the
Washington political community, ruminates on the problems that prime
ministers encounter in getting people to work for them.*

Few other Americans, if any, have the depth of knowledge and
understanding of the British political system, and especially of
the inner workings of Whitehall, possessed by Professor
Neustadt. He first hit the headlines when President John F.
Kennedy after his election in 1960 said publicly that he had
been using Neustadt's book *Presidential Power* to help him
organise the White House. In fact, he had gone further, he had
asked Neustadt, after having read his book, to prepare a special
memorandum for him with more specific recommendations on
not only how to organise the White House, but whom to

appoint to the key positions. Neustadt at that time was Professor of Government at Columbia University, but it was in the Truman administration, as an assistant to the president, that he had gained practical, first-hand knowledge about the meaning of presidential power and its application. Later during a year in Oxford, at Nuffield College, he widened his knowledge of government organisation by learning more about the mysteries of the corridors of power in Whitehall. He deepened that knowledge when President Kennedy sent him to London in the spring of 1963 to prepare for him a study of the Skybolt crisis which had seriously threatened Anglo-American relations in spite of the fact that President Kennedy had an unusually close relationship with Lord Harlech, the then British ambassador, and with Mr Harold Macmillan, then prime minister. Kennedy wanted to know what mistakes had been made and where, in order to prevent such a situation from happening again. And in November 1964 Neustadt became something of a secret emissary for President Johnson when he was sent to London on the eve of Mr Harold Wilson's visit to Washington as prime minister to make certain there would not be another Anglo-American misunderstanding over the multilateral and Atlantic nuclear fleet proposals. Meanwhile Neustadt has become Professor of Government and Director of the Institute of Politics, which Harvard University has established as a part of the John F. Kennedy memorial in Cambridge.

October 1964

Brandon   There's a great deal of controversy in Britain as to whether 10 Downing Street is sufficiently well staffed and organised to cope with the needs of our times. You can draw from your own experience in the White House under President Truman; you've written a book on presidential power and the politics of leadership; and President Kennedy invited you to assist him in organising the White House. In addition you are also a student of the inner workings of the British government. Do you think 10 Downing Street needs to be modernised?

Neustadt   I do think so. Of course I express that view with all the qualifications suitable to a foreign observer. It seems to me that the only circumstance under which 10 Downing Street can remain what it has been – a private office in the strictest and smallest sense – is if you had consistently a prime minister of the most orthodox and passive sort, content to be 'presiding officer' in the cabinet. But particularly in the last quarter of a century this has not seemed to be the dominant trend. If the Churchill and Macmillan precedents are any guide to the dominant trend, as they certainly seem to be for Harold Wilson, then 10 Downing Street is plainly inadequate as a personal arm for the PM.

Brandon How do you think a PM should go about turning 10 Downing Street into a 'power-house of ideas' to use Harold Wilson's phrase?

Neustadt '10 Downing Street' is an ambiguous term in that connection. Does it mean the PM's private office alone, or does it encompass the Cabinet Office as well? The first may be too 'private' to become a 'power-house'. The second might be hard to make exclusively a 'power-house' for *him*.

Let me try to sort this out. An active prime minister has a strong personal interest in major lines of policy, foreign and domestic. He also has a strong personal interest in political strategy and parliamentary tactics and political appointments and, if he's wise, in civil service appointments too. When I say 'personal' I mean he will want to put the stamp of his own judgement on the outcome.

Now, such a man must have some helpers whom he can call his own. For one thing, he'll need personal aides devoted to his interests, mindful of his own perspective and priorities; who monitor his daily schedule, man his door, keep his papers, run his errands and the like. This is the traditional private office function. It sounds simple, but at the PM's level this function calls for skills of a high order from very able people: 'generalists' as we would say, and thoroughly experienced in government, and also absolutely loyal to the PM.

But in my very limited observation there are two things wrong with recent practice. For one, it's evidently a mistake to draw these people from the civil service with the expectation they can go back there. I'm not suggesting that one can't find the ability there; obviously one can. But in the rarefied, highly charged political environment of Number 10 an able civil servant who gives loyalty as he should may not be able to go back into the bureaucracy. Recent examples are suggestive: Sir Timothy Bligh, Sir Philip de Zulueta. Among the changes which are needed is the recognition that such jobs are not civil service careers. Another change, I should think, will be eventual enlargement of the number of people in the private office.

Mr Wilson at one time suggested that a prime minister should have staff to probe the bureaucracy, the officialdom, for ideas, new conceptions, new solutions; and to reach outside of Whitehall into universities and other private sources for what Franklin Roosevelt once called 'happy thoughts' – feeding in ideas for prospective government programmes, and that this staff should keep a prime minister continuously abreast of what is going on around him in government.

To an American this makes great sense. We have had staff work of that sort done for a president ever since the middle 1930s. It hasn't always been adequate or successful, of course, but it has always had the objective I think Mr Wilson seeks: to give the chief of government the wherewithal – ideas and information – so that he can make his judgement count on matters of concern to him and not be a mere ratifier of other people's judgements; not having to decide on two-page briefs at the end of the argument but, rather, getting into the details at the beginning.

In Washington this sort of staff work is directed from the White House itself, but much of it is done by other presidential staffs, less intimate and personal, in what we call the Executive Office of the President. That's quite a large entity, composed in major part of civil servants, which constitutes virtually a 'president's department' and includes a number of the current functions of your Treasury relating to supply, economic advice and establishments. It's natural that we should come to this since ours is not, in any sense, a cabinet system. But with you, of course, creation of a comparable 'prime minister's department' would be a great constitutional departure. I doubt that Mr Wilson has anything so drastic in mind.

To enlarge the private office to the point where it could do the whole job seems a difficult and dangerous course. Ministers might mutiny. Worse, civil servants would regard it with disdain, distaste and horror. But they run the machine. Do you suppose a sensible prime minister would take the risk of driving them distracted? I think not.

Brandon What is the alternative?

Neustadt It is to build up the capabilities – not of Number 10 *per se*, not of the private office, but of the Cabinet Office making it the main source of the programmatic staff work on ideas and information. What one could do, I take it, is to staff the major cabinet committees – the Defence Policy Committee for example, with a few high-level, keen effective generalists who have high sensitivity to policy; no narrow experts but broad-gauge people. One could find them presumably in the administrative class and detach them from departmental work for a tour of cabinet duty, as one does with the present cabinet secretariat. And, presumably, one could draw some people in from universities or business for fixed periods, as with the present Economic Section.

But here's where the dilemma comes, here is where I'm puzzled because there's an essential ambiguity in this from a prime minister's point of view. The whole doctrine of staff work under which the cabinet secretariat now operates is service to the cabinet as a whole, respecting the equality and collectivity of all members. The secretariat acknowledges the PM's special role as maker-of-agenda and enunciator of decisions – he is its administrative boss – but in its own actions it thinks of itself as loyal to the collectivity. Yet the PM's personal interests are not necessarily those of the collectivity. If you visualise the cabinet secretariat as a personal policy staff for the PM, you interfere with the whole doctrine under which it operates. But if you build up the secretariat without changing its doctrine, you get something other than personal service. An outsider cannot help but wonder if 'collective responsibility' would not have disappeared long since except for Lloyd George's invention of the cabinet secretariat, and the chain of conventions surrounding it. But the doctrine thrives; the secretariat helps to sustain it. As a result a prime minister who wants to build a personal staff will buttress his resources through the Cabinet Office at some cost to himself in terms of loyalty and staff service. If he doesn't want to pay that cost, but also doesn't want to run the risk of building up an outsize private office, he may have to alter the whole orientation of the Cabinet Office – which raises similar risks.

I once was told by an experienced and well-placed civil servant something I've been at great pains to remember: that the members of a PM's private office – those four men at 10 Downing Street seconded from the civil service – feel themselves at liberty to call ministers in the PM's name and talk very firmly indeed. That's indicative of the PM's relation with the ministers. But on the other hand these same private secretaries, according to my informant, feel themselves impelled to speak with discretion, courtesy, care and respect to senior civil servants.

The atmosphere at Number 10 is evidently so political, and the Palace – as with us – is so heady a place to be and the PM's need for confidants is so great in his relative isolation from departments, that any good civil servant who spends many years as a PM's personal aide is, as with us, unlikely to drop back into the service. There is a real qualitative difference between Number 10 and other ministerial positions. PMs may not be 'presidential', but they are something more and different from *primus inter pares*.

Brandon   This perhaps is also one reason why a civil servant who is taken out of the ministry and is expected to go back into the ministry cannot provide the PM with the kind of close confidential relationship that is perhaps necessary at that place.

Neustadt   Well, I would assume that the departure of two long-term holders of such positions is very indicative. In the US most of our political executives, heads of department or presidents, seem to operate with two kinds of staff: one kind is oriented to their personal needs, to their ways of doing business, the others are oriented to the office and the institution for the sake of making sure that the work of the others reflects the personal interests of the top man. This is the real distinction between White House staff and career staffs in the Executive Office. Most American executives are very conscious that they need both kinds of service. But obviously a PM needs the first kind almost more than anybody because he alone has no department. Who can he talk to? No departmental civil servants work for him and ministers can scarcely be his confidants. He just has to talk to those who have been seconded to him and once they've gone through that experience for a very long time, they're not fit for anything else. I would suggest that, at least at this level, something is lacking in your system. I suspect deliberately.

Brandon If we could be more specific on how to organise the personal staff, how would you divide the functions that are now shouldered by the PM's four private secretaries?

Neustadt I doubt that one would wish to create at Number 10 fixed, irrevocable divisions of responsibility. In White House experience the best organising principle has been to give each assistant continuing responsibility for particular sorts of actions to be taken by the president. So in Mr Kennedy's time, Ted Sorensen was continuously involved with preparation of the public documents through which the president enunciated programmes: speeches, messages to Congress, statements on enrolled bills, legislative drafts – that sort of thing; while McGeorge Bundy played the same role with respect to action issues stemming from the operational cables, diplomatic and military, in the sphere of overseas affairs. Both these men dealt with a recurring stream of actions requiring decision. The specialisation between them was not by subject-matter so much as it was by type of action. In the present private office in a very loose, informal way something of the same sort has been traditional. The private secretary seconded from the Foreign Office has tended to be the man through whom certain kinds of actions got attended to. The man seconded from the Home Office has dealt with domestic counterparts; the principal private secretary seems to a considerable extent to have dealt with what on our side would be called personality issues: interrelationships at the political level. And then, it has been traditional or at least characteristic for some time to have one member of the entourage who dealt regularly with party matters. An enlarged private office would not so much change as buttress this division of labour.

It's important to understand, and very hard for an American to remember, that the only departmental people who can be said to work for the PM in a sharp, direct way are other ministers. Departmental civil servants do not work for him. His day-by-day relations with departments are either through the cabinet secretariat or through direct connections with ministers. His personal secretaries, civil servants though they are, continuously get involved in making those connections from politician to politician. Perhaps part of the strengthening that Mr Wilson talked about would be achieved not only by enlarging the number of private secretaries, but by introducing into the private office some aides who had some status of their own as politicians.

Brandon   Or as experts.

Neustadt   Now you come to experts. I can conceive that within the framework of this private office, and apart from the Cabinet Office, one could have a few broad-gauged, personally loyal, politically oriented people with a great deal of substantive experience in particular areas, who would not have continuing action issue assignments of the sort I've described. They wouldn't be regular secretaries but, rather, special aides on *ad hoc* assignments. There is some precedent for this: the present Economic Section had its origins in *ad hoc* arrangements that Mr Churchill made during the war. In the White House we have had a few such people, personal experts if you will, attached directly to the personal staff. And if Mr Wilson means no more than that he would have two or three such men with economic backgrounds, and a comparable man or two with scientific backgrounds given roving assignments to watch, to make connections in officialdom and with the universities, to put proposals and ideas to him outside normal channels as a way of balancing against advice through official channels – if this is all he has in mind I think it might well work, at least for a while. But our experience has been that when you have such people in a personal entourage for very long, one of two things happens: either they carve out a role in action issues which begin to come to them routinely, and so settle down to being regular staff doers, not thinkers; or they begin to assemble staffs of their own in order to allow them to think better. If they do that, pretty soon they lose intimacy with the boss, begin to irritate the boss by virtue of the very number of people they have working for them, the number of bureaucratic fights that their people get into, the number of second-level matters they pursue. Then they either have to be got rid of, or they need be given a regular place outside the immediate entourage.

One fairly recent example with us is the science adviser's office, which began in the White House because Mr Eisenhower felt a tremendous need for a personal expert who had no axe to grind. By Mr Kennedy's time this man had taken on a lot of less intimate functions, things of a continuing governmental character. The science adviser kept his title as a personal aide and was so used from time to time, but a step removed from the president. It might be better to start the whole thing over . . . Perhaps you start with a Lord Cherwell and then as the personal connection dissipates and the big institutional relationships develop you let these people drift away, keep moving a few of them about, and when you want another Cherwell start again at Number 10 knowing that he, too, should be sloughed off in due course.

As an alternative to putting such people into Number 10 there remains the possibility of connecting them to the career staffs of cabinet committees. I'm not sure how it would operate to the prime minister's advantage unless the Cabinet Office became thoroughly identified as second-level staff to him, like our Executive Office of the President. I can conceive of this happening under a strong PM so far as members of a cabinet are concerned. But, as I said before, I think your officials would resist it. 'Collective responsibility' serves *them*. They've got the biggest stake in it. If I have the British system right, the great boon in the cabinet system for the civil servant is that through his minister, who needs his advice, it secures him a voice in the decisions he must carry out.

Brandon   Do you then suggest enlarging the cabinet secretariat or Number 10?

Neustadt   You don't face the same clear-cut situation we faced in Washington. If in the 1930s we had not developed a White House staff, a personal staff outside the civil service and also an Executive Office, our presidency would have been incapable of operating since the Second World War. But the choice is not so clear with you. You have what is called a cabinet system which in recent decades has often shown signs of becoming more rather than less prime-ministerialised. It would be possible to enlarge the private office and reorient the

Cabinet Office in such a way, really, as to presidentialise the system. I don't doubt the possibility. It would be a great wrench for civil servants. It would be enormously irritating to ministers. The PM's hold on ministers at most times is so great that he can have his way with them in matters of this sort if he is determined to. On the other hand his hold on civil servants is tenuous, and that's the real separation of power in the British system, as I understand it.

I think their mechanisms of resistance would be twofold: insistence on the present doctrines of the cabinet system and insistence on the relative autonomy of the establishments' work in the Treasury. The PM, as I understand it, does have a right of review over senior appointments to ministries. But he has no independent source of advice, save his own knowledge and the knowledge of his ministerial associates, so far as I know. This suggests that if a PM really wished to make himself the master of the government machine he could do it by selective use of his own non-career people. But he'd have to be ruthless and he'd make a lot of trouble and I wonder if it's worth it. Clearly there's no absolute necessity. The machine can and does operate with a relatively passive prime minister.

Brandon   How good do you think an instrument is Whitehall today?

Neustadt   Whitehall is not, I think, the perfect instrument Americans have so often thought it. I have found senior officials worried about its relative decline. But perhaps it never was as perfect an instrument as it seems in retrospect. Certainly it does not have the great advantage of our system, the lateral movement of officials in and out, from government to the academic institutions and business – and back again. It therefore lacks a certain freshness. But it does have a number of extremely skilled, broad-gauged, inventive people. A wholesale assault on its internal ways of life and operation would, at least temporarily, deprive the assaulter of those services – or anyway disrupt them. I daresay a politician coming in would think two or three times about that.

Brandon   You said in your book *Presidential Power* that the most essential need for the president is to be his own director of his own central intelligence, that much of what he needs will not be volunteered by his official advisers. Now how would you protect that need under the British system? Because the American president is really a much more free-wheeling individual than the PM.

Neustadt   I would think the need is there for the PM also. Short of an attack on the whole system I would think him obviously much less free than our man to establish and manage an information net throughout the government, throughout official ranks. But I should think with enough skill a good deal might be done, even in the framework of the present system. What it takes is people who are both very knowledgeable and very discreet, who also have no obligations other than to serve the PM; with no particular departmental or personal axe to grind except his own. It takes several such people in the private office and one or two such people in the major cabinet committees. And these have to be people whose networks of acquaintance with able civil servants are such that the connections could be made there. But you can only bring in a few. Then rapidly but quietly you'd have to use prime ministerial authority over the posting of senior civil servants to ensure not passive subordinates but, rather, people of such temperamental affinity that your own people and they will work together easily. It has to be done very delicately, though. To start interfering wholesale with appointments of a career service, and with its own sense of its own proper movement of its people, is to do enormous damage to morale; also, men you favour can in the process get marked for future sacrifice.

Brandon   I think the Roosevelt method of creating competition between people and keeping jurisdictions uncertain is not very adaptable to the British system.

Neustadt   No, it isn't. The greatest competition, I take it – and this is a crude over-simplification – is between civil service ranks and ministerial ranks; or really, perhaps, between Treasury types screened by their ministers and an active prime minister. There is of course a great deal of strain between departments, at least until a government decision has been taken. But it is not the kind of strain a prime minister can readily exploit because the civil servants who are fighting have every incentive, if I understand the system, to keep their fights below his level – below cabinet level. They may have more to lose than to gain by prematurely carrying their own wars up to a level they less readily control. Of course there are the personal competitions between ministers, and these no doubt a PM sometimes can exploit; sometimes, I take it, that's how he survives.

Brandon   You wrote once that the needs of bureaucrats and presidents are incompatible. Would it be true to say for Whitehall, too, that the better one is served the worse will be the other?

Neustadt   Well, there's bound to be a certain amount of conflict between a career service and a political service if I can coin that phrase. But I don't think our systems are very much alike. I think the essential difference is that your system, as I perceive it, is constructed out of a set of tacit treaties or agreements in which all the players co-operate with one another to reduce to an irreducible minimum the insecurities of personal and institutional position. Your civil service has a tradition of loyal execution of government decisions. By our standards it is astonishing. In return for loyal execution, the governing politicians in your system, the cabinet ministers, have a tradition, rarely violated, of consulting civil servants, of protecting their anonymity, of respecting their co-optative system, and of assuring their honorific status in society. Now that's quite a reasonable treaty, a good trade. Sometimes, when I feel most American, I am tempted to think that this leaves nothing to quarrel about except policy; and whoever could seriously care about that as long as his position and his service were secure?

What gives the real bite and passion and innovation to policymaking in our system are the personal and institutional insecurities of everybody. Neither the civil servants nor their departmental superiors, least of all the president, can be sure for one moment of the security of his programme, his organisation, his personal authority. And this insecurity, although it causes great confusion and enormous rows, does put a spur under people; it adds to their ingenuity and it makes them more passionate about policy. Every policy fight is also a fight over personal and institutional status. To some extent perhaps this adds to the inventiveness of policy. To a large extent of course it adds to the chaos of administration – which is a considerable price to pay.

Brandon   And the internal pressures?

Neustadt   The internal pressures are all maximised. Now with you, the civil servants have every incentive to execute anything their political masters can agree on. One gets the impression from outside that they are also capable of taking considerable steps to make sure their masters don't agree on things they very seriously disapprove of. Your ministers, being assured that if they can agree they'll get results, are in a much more relaxed position than our political people; and at the same time, by virtue of their tacit treaties with their own backbenchers, your people are assured a much easier road where legislation is concerned. Your governing politicians – the cabinet politicians – do not need to worry every minute of the day, as ours do, that what they want may not be put in operation. On the other hand the price they pay for this is that they must consult the civil servants; they must in their fashion be loyal to civil service rights and privileges; they must keep their ears attuned to backbench grumbling, and they must keep up a show of decorum among themselves. 'Non-arbitrariness', except when he's dismissing them, is evidently in their tacit treaty with each other and the PM. These probably are rather heavy prices for politicians, and no doubt inhibit them greatly. Given these restraints, their ability to agree on innovative ideas is probably rather limited. I've often wondered if this is one of the reasons why British policy frequently has not been very innovative. But that's an ill-tempered American supposition, not too seriously meant.

Brandon   That really brings us back to the need perhaps of the reorganisation of the PM's office, in order to give it this new, innovative quality.

Neustadt   Well, if you start from an American point of view, which is of course what I start from and which is very dangerous to export, then you would be inclined to say that competition is the life of trade. Personal insecurity, with government officials as with entrepreneurs, is a spur to thought. The interjection of outsiders near the top would certainly increase the discomfort of everybody in the system. It also could be – and one has to admit it – very dangerous if overdone. Moreover, I don't think that the establishment, if there is such a thing, or the general public either, much likes fuss. The only untidiness that is really liked is the untidiness of tradition. But the unseemliness of bureaucratic and political haggling, American style, would not I think be politically very advantageous to a PM in Britain. I could be wrong about this.

But if I'm right, that's another limitation.

Reference

1. Reprinted from *Conversations with Henry Brandon* (London: Deutsch, 1966) pp. 98–111, with the permission of the publisher.

6

White House and Whitehall

RICHARD E. NEUSTADT[1]

On the face of it, the British prime ministership is by no means a suitable candidate for comparison with the United States presidency. The British and American constitutions differ in almost every particular, and 10 Downing Street as a piece of administrative apparatus is miniscule compared with the staff that an American president has available in the White House. Nevertheless, as Professor Neustadt points out in this chapter, originally written for an American audience, a careful comparison between the two offices — one that does not confuse function with form — can reveal a considerable amount about the political dynamics of both.

'Cabinet government', so-called, as practised currently in the United Kingdom, differs in innumerable ways, some obvious, some subtle, from 'presidential government' in the United States. To ask what one can learn about our own machine by viewing theirs — which is the question posed for me this morning – may seem far-fetched, considering those differences. But actually the question is a good one. For the differences are matters of degree and not of kind.

Despite surface appearances these two machines, the British and American, are not now at opposite poles. Rather they are somewhat differently located near the centre of a spectrum stretching between ideal types, from collective leadership to one-man rule. Accordingly, a look down Whitehall's corridors of power should suggest a lot of things worth noticing in Washington. At any rate, that is the premise of this paper.

For a president-watcher, who tries to understand the inner politics of our machine and its effects on policy by climbing inside now and then and learning on the job, it is no easy matter to attempt comparison with the internal life of Whitehall. How is one to get a comparable look? Those who govern Britain mostly keep their secrets to themselves. They rarely have incentive to do otherwise, which is among the differences between us. Least of all are they inclined to satisfy curiosities of *academics*, especially not English academics. But even we colonials, persistent though we are and mattering as little as we do, find ourselves all too frequently treated like Englishmen and kept at bay by those three magic words, 'Official Secrets Act'. Why not? Nothing in the British constitution says that anyone outside of Whitehall needs an inside view. Quite the reverse. If academics knew, then journalists might learn, and even the backbenchers might find out. God forbid! That could destroy the constitution. Governing is *meant* to be a mystery.

And so it is, not only in the spoken words of those who do it but also, with rare exceptions, in the written words of journalists and scholars. Only in the memoirs of participants does one get glimpses now and then of operational reality. And even the most 'indiscreet' of recent memoirs veil the essence of the modern system: the relations between ministers and civil servants in the making of a government decision.[2] Former civil servants have at least as great a stake as former ministers in shielding those relationships: the stake of loyalty to their own professional successors in the governing of Britain. What could matter more than that?

For four years I have made a hobby of attempting to poke holes in their defences, and to take a closer look than either interviews or books afford. Partly this has been a 'busman's holiday': having roamed one set of corridors I find it irresistible to look around another set. Partly, though, I have been tempted by the thought which prompted those who organised this panel: namely, that comparison of likenesses and differences would add a new dimension to president-watching.

To test that proposition I have taken every look at Whitehall I could manage by a whole variety of means. Happily for me, White House assignments have contributed to this endeavour. In 1961 when I enjoyed the hospitality of Nuffield College and began my inquiries in Whitehall, the vague status of sometime-Kennedy-consultant opened many doors. It helps to be an object of curiosity. It also helps to have been an official, even in another government: one then 'talks shop'. In 1963 President Kennedy asked me for a confidential report on the evolution of the Skybolt crisis in both governments. Prime Minister Macmillan co-operated. I learned a lot. In 1964 President Johnson asked me to help facilitate communications between governments in preparation for his first meeting with Harold Wilson as prime minister. Wilson then had just come into office. Whitehall was in transition. Again, I learned a lot. Each time I go to London now I learn a little more.

If this strikes you as a hard way, or an odd way, to do 'research', I should simply say that I have found no better way to study bureaucratic politics. While the specifics of official business remain classified, perceptions of behaviour in the doing of the business become grist for our academic mill. I shall draw on such perceptions in this paper. You will understand, of course, that I am still a novice Whitehall-ogist. It would take ten years of such 'research' before I came to trust my own perceptions. This, perforce, is but an interim report on insufficient evidence from an unfinished study.

What I shall do this morning is to raise two simple points of difference between their machine and ours, with an eye to implications for the study of *our* system:

First, we have counterparts for their top civil servants – but not in our own civil service.

Second, we have counterparts for their cabinet ministers – but not exclusively or even mainly in our cabinet.

If I state these two correctly, and I think I do, it follows that in our conventional comparisons we students all too often have been victims of semantics. Accordingly, in our proposals for reform-by-analogy (a favourite sport of this association since its founding) we all too often have confused function with form. I find no functions in the British system for which ours lacks at least nascent counterparts. But it is rare when institutions with the same names in both systems do the same work for precisely the same purpose. We make ourselves much trouble, analytically, by letting nomenclature dictate our analogies. Hopefully, this paper offers something of an antidote.

For the most important things that I bring back from my excursioning in Whitehall are a question and a caution. The question: what is our functional equivalent? The caution: never base analysis on nomenclature. With these I make my case for a comparative approach to American studies. These seem to be embarrassingly obvious. But that is not the way it works in practice. By way of illustration let me take in turn those 'simple' points of difference between Whitehall and Washington.

I

'Why are your officials so passionate?' I once was asked in England by a bright young Treasury official just back from Washington. I inquired with whom he had been working there; his answer 'Your chaps at the Budget Bureau'.

To an American those 'chaps' appear to be among the most dispassionate of Washingtonians. Indeed, the budget staff traditionally prides itself on being cool, collected, and above the struggle, distant from emotions churning in the breasts of importunate agency officials. Yet to my English friend, 'They took themselves so seriously . . . seemed to be crusaders for the policy positions they thought made sense . . . seemed to feel that it was up to them to save the day'. If this is how the Budget Bureau struck him, imagine how he would have felt about some circles in our Air Force, or the European Bureau of the State Department, or the Office of Economic Opportunity, or the Forest Service, for that matter, or the Bureau of Reclamation, or the National Institutes of Health!

His question is worth pondering, though that is not my purpose here.[3] I give it you gratis to pursue on your own time. What I should rather do is to pursue two further questions which his inquiry suggests. First, out of what frame of reference was he asking? And second, is it sensible of him (and most of us) to talk of our own budgeteers as though they were his counterparts? I ask because I think that we are very far from candid with ourselves about the way we get *his* work done in *our* system.

This young man was a principal-with-prospects at the Treasury. By definition, then, he was a man of the administrative class, elite corps of the British civil service. More importantly, he was also apprentice member of the favoured few, elite-of-the-elite, who climb the ladder *in* the Treasury. With skill and luck and approbation from his seniors he might someday rise to be a mandarin. And meanwhile he would probably serve soon as personal assistant to a cabinet minister. In short, he had the frame of reference which befits a man whose career ladder rises up the central pillar of the whole Whitehall machine toward the heights where dwell the seniors of all seniors, moulders of ministers, heads of the civil service, knights in office, lords thereafter: permanent secretaries of the cabinet and Treasury.

English civil servants of this sort, together with their Foreign Office counterparts, comprise the inner corps of 'officials', civilian careerists, whose senior members govern the United Kingdom in collaboration with their ministerial superiors the front bench politicians, leaders of the parliamentary party which commands a House majority for the time being. Theirs is an intimate collaboration grounded in the interests and traditions of both sides. Indeed it binds them into a society for mutual benefit: what they succeed in sharing with each other they need share with almost no one else, and governing in England is a virtual duopoly.

This is the product of a tacit treaty, an implicit bargain, expressed in self-restraints which are observed on either side. The senior civil servants neither stall nor buck decisions of the government once taken in due form by their political masters. 'Due form' means consultation, among other things, but having been consulted these officials act without public complaint or private evasion, even though they may have fought what they are doing up to the last moment of decision. They also try to assure comparable discipline in lower official ranks, and to squeeze out the juniors who do not take kindly to it. The senior politicians, for their part – with rare and transient exceptions – return the favour in full measure.

The politicians rarely meddle with official recruitment or promotion; by and large, officialdom administers itself. They preserve the anonymity of civil servants both in parliament and in the press. Officials never testify on anything except 'accounts', and nobody reveals their roles in shaping public policy. Ministers take kudos for themselves, likewise the heat. They also take upon themselves protection for the status of officialdom in the society: honours fall like gentle rain at stated intervals. They even let careerists run their private offices, and treat their personal assistants of the moment (detailed from civil service ranks) as confidentially as our department heads treat trusted aides imported from outside. More importantly, the politicians *lean* on their officials. They *expect* to be advised. Most importantly, they very often do what they are told, and follow the advice that they receive.

This is an advantageous bargain for both sides. It relieves the politicians of a difficult and chancy search for 'loyal' advisers and administrators. These are there, in place, ready to hand. And it relieves officials of concern for their security in terms both of profession and of person. No wonder our careerists appear 'passionate' to one of theirs; they have nothing at stake [in Britain] except policy!

So a Treasury-type has everything to gain by a dispassionate stance, and nothing to lose except arguments. Since he is an elitist, ranking intellectually and morally with the best in Britain, this is no trifling loss. If parliamentary parties were less disciplined than they now are, or if he had backbenchers who identified with him, he could afford to carry arguments outside official channels, as his predecessors sometimes did a century ago, and *military* officers still do, on occasion.[4] But party discipline calls forth its counterpart in his own ranks. And party politicians on back benches have no natural affinities for *civil* servants – quite the contrary. He really has no recourse but to lose his arguments with grace and wait in patience for another day, another set of ministers. After all, he stays, they go. And while he stays he shares the fascinating game of power, stretching his own mind and talents in the service of a reasonably grateful country.

The Treasury-type is a disciplined man, but a man fulfilled, not frustrated. His discipline is what he pays for power. Not every temperament can take it; if he rises in the Treasury he probably can. Others are weeded out. But there is more to this than a cold compromise for power's sake. Those who rise and find fulfilment in their work do so in part because they are deliberately exposed at mid-career to the constraints, the miseries, the hazards which afflict the human beings who wield power on the political side. They know the lot of ministers from observation at first hand. Exposure makes for empathy and for perspective. It also makes for comfort with the civil servant's lot. Whitehall's elitists gain all three while relatively young. It leaves them a bit weary with the weight of human folly, but it rids them of self-righteousness, the bane of *our* careerists – which is, of course, endemic among budgeteers.

A Treasury-type gains this exposure through that interesting device, the tour of duty in a minister's private office as his personal assistant ('dogsbody' is their term for it). The private secretary, so called, now serves his master-of-the-moment as a confidential aide, minding his business, doing his chores, sharing his woes, offering a crying towel, bracing him for bad days in the House, briefing him for bad days in the office. Etcetera. Remarkably, by our standards, the civil service has pre-empted such assignments for its own. (Do not confuse these with mere *parliamentary* private secretaries.) Still more remarkably, the politicians feel themselves well served and rarely dream of looking elsewhere for the service. I know an instance where a minister confided in his private secretary a secret he told no one else save the prime minister, not even his permanent secretary, the career head of department, 'lest it embarrass him to know'. The permanent secretary was the private secretary's boss in career terms. Yet the secret was kept as a matter of course. This, I am assured, is not untypical: 'ministerial secrets' are all in the day's work for dogsbodies.

Accordingly, the one-time private secretary who has risen in due course to be a permanent secretary of a department, knows far more of what it feels like to perform as politician than his opposite number, the department's minister, can ever hope to fathom in reverse. A William Armstrong, for example, now joint head of the Treasury, whose opposite number is the chancellor of the exchequer, spent years as private secretary to a previous chancellor who was among the ablest men in cabinets of his time. Consider the ramifications of that![5] And draw the contrast with our own careerists!

Our budgeteers imagine that they are the nearest thing to

Treasury civil servants. For this no one can blame them. Much of our literature suggests that if they are not quite the same as yet, a little gimmickry could make them so. Many of our colleagues in this association have bemused themselves for years with plans to borrow nomenclature and procedures from the British side, on the unstated premise that function follows form. But it does not.

Functionally, our counterparts for British Treasury-types are *non*-careerists holding jobs infused with presidential interest or concern – 'in-and-outers' from the law firms, banking, business, academia, foundations, or occasionally journalism, or the entourages of successful governors and senators – along with up-and-outers (sometimes up-and-downers) who relinquish, or at least risk, civil service status in the process. Here is the elite-of-the-elite, the upper-crust of *our* 'administrative class'. These are the men who serve alongside our equivalents for ministers and share in governing. One finds them in the White House and in the *appointive* jobs across the street at the Executive Office Building. One finds them also on the seventh floor of State, and on the third and fourth floors of the Pentagon: these places among others. If they have not arrived as yet, they probably are trying to get in (or up). If they have gone already, they are likely to be back.

Let me take some names at random to suggest the types. First, the prototype of all: Averell Harriman. Second, a handful of the currently employed: David Bell, both Bundys (by their different routes), Wilbur Cohen, Harry McPherson, Paul Nitze. Third, a few fresh 'outers' almost certain to be back, somehow, sometime: Kermit Gordon, Theodore Sorensen, Lee White. Fourth, a long-time 'outer' who is never back but always in: Clark Clifford. Three of these men got their start as government careerists, two as academics, one in banking, two in law, and two on Capitol Hill. The numbers are but accidents of random choice; the spread is meaningful.

The jobs done by such men as these have no precise equivalents in England; our machinery is too different. For example, McGeorge Bundy as the President's Assistant for National Security Affairs is something more than principal private secretary to the prime minister (reserved for rising Treasury-types), a dogsbody-writ-large, and something different from the secretary of the cabinet (top of the tree for them), a post 'tradition' turns into an almost constitutional position, certainly what we call an 'institutional' one. Yet the men in those positions see a Bundy as their sort of public servant. They are higher on the ladder than my young friend with the question; they do not take budgeteers to be their counterparts: they know a senior civil servant when they see one.

A Bundy *is* one in their eyes – and they are right. For so he is in American practice. I mention Bundy whom they actually know. But if they knew a Sorensen, a Moyers, or the like, I have no doubt that they would see them much the same.

Every detail of our practice is un-English, yet the general outline fits. One of our men appears on television; another testifies against a bill; a third and fourth engage in semi-public argument; a fifth man feeds a press campaign to change the president's mind; a sixth disputes a cabinet member's views in open meeting; a seventh overturns an inter-agency agreement. So it goes, to the perpetual surprise (and sometimes envy?) of the disciplined duopolists in Britain. Yet by *our* lights, according to *our* standards, under *our* conditions, such activities may be as 'disciplined' as theirs, and as responsive to political leadership. The ablest of our in-and-outers frequently display equivalent restraint and equal comprehension in the face of the dilemmas which confront our presidential counterparts for cabinet politicians.

The elite of our officialdom is not careerist in the British sense (although, of course, our in-and-outers have careers); why should it be? Neither is the president with his department heads. They too are in-and-outers. We forget that the duopoly which governs Britain is composed of *two* career systems, official and political. Most ministers who will take office through the next decade are on the scene and well identified in Westminster. The permanent secretaries who will serve with them are on the Whitehall ladders now; a mere outsider can spot some of them. Contrast our situation – even the directorships of old-line bureaus remain problematical. Who is to succeed J. Edgar Hoover?

We have only two sets of true careerists in our system. One consists of senators and congressmen in relatively safe seats, waiting their turn for chairmanships. The other consists of military officers and civil employees who are essentially technicians manning every sort of speciality (including 'management') in the executive establishment. Between these two we leave a lot of room for in-and-outers. We are fortunate to do so. Nothing else could serve as well to keep the two apart. And *their* duopoly would be productive not of governance but of its feudal substitute, piecemeal administration. We can only hope to govern in our system by and through the presidency. In-and-outers are a saving grace for presidents.

II

Since 1959, English commentators frequently have wondered to each other if their government was being 'presidentialised'. In part this stemmed from electoral considerations following the 'personality contest' between Harold Macmillan and Hugh Gaitskell at that year's general election. In part it stemmed from operational considerations in the wake of Macmillan's active premiership – reinforced this past year by the sight of still another activist in office, Harold Wilson.

Despite their differences of style, personality, and party, both Macmillan and Wilson patently conceived the cabinet room in Downing Street to be the PM's office, not a mere board room. Both evidently acted on the premise that the PM's personal judgement ought, if possible, to rule the day. Both reached out for the power of personal decision on the issues of the day. Macmillan did so through off-stage manoeuvre, while avowing his fidelity to cabinet consensus as befits a man beset by the conventions of committee government. With perhaps a bit more candour, Wilson does the same. But what alerts the commentators is that both have done it. Hence discussion about trends toward presidential government.

Yet between these two prime ministers there was another for a year, Sir Alec Douglas-Home. And by no stretch of the imagination could his conduct of the office have been characterised as presidential. On the contrary, by all accounts he was a classic 'chairman of the board', who resolutely pushed impending issues *out* of Number 10, for initiative elsewhere by others. He managed, it is said, to get a lot of gardening done while he resided there. I once asked a close observer what became of the initiatives, the steering, the manoeuvring, which Home refused to take upon himself. He replied:

> When ministers discovered that he really wouldn't do it, they began to huddle with each other, little groups of major figures. You would get from them enough agreement or accommodation to produce the main lines of a government position, something they could try to steer through cabinet. Or if you didn't get it, there was nothing to be done. That's how it began to work, outside of Number 10, around it.

That is how it would be working now, had there been a slight shift in the popular vote of 1964.

The British system, then, has *not* been presidentialised, or not at least in operational terms. For as we learned with Eisenhower, the initiatives a president must take to form 'the main lines of a government position' cannot be kept outside the White House precincts. Toss them out and either they bounce back or they do not get taken. A president may delegate to White House aides ('OK, S.A.'), or to a Foster Dulles, but only as he demonstrates consistently, day-in-and-out, that they command his ear and hold his confidence. Let him take to his bed behind an oxygen tent and they can only go through motions. Eisenhower's White House was a far cry from 10 Downing Street in the regime of Douglas-Home. That remains the distance Britain's system has to travel towards a presidential status for prime ministers.

But even though the system did not make an activist of Douglas-Home, his predecessor and successor obviously relished the part. The system may not have required it but they pursued it, and the system bore the weight of their activity. In externals Number 10 looks no more like the White House under Wilson than it did a year ago. But in essence Wilson comes as close to being 'president' as the conventions of his system allow. He evidently knows it and likes it. So, I take it, did Macmillan.

How close can such men come? How nearly can they assert 'presidential' leadership inside a cabinet system? Without endeavouring to answer in the abstract, let me record some impressions of concrete performances.

First, consider Britain's bid for Common Market membership four years ago, which presaged an enormous (if abortive) shift in public policy, to say nothing of Tory party policy. By all accounts this 'turn to Europe' was Macmillan's own. The timing and the impetus were his, and I am told that his intention was to go whole-hog, both economically and politically. As such this was among the great strategic choices in the peacetime politics of Britain. But it never was a government decision. For those, by British definition, come in cabinet. Macmillan never put the issue there in terms like these. Instead he tried to sneak past opposition there – and on back benches and in constituencies – by disguising his strategic choice as a commercial deal. The cabinet dealt with issues of negotiation, *en principe* and later in detail, for making Britain part of Europe's economic union without giving up its Commonwealth connections (or farm subsidies). One minister explained to me:

> Timing is everything. First we have to get into the Common Market as a matter of business, good for our economy. Then we can begin to look at the political side . . . Appetites grow with eating. We couldn't hold the Cabinet, much less our back-benchers, if we put this forward now in broader terms . . .

Accordingly, the move toward Europe had to be played out in its ostensible terms, as a detailed negotiation of commercial character. This took two years, and while the tactic served its purpose within Tory ranks these were the years when France escaped from the Algerian war. By the time negotiations neared their end, Charles de Gaulle was riding high at home. Macmillan tiptoed past his own internal obstacles, but took so long about it that his path was blocked by an external one, the veto of de Gaulle.

Second, take the Nassau Pact of 1962, which calmed the Skybolt crisis between Washington and London even as it gave de Gaulle excuses for that veto. Macmillan was his own negotiator at the Nassau conference. He decided on the spot to drop his claim for Skybolt missiles and to press the substitution of Polaris weaponry. He wrung what seemed to him an advantageous compromise along those lines from President Kennedy. Then and only then did he 'submit' its terms to the full cabinet for decision (by return cable), noting the concurrence of three potent ministers who had accompanied him: the foreign, commonwealth, and defence secretaries. With the president waiting, the cabinet 'decided' (unenthusiastically by all accounts) to bless this virtual *fait accompli*. What else was there to do? The answer, nothing – and no doubt Macmillan knew it.

Third, consider how the present Labour government reversed its pre-election stand on Nassau's terms. Within six weeks of taking office Wilson and his colleagues became champions of the Polaris programme they had scorned in opposition. Their backbenchers wheeled around behind them almost to a man. It is no secret that the PM was the source of this reversal, also its tactician. So far as I can find, it was his own choice, his initiative, his management, from first to last. He got it done in quick time, yet he did it by manoeuvring on tiptoe like Macmillan in the Common Market case (with just a touch of shot-gun like Macmillan in the Nassau case). When Wilson let Polaris reach the cabinet for 'decision', leading ministers, both 'right' and 'left', already were committed individually through things they had been led to say or do in one another's presence at informal working sessions. By that time also, Wilson had pretested backbench sentiment, 'prematurely' voicing to an acquiescent House what would become the rationale for cabinet action: keeping on with weapons whose production had already passed a 'point of no return'.[6]

Superficially, such instances as these seem strikingly *un*presidential. In our accustomed vision, presidents do not tiptoe around their cabinets, they instruct, inform, or ignore them. They do not engineer *faits accomplis* to force decisions from them, for the cabinet does not make decisions, *presidents* decide. A Kennedy after Birmingham, a Johnson after Selma, deciding on their civil rights bills, or a Johnson after Pleiku, ordering the bombers north, or Johnson last December, taking off our pressure for the multilateral force, or Kennedy confronting Moscow over Cuba with advisers all around him but decisions in his hands – what contrasts these suggest with the manoeuvres of a Wilson or Macmillan!

The contrasts are but heightened by a glance at their work forces: presidents with 20-odd high-powered personal assistants, and 1,000 civil servants in their Executive Office – prime ministers with but four such assistants in their private office (three of them on detail from departments) and a handful more in Cabinet Office which by definition is not 'theirs' alone. Differences of work place heighten the effect still more: 10 Downing Street is literally a house, comparing rather poorly with the White House before Teddy Roosevelt's time. The modern White House is a palace, as Denis Brogan keeps reminding us, a physically-cramped version of the Hofburg, or the Tuileries.[7]

Yet beneath these contrasts, despite them, belying them, Americans are bound to glimpse a long-familiar pattern in the conduct of an activist prime minister. It is the pattern of a president manoeuvring around or through the power men in his administration *and* in Congress. Once this is seen all contrasts become superficial. Underneath our images of presidents-in-boots, astride decisions, are the half-observed realities of presidents-in-sneakers, stirrups in hand, trying to induce particular department heads, or congressmen, or senators to climb aboard.

Anyone who has an independent power base is likelier than not to get 'prime ministerial' treatment from a president. Even his own appointees are to be wooed, not spurred, in the degree that they have their own attributes of power: expertise, or prestige, or a statute under foot. As Theodore Sorensen reported while he still was at the White House:

> In choosing between conflicting advice, the President is also choosing between conflicting advisers . . . He will be slow to overrule a Cabinet officer whose pride or prestige has been committed, not only to save the officer's personal prestige but to maintain his utility . . . Whenever any President overrules any Secretary he runs the risk of that Secretary grumbling, privately, if not publicly, to the Congress, or to the Press (or to his diary), or dragging his feet on implementation, or, at the very worst, resigning with a blast at the President.[8]

But it is men of Congress more than departmental men who regularly get from Pennsylvania Avenue the treatment given cabinet ministers from Downing Street. Power in the Senate is particularly courted. A Lyndon Johnson when he served there, or a Vandenberg in Truman's time, or nowadays an Anderson, a Russell, even Mansfield, even Fulbright – to say nothing of Dirksen – are accorded many of the same attentions which a Wilson has to offer a George Brown.

The conventions of 'bipartisanship' in foreign relations, established under Truman and sustained by Eisenhower, have been extended under Kennedy and Johnson to broad sectors of the home front, civil rights especially. These never were so much a matter of engaging oppositionists in White House undertakings as of linking to the White House men from either party who had influence to spare. Mutuality of deference between presidents and leaders of congressional opinion, rather than between the formal party leaderships, always has been of the essence to 'bipartisanship' in practice. And men who really lead opinion on the Hill gain privileged access to executive decisions as their customary share of 'mutual defer- ence'. 'Congress' may not participate in such decisions, but these men often do: witness Dirksen in the framing of our recent Civil Rights Acts, or a spectrum of senators from Russell to Mansfield in the framing of particular approaches to Vietnam. Eleven years ago, Eisenhower seems to have kept our armed forces out of there when a projected intervention at the time of Dien Bien Phu won no support from Senate influentials. Johnson now manoeuvres to maintain support from 'right' to 'left' within their ranks.

If one seeks our counterparts for Wilson or Macmillan as cabinet tacticians one need look no farther than Kennedy or Johnson manoeuvring among the influentials both downtown *and* on the Hill (and in state capitals, steel companies, trade unions, for that matter). Macmillan's caution on the Common Market will suggest the tortuous, slow course of J. F. Kennedy toward fundamental changes in our fiscal policy, which brought him only to the point of trying for a tax cut by the start of his fourth year. Macmillan's *fait accompli* on Polaris brings to mind the South-East Asia resolution Johnson got from Con- gress after there had been some shooting in the Tonkin Gulf – and all its predecessors back to 1955 when Eisenhower pioneered this technique for extracting a 'blank cheque'.

Wilson's quiet, quick arrangement for the Labour party to adopt Polaris has a lot in common with the Johnson coup a year ago on aid to education, where a shift in rationale took all sorts of opponents off the hook.

British government may not be presidential but our government is more prime ministerial than we incline to think. Unhappily for thought, we too have something called a cabinet. But that pallid institution is in no sense the equivalent of theirs. Our equivalent is rather an informal, shifting aggregation of key individuals, the influentials at both ends of Pennsylvania Avenue. Some of them may sit in what we call the cabinet as department heads; others sit in back rows there, as senior White House aides; still others have no place there. Collectively these men share no responsibility nor any meeting ground. Individually, however, each is linked to all the others through the person of the president (supported by his telephone). And all to some degree are serviced – also monitored – by one group or another on the White House staff. The 'Bundy Office', and the former 'Sorensen Shop', which one might best describe now as the Moyers 'sphere of influence', together with the staff of legislative liaisoners captained until lately by Lawrence O'Brien – these groups although not tightly interlocked provide a common reference point for influentials everywhere: 'This is the White House calling . . .'. While we lack an institutionalised cabinet along British lines, we are evolving an equivalent of Cabinet Office. The O'Brien operation is its newest element, with no precursors worthy of the name in any regime earlier than Eisenhower's. Whether it survives, and how and why, without O'Brien become questions of the day for presidency-watchers. Doctoral candidates take note!

The functional equivalence between a British cabinet and our set of influentials – whether secretaries, senators, White House staffers, congressmen, or others – is rendered plain by noting that for most intents and purposes their cabinet members do the work of our congressional committees, our floor leaderships, and our front-offices downtown, all combined. The combination makes for superficial smoothness; Whitehall seems a quiet place. But once again appearances deceive. Beneath the surface this combine called 'cabinet' wrestles with divergencies of interest, of perspective, of procedure, personality, much like those we are used to witnessing above ground in the dealings of our separated institutions. Not only is the hidden struggle reminiscent of our open one, but also the results are often similar: 'bold, new ventures' actually undertaken are often few and far between. Whitehall dispenses with the grunts and groans of Washington, but both can labour mightily to bring forth mice.

It is unfashionable just now to speak of 'stalemate' or of 'deadlock' in our government, although these terms were all the rage two years ago and will be so again, no doubt, whenever Johnson's coattails shrink. But British government is no less prone to deadlock than our own. Indeed I am inclined to think their tendencies in that direction more pronounced than ours. A keen observer of their system, veteran of some seven years at cabinet meetings, put it to me in these terms:

> The obverse of our show of monolithic unity behind a government position when we have one is slowness, ponderousness, deviousness, in approaching a position, getting it taken, getting a 'sense of the meeting'. Nothing in our system is harder to do, especially if press leaks are at risk. You Americans don't seem to understand that.

In the Common Market case, to cite but one example, the three months from October to December 1962 were taken up at Brussels, where negotiations centred, by a virtual filibuster from the British delegation. This drove some of the Europeans wild and had them muttering about 'perfidious Albion'. But London's delegates were not engaged in tactical manoeuvring at Brussels. All they were doing there was to buy time for tactical manoeuvring back home, around the cabinet table. The three months were required to induce two senior ministers to swallow agricultural concessions every student of the subject knew their government would have to make. But Britain could not move until those influential 'members of the government' had choked them down. The time-lag seemed enormous from the vantage point of Brusssls. Significantly it seemed short indeed to Londoners. By Whitehall standards this was rapid motion.

One of the checks and balances in Britain's system lies

between the PM and his colleagues as a group. This is the check that operated here. A sensible prime minister, attuned to his own power stakes, is scrupulous about the forms of collective action: over-reaching risks rejection; a show of arbitrariness risks collegial reaction; if they should band together his associates could pull him down. Accordingly, the man who lives at Number 10 does well to avoid policy departures like the plague, unless, until, and if, he sees a reasonable prospect for obtaining that 'sense of the meeting'. He is not without resources to induce the prospect, and he is at liberty to ride events which suit his causes. But these things take time – and timing. A power-wise prime minister adjusts his pace accordingly. So Macmillan did in 1962.[9]

Ministerial prerogatives are not the only source of stalemate or slow motion in this system. If members of the cabinet were not also heads of great departments, then the leader of their party in the Commons and the country might be less inclined to honour their pretensions in the government. A second, reinforcing check and balance of the system lies between him and the senior civil servants. To quote again, from the same source:

> The PM has it easier with ministers than with the civil servants. The ranks of civil servants do not work for him. They have to be brought along. They are loyal to a 'government decision' but that takes the form of action in Cabinet, where the great machines are represented by their ministers.

The civil servants can be his allies, of course, if their perceptions of the public interest square with his and all he needs is to bring ministers along. Something of this sort seems to have been a factor in the Labour government's acceptance of Polaris: Foreign Office and Defence officials urged their masters on; Treasury officials remained neutral. The PM who first manages to tie the civil servants tighter to his office than to their own ministries will presidentialise the British system beyond anything our system knows. But that day is not yet. For obvious reasons it may never come.

So a British premier facing cabinet is in somewhat the position of our president confronting the executive departments and Congress combined. Our man, compared to theirs, is freer to take initiatives and to announce them *in advance* of acquiescence from all sides. With us, indeed, initiatives in public are a step toward obtaining acquiescence, or at least toward wearing down the opposition. It is different in Downing Street. With us, also, the diplomatic and defence spheres yield our man authority for binding judgements on behalf of the whole government. Although he rarely gets unquestioning obedience and often pays a price, his personal choices are authoritative, for he himself is heir to royal prerogatives. In Britain these adhere to cabinet members as a group, not the prime minister alone. Unless they stop him he can take over diplomacy, as Neville Chamberlain did so disastrously, and others since, or he can even run a war like Winston Churchill. But Chamberlain had to change foreign secretaries in the process, and Churchill took precautions, making himself minister of defence.

Still, despite all differences, a president like a prime minister lives daily under the constraint that he must bring along *his* 'colleagues' and get action from *their* liege men at both ends of the Avenue. A sensible prime minister is always counting noses in cabinet. A sensible president is always checking off his list of 'influentials'. The PM is not yet a president. The president, however, is a sort of super prime minister. This is what comes of comparative inquiry!

References

1. Reprinted in abridged form from a paper delivered at the 1965 Annual Meeting of the American Political Science Association, Washington, D.C., 8–11 September 1965, with the permission of the American Political Science Association and *The Public Interest* (New York). A slightly revised version of the paper appeared in *The Public Interest 2* (Winter 1966), pp. 55–69.
2. See for an example of a 'frank' political memoir, Hugh Dalton, *Memoirs*, vol. ii: *High Tide and After* (London: Muller, 1962). For an example on the civil service side see Edward, Lord Bridges, *The Treasury* (New Whitehall Series No. 12; London: Allen & Unwin, 1964).

3. I have suggested at least a partial answer in 'Politicians and Bureaucrats', *The Congress and America's Future* (New York: Prentice-Hall, 1965), pp. 115–16.

4. Regarding civil servants of an earlier era, when aristocratic patronage opened the way to careers, it is delightful to note that Sir Charles Trevelyan, one of the creators of the modern civil service, was accustomed to 'sound off' on issues of the day, with which he was concerned as an official of the Treasury, in letters to the press. See Cecil Woodham-Smith. *The Great Hunger* (New York: Harper, 1962).

   Regarding the military, I am indebted to Hugh Gaitskell, in a conversation three years ago, for the observation that the opposition was the target of confidential griping from senior service officers to a degree 'absolutely unknown' on the civilian side, 'perhaps for the reason that the army and navy are so much older than the civil service and quite a lot older than cabinet government. This gives a certain confidence . . . They still rather regard themselves as "servants of the crown" *apart* from the government. The civil servants wouldn't dare; theirs is a "junior" service . . . under cabinet from the start'.

5. There is some question whether the diet of a private secretary is not altogether too rich for a man on his way up civil service ladders in the rather special case of the prime minister's private office. Macmillan's private secretaries, both from the Treasury and from the Foreign Office, went not up but out. They had been too intimately and confidentially involved with too much power to resume the civil servant's climb within the ranks. I once speculated publicly that this might be the usual result, henceforth, given the heady atmosphere of Number 10 (*Sunday Times*, 8 November 1964, p. 41). This speculation drew a wager from the present PPS to the PM that *he*, unlike his predecessor, would be prepared to go back in and climb. When the time comes we shall see who wins that bet.

6. From the prime minister's statement to the House of Commons, defence debate, 23 November 1964.

7. Sir Denis Brogan, 'The Presidency', in *American Aspects* (London: Hamish Hamilton, 1964), pp. 5–6.

8. Theodore Sorensen, *Decision-Making in the White House* (New York: Columbia, 1963), pp. 79–80.

9. A man who seems to have made every mistake in the book on these scores, among others, is Anthony Eden, before, during, and after the Suez invasion of 1956.

7

Prime Ministerial Government

R. H. S. CROSSMAN[1]

As Professor Neustadt indicated in the previous two chapters, a debate has been going on in Britain for many years about whether the British system of government deserves any longer to be called 'cabinet government'. Have not the historic constitutional prerogatives of the cabinet as a whole been usurped by a succession of powerful incumbents of Number 10? The classic statement of the view the British government should now be called 'prime ministerial government' is set out in this chapter by R. H. S. Crossman. Crossman was a Labour frontbench spokesman when he wrote this chapter. He subsequently became a cabinet minister under Harold Wilson. He claimed that his experiences as a cabinet minister only reinforced the views that he had formed in opposition. An obvious question immediately arises: does the theory of prime ministerial government expounded in this chapter conform, or not conform, to the experience of British government under Margaret Thatcher described in chapter 4?

It seems to me that *The English Constitution* can still be read as the classical account of the classical period of parliamentary government. The secret which Bagehot claimed to have discovered between the dignified and efficient parts of the constitution does indeed provide the correct explanation of the relationship between the Commons and the cabinet as it emerged between 1832 and 1867.

It was not until well after Bagehot's death that this system was fundamentally transformed by the transfer of effective power from the floor of the Commons to the great party machines and the bureaucracy in Whitehall. Yet this was the very period when *The English Constitution* was finally accepted, not only as the *locus classicus* for the *mores* of Whitehall and Westminster, but as the definitive and authoritative account of how, in a democracy, power is divided between the electorate, the Commons and the cabinet. Once he was safely dead and buried, the sceptic whose chief pleasure was the deflating of myths and the exposure of democratic pretensions, was himself admitted to the literary establishment; and the book in which he achieved such an exact separation of political myth from political reality became a part of the dignified façade behind which a new 'efficient secret' could operate.

This absorption of Bagehot's anti-democratic analysis into the myth of democracy was not performed by the conservative opponents of change. It was a long line of radical theorists and left-wing reformers who wilfully misunderstood the lessons of *The English Constitution*, seeing it not as a model of how to pry behind the façade and observe the technique of power, but as the classical account of how a British democracy does work and ought to work.

The most recent examples of this misreading are to be found in the writings of Harold Laski and Lord Morrison. In the last lectures he ever delivered, Laski rebuked Amery for daring to criticise Bagehot, and once again expounded the 'efficient secret' as though it were a true account of what really happens, and not a hoary legend. 'I see no danger', he wrote, 'to the supremacy of the House of Commons in the new phase of its long life upon which it has entered'. And four pages later, we read: 'The Cabinet remains, in essence, a committee of the party or parties with a majority in the House of Commons'.[2]

Despite Lord Morrison's dislike of socialist intellectuals, we find Laski's uncritical acceptance of Bagehot's analysis repeated in the few passages of *Government and Parliament*, where Lord Morrison tries to relate his practical experiences in the cabinet to first principles. Both books are written on Mill's and Bagehot's liberal assumption that real sovereignty resides in the House of Commons, and that the cabinet is created by and responsible to the Commons. Yet having made their obeisance to the democratic appearance, both Lord Morrison and Laski proceed to give us detailed descriptions of how cabinet and parliament have operated since the war, which show that these appearances no longer bear much relation to fact. Bagehot's ingenious and shocking revelation has become part of the respectable legend that now obscures the way in which power is really wielded and decisions are really taken in the modern state.

When Bagehot, for example, described the Commons as the place where 'ministries are made and unmade' and Congress as the place where 'the debates are prologues without a play', the contrast was valid because the House of Commons in the 1860s still enjoyed effective sovereignty. But the contrast has become less and less true, as the suffrage was extended in this country and the modern party system developed. The right to appoint the prime minister, which Bagehot and Mill agreed to be the most important constitutional power belonging to the Commons, was gradually removed from it and shared between the parties and the monarch. And once it had lost its status as an 'electoral college' the House of Commons began to lose its collective will and finally became merely the forum of debate between well-disciplined political armies. Britain had left the epoch of classical parliamentary government, and entered a new epoch of bureaucratic democracy – with its new division between the dignified and efficient elements in the constitution.

The growth of party was of course directly related to the extension of the suffrage that began in the year *The English Constitution* was published. Once votes became too numerous to buy, organised corruption was gradually replaced by party organisation; and the voter was wooed not with offers of ready cash but with promises of state benefits to come. The party which, up to now, had been a weak organisation, functioning informally in the lobbies and political clubs, became a centralised, extra-parliamentary machine, constantly seeking to impose its discipline and its doctrine on the member of parliament as well as on the party worker. By the turn of the century, when the party caucuses were firmly entrenched, the efficient secret of the constitution was no longer the fusion of the executive and the legislature, in that supreme committee of the House of Commons called the cabinet, but the secret links that connected the cabinet with the party on the one side and with the civil service on the other.

Of the modern party, Bagehot had not even a premonition – partly because he had never visited America where it was already dominant when he wrote. Throughout *The English Constitution*, he describes party organisation as weak at Westminster and almost non-existent outside. 'At present the member is free', he remarks, 'because the constituency is not in earnest; no constituency has an acute, accurate doctrinal creed in politics'. One of his main reasons for opposing an extension of the suffrage was his correct premonition that this would bring as its consequence a growth of constituency government, i.e. party machines. 'Constituency government', he observes, 'is the precise opposite of Parliamentary government. It is the government of immoderate persons far from the scene of action, instead of the government of moderate persons close to the scene of action'.

What he liked most about parliament was the existence of a solid centre, composed of the majority of solid, sensible independent MPs, collectively able to make and unmake ministries, to defy when necessary their own whips, and above all to frustrate the growth of 'constituency government' outside. True, he emphasised the need for 'party' under a system where the government has to sustain its majority in order to endure. But the kind of party organisation he wanted was more like a club than a modern machine. It will work well, he remarks, precisely 'because it is not composed of warm partisans. The body is eager, but the atoms are cool. If it were otherwise, Parliamentary government would become the worst of governments – a sectarian government'. By Bagehot's standards, therefore, parliamentary government has long since ceased to exist in this country. Ever since the party machines took over the 'electoral' powers previously exercised by the House of Commons, we have been living under 'sectarian government'.

The first impact of the modern mass party on classical parliamentary democracy was made by Joseph Chamberlain's

Birmingham caucus.[3] But it was not until the rise of working-class parties, based on trade unions and disciplined according to their canons of working-class solidarity, that the 'iron law of increasing oligarchy'[4] completed the transformation of the system. Until then, parliament had been dominated by the middle classes, and parties had really been electoral organisations at the service of groups of MPs, still arguing within the social oligarchy. Though partially enfranchised, the working class were effectively though precariously excluded from government, which was still the monopoly of the aristocracy and the business community. When the Labour party was formed at the beginning of the century, what Bagehot wrote in the introduction to his second edition was still largely true:

> The issue put before these electors was, Which of two rich people will you choose? And each of those rich people was put forward by great parties whose notions were the notions of the rich – whose plans were their plans. The electors only selected one or two wealthy men to carry out the schemes of one or two wealthy associations . . . They were just competent to make a selection between two sets of superior ideas; or rather – for the conceptions of such people are more personal than abstract – between two opposing parties, each professing a creed of such ideas . . . They were competent to decide an issue selected by the higher classes, but they were incompetent to do more.

The irruption into politics of the labour movement ended this phase. In order to break down the walls of social oligarchy which surrounded parliament, a battering ram was required and the Labour party was created for this purpose. Its structure was determined by three conditions. First it must have very large funds at its disposal; hence the reliance on trade union financing which led to the sponsoring of trade union candidates by particular unions. Secondly, since it could not afford, like its opponents, to maintain a large army of paid party workers, the Labour party required militants – politically conscious socialists to do the work of organising the constituencies. But since these militants tended to be 'extremists', a constitution was needed which maintained their enthusiasm by apparently creating a full party democracy while excluding them from effective power. Hence the concession in principle of sovereign powers to the delegates at the annual conference, and the removal in practice of most of this sovereignty through the trade union block vote on the one hand, and the complete independence of the parliamentary Labour party on the other. Thirdly, since its avowed aim was social revolution, the Labour party from the first accepted the semi-military discipline of democratic centralism, based on the enforcement of majority decision. Hence its intolerance of minority opinion.

In any modern mass party, power tends to be concentrated in the hands of the parliamentarians, and the professional machine politicians. In working-class parties, the spirit of trade unionism intensifies this process. The emergence of Labour as the alternative government had an important effect on its opponents. The Conservative party was compelled in certain respects to copy it. Gradually it was transformed from an old-fashioned caucus, with old-fashioned electoral machinery, into a modern, carefully disciplined mass party. The two great machines began to resemble each other. In his *British Political Parties*, Robert McKenzie has described in great detail this process of approximation. In so doing he seems to me to have very gravely underestimated the differences both in social structure, group behaviour, organisation and discipline that still divide the Conservative and Labour parties. Nevertheless the picture he painted in 1954 was in one important respect completely accurate. The British political scene was indeed dominated by two great party oligarchies which had usurped and divided between them most of the sovereign powers Bagehot ascribed to the Commons.

In order to see the difference between his English constitution and that under which we now live, it may be useful to summarise these changes.

The Effect of Party on the Individual MP

In Bagehot's day, the private member was genuinely free to defy the whip, genuinely responsible to his own conscience and his constituents, and genuinely at liberty, within wide limits, to speak as he wished. It was this independence of the private member that gave the Commons its collective character and made it the most important check on the executive. Now the prime responsibility of the member is no longer to his conscience or to the elector, but to his party. Without accepting the discipline of the party he cannot be elected; and, if he defies that discipline, he risks political death. Even 40 years ago it was still possible to cross the floor and survive. But today the member who loses the whip may win the next election, but after that the party machine will destroy him. Party loyalty has become the prime political virtue required of an MP, and the test of that loyalty is his willingness to support the official leadership when he knows it to be wrong.

One result of the virtual disappearance of the MP's independence is that the point of decision has now been removed from the division lobby to the party meeting upstairs. The debate on the floor of the House becomes a formality, and the division which follows it a foregone conclusion. It is what is said and done in the secrecy of the party meeting which is now really important – though the public can only hear about it through leaks to the press.

The Effect of Party on Parliamentary Control of the Executive

Parliamentary control becomes a fiction with the disappearance of that solid centre of independent and independent-minded members, on which Bagehot relied to ensure that party government was always 'mild'. Once the party leadership runs a modern machine and can discipline its MPs, government control of parliament and its business becomes absolute. The Commons, which in Bagehot's day had a real collective life and a general will, is split into two sectarian armies – the cabinet with its phalanx of supporters, and the shadow cabinet also with its phalanx.

The Effect of Party on the Task of Opposition

Theoretically, the task of checking and controlling the

executive, which previously belonged in a real sense to the House as a whole, has now passed to the opposition. But the opposition is incapable of adequately fulfilling it. For with good management and even a moderate sized majority, any modern government can survive, whatever the opposition may do, until the prime minister decides to dissolve. Modern oppositions are often accused of ineffectiveness, and rebuked for shadow-boxing. But this is all they can do – unless they are willing over a period of months to obstruct legislation and so halt the process of government. But by taking opposition to this level, an opposition lays itself open to the charge of extremism and irresponsibility, and may well lose the support of that mass of floating voters which it must hope to win in order to turn out the government. Hence the tendency of the modern opposition to play safe.

It is not the opposition but the electorate whose views, as revealed in by-elections and Gallup polls, the government solicitously watches, and is often ready to appease. Indeed the opposition normally has less power to exert a check on the executive, or to modify government policy, than a dissident group on the government's back benches. The government knows that it could be undermined from inside by the dissident group, whereas it cannot be defeated by an attack across the floor from the opposite front bench. That is why a government tends to pay much more attention to the private approaches from its own back benchers than it does to the public onslaught of the opposition. For even if the shadow cabinet triumphs in the debates day after day, the government knows that it cannot be brought down except by disloyalty among its own supporters. Thus it is no exaggeration to say that, very often at Westminster, more effective opposition can be exercised by dissident groups of government supporters than by Her Majesty's Loyal Opposition.

The Effect of Party on the Struggle for Power

Just as the important debates have been removed from the floor of the Commons to the secrecy of the committee rooms upstairs, so the struggle for power which gives meaning to democratic politics has also been hidden from the public eye. Today the struggle for real power takes place secretly inside the government party, and for shadow power inside the opposition. Driven underground by the requirements of party discipline, it is normally a conspiratorial matter of cliques and cabals. Groups are formed to fight for causes or uphold principles, only to be disintegrated from above by threats of expulsion and offers of preferment. In our modern party politics, there is no 'loyal' way either of removing a disastrous leader or of promoting to power a saviour at loggerheads with the machine.

In the classical parliamentary system, the debates were public, the issues were known and the personal struggle for power could take place on the floor of the House or on the hustings. The elector could see something at least of the issues at stake in the clash of personalities. In our modern system, all he can usually see is the shadow fight between the selected champions of the two party phalanxes on the floor of the chamber. Of the struggle between personalities and the conflict of ideas that takes place inside each great party machine, he can only hear the garbled versions leaked to the press by interested parties. Thus he can never know for certain why a cabinet has been suddenly reconstructed, why a policy defended for years is now dropped, and what importance should really be attached to the various items in a programme. Politics is inevitably personified and simplified in the public mind, into a battle between two super-leaders – appointed for life or until they are removed by intra-party *coup d'état*.

The Effect of Party on Ministerial Responsibility

So long as parties were little more than electoral caucuses, the responsibility of the minister to parliament was an important check on bureaucratic incompetence. If departments were bad, ministers could be sacked; if ministers disagreed with their colleagues, they could resign without losing caste. But now that the government party controls parliament, both resignations on principle and dismissals for incompetence have become rare. Indeed the incompetent minister with a departmental muddle to cover up may be kept in office for years; and the louder the demand for his dismissal, the more loyally the party oligarchy will usually support him, rightly calculating that more votes will be lost in a general election by admitting ministerial incompetence than by concealing it.

The Reduced Role of Parliament

The Commons still have a useful job to do. But today it is not very much more useful than the job allotted by Bagehot to the House of Lords. If the peers provide one reservoir from which governments are drawn, the House of Commons is a much more important one. Although a premier can co-opt an outsider to his cabinet, anyone ambitious for a political career is still well advised to obtain a seat in the Commons, and there to prove his suitability for high office by a longish period of safe party speeches and loyal adherence to the party line. In the sense that both cabinet and shadow cabinet are steeped in parliamentary tradition, and manned overwhelmingly by loyal party men who are also loyal parliamentarians, we can still call our system of government 'parliamentary democracy'. We can still be proud of question time and of the work of the public accounts and estimates committees. We can still claim that even a government with a substantial majority must remain sensitive to the climate of parliamentary opinion. But the fact remains that in a period when effective power in all spheres of life – economic, social, political – is being concentrated in fewer and fewer hands, parliamentary control of the executive has been steadily decreasing, without being replaced by other methods of democratic control.

The danger into which we are drifting has been well described by one acute French observer. In his *Political Parties*, M. Duverger reminds us how far we have moved from the system described by Bagehot:

Officially Great Britain has a parliamentary system . . . in practice the existence of a majority governing party transforms this constitutional pattern from top to bottom. The party holds in its own hands the essential prerogatives of the legislature and the executive . . . Parliament and Government are like two machines driven by the same motor – the party. The regime is not so very different in this respect from the single party system. Executive and legislature, Govern-

ment and Parliament are constitutional façades: in reality
the party alone exercises power.

In this passage, M. Duverger no doubt was being deliberately
onesided in order to point out a very real danger. What makes
his description unbalanced is the existence of a second
countervailing factor, rivalling that of the modern party, which
was given just as little importance in *The English Constitution*.
This factor is the vast apparatus of power and public service
which the state now administers centrally and locally, and
whose emergence Bagehot failed to foresee. As parliament has
been reduced to a new and more submissive role by the modern
party machine, so the powers of the cabinet have been eroded
by the growing ascendancy of Whitehall. Bagehot, as we have
seen, was profoundly suspicious of J. S. Mill's proposal to
create an administrative elite, selected strictly by competitive
public examination, which would take over the job of state
management. No business, he tells us, selects its personnel in
this way. And though the argument sounds naïve today, it
seemed conclusive enough to a Victorian banker who liked the
cabinet precisely because it functioned like a board of directors.

> The truth is that a skilled bureaucracy – a bureaucracy
> trained from early life to its special avocation – is, though it
> boasts of an appearance of science, quite inconsistent with
> the true principles of the art of business . . . One of the most
> sure principles is, that success depends on a due mixture of
> special and non-special minds – of minds which attend to the
> means, and of minds which attend to the end.

Bagehot believed that a civil service of the kind Mill desired
would very soon arrogate to itself the common-sense business
decisions which in *The English Constitution* are reserved to the
inexpert minister in his department, and to the secret informal
meetings of the cabinet. He did not deny that Napoleon in
France and Frederick the Great in Germany had created far
more efficient public administration than anything we knew in
Britain. Indeed, he was prepared to admit that any dictatorial
or revolutionary regime 'is likely, whatever be its other defects,
to have a far better and abler administration than any other

government . . . The dictator dare not appoint a bad minister if he would . . . He will know how to mix fresh minds and used minds better; he is under a stronger motive to combine them well'. But he concluded very firmly 'that the revolutionary selection of rulers obtains administrative efficiency at a price altogether transcending its value'.

Cabinet government of this type could only function so long as state activity and the public services remained on a very small scale. Even so, as Bagehot frankly admitted, the price the business community paid for freedom from bureaucratic tyranny was the fantastic degree of incompetence revealed in the Crimean war. After 1868 both the powers of the state and the efficiency of the civil service increased very rapidly; and if cabinet government of the classical type lasted far longer into this century than the parliamentary system to which it was linked, the reason is to be found in the readiness of the business community to tolerate, at least in peace time, a high degree of incompetence in the highest places.

The first major change in the system was the ending of cabinet informality by the creation of a secretariat to keep the minutes and circulate papers. This took place in the First World War when Lloyd George was leading a small war cabinet, in which all important decisions were centralised. But old-fashioned cabinet government was re-established in the 1920s in a form not very different from that described in *The English Constitution*. In describing the Labour government of 1929, where he had his first experience as a cabinet minister, Lord Morrison makes it clear that normally decisions were still taken collectively by the full cabinet. He also suggests – probably rightly – that this was one cause at least of the Labour government's failure to cope with the economic crisis.[5]

Already, in fact, by 1931 cabinet government in Bagehot's sense of the word had become an anachronism. It finally disappeared under the Churchill war regime. Once Sir Winston had accepted the leadership of the Conservative party, his ascendancy became unchallengeable. As party leader, he controlled the Conservative machine inside and outside parliament, and could therefore dictate his terms, not merely to the House of Commons but to the Labour members of his cabinet. As prime minister and minister of defence, he was the apex of a pyramid of power, exerting a personal control over the whole of the war effort through a vastly expanded cabinet secretariat, and a network of cabinet committees, under the chairmanship of ministers who had become his agents. Over wide fields of policy and administration cabinet government lapsed altogether, and the informal discussions of policy which had been its lifeblood now took place exclusively between the premier and his entourage.

When Mr Attlee took over in 1945, he was determined that there should be no 'return to normalcy' as there was in 1918. Under his premiership, a well-organised system of centralised decision taking replaced the rather haphazard personal auto-cracy of Sir Winston. Despite his mild appearance, however, Mr Attlee had no intention of becoming chairman of a large traditional cabinet. The wartime centralisation of power in the person of the premier was in no way reduced by Mr Attlee; and under him the enlarged cabinet secretariat and the elaborate system of cabinet committees were maintained and reorganised for peacetime purposes. In this way, the point of decision, which in the 1930s still rested inside the cabinet, was now permanently transferred either downwards to these powerful cabinet committees, or upwards to the prime minister himself.

The same forces which produced these changes in the structure and functions of the cabinet were simultaneously responsible for an equally important but far less noticeable revolution in Whitehall. Since 1919 the civil service has been subjected to a double process of expansion and centralisation, which has transformed it from a collection of self-recruiting and autonomous departments into an ever more homogeneous bureaucracy controlled by a closely knit central directorate with its centre in the Treasury.

Until the end of the First World War, the civil service had remained decentralised. Young men who joined a department expected to stay there. Moreover, because each department recruited its own staff under a permanent under-secretary responsible to and appointed by the departmental minister, there was no difficulty in adding to the non-specialist civil servants recruited by the normal examination experts, techni-cians, and other specialists from outside.

All this was changed as the result of a decision promulgated by Lloyd George on 4 September 1919.[6] Apparently the wartime premier was persuaded by the then secretary of the Treasury, Warren Fisher, that the only way of making available the best talents of all departments for postwar reconstruction was to unify the service, and recognise the secretary of the Treasury as its head. This ruling was followed by a further regulation laying down that the consent of the premier (which in practice meant the head of the civil service) would be required in all departments to the appointment of the permanent heads and their deputies.

As a result of these two regulations, it has by now become the exception rather than the rule for the head of a department to be a man with life-long service within it. A circulation of elites from ministry to ministry has replaced vertical promotion to the top of a single ministry. Instead of a cluster of departments, each with its own traditions, characteristics, and standards of recruitment, there has emerged a new horizontal stratification, with the heads forming a single, like-minded group of super bureaucrats, each confident that he can take charge at a few weeks' notice of a ministry of which he has had no previous experience. One inevitable by-product of this process has been the tendency to give technicians and experts a lower status, and to resent any attempt by a minister to introduce 'outsiders' even into his private office. The system is more democratic if by democracy we mean the possibility of rising from the humblest clerical work to a permanent under-secretaryship. But the price to be paid for this democracy is the surrender of leadership in Whitehall to 'the Treasury mind', and an ever-increasing uniformity of outlook and resistance to outside influences and new ideas.

Unification and centralisation have had two important political effects. Firstly, they have made it even more difficult for departmental ministers to get their way against their senior officials, or where necessary to dismiss them. In our new kind of civil service, the minister must normally be content with the role of public relations officer to his department, unless the premier has appointed him with the express purpose of carrying our reforms. Secondly, the centralisation of authority, both for appointments and for policy decisions, under a single head of the civil service (quite recently the task has been given to a committee of three) responsible to Downing Street, has brought with it an immense accretion of power to the prime minister. He is now the apex not only of a highly centralised political machine, but also of an equally centralised and vastly more powerful administrative machine. In both these machines, loyalty has become the supreme virtue, and independence of thought a dangerous adventure.

The postwar epoch has seen the final transformation of cabinet government into prime ministerial government. Under this system the 'hyphen which joins, the buckle which fastens, the legislative part of the state to the executive part' becomes one single man. Even in Bagehot's time it was probably a misnomer to describe the premier as chairman, and *primus inter pares*. His right to select his own cabinet and dismiss them at will; his power to decide the cabinet's agenda and announce the decisions reached without taking a vote; his control, through the chief whip, over patronage – all this had already before 1867 given him near-presidential powers. Since then his powers have been steadily increased, first by the centralisation of the party machine under his personal rule, and secondly by the growth of a centralised bureaucracy, so vast that it could no longer be managed by a cabinet behaving like the board of directors of an old-fashioned company.

Under prime ministerial government, secondary decisions are normally taken either by the department concerned or in cabinet committee and the cabinet becomes the place where busy executives seek formal sanction for their actions from colleagues usually too busy – even if they do disagree – to do more than protest. Each of these executives, moreover, owes his allegiance not to the cabinet collectively but to the prime minister who gave him his job, and who may well have dictated the policy he must adopt. In so far as ministers feel themselves to be agents of the premier, the British cabinet has now come to resemble the American cabinet.

Every Cabinet Minister is in a sense the Prime Minister's agent – his assistant. There's no question about that. It is the Prime Minister's Cabinet, and he is the one person who is directly responsible to the Queen for what the Cabinet does.

If the Cabinet discusses anything it is the Prime Minister

who decides what the collective view of the Cabinet is. A Minister's job is to save the Prime Minister all the work he can. But no Minister could make a really important move without consulting the Prime Minister, and if the Prime Minister wanted to take a certain step the Cabinet Minister concerned would either have to agree, argue it out in Cabinet, or resign.[7]

But there is one important difference. The old doctrine of collective cabinet responsibility is scrupulously maintained and enforced, even though many of the decisions for which members must assume responsibility have been taken above their heads and without their knowledge. And this collective responsibility now extends downwards from the cabinet through the ministers outside the cabinet to the parliamentary secretaries and even the parliamentary private secretaries.

Under this doctrine, today, about a third of the government's parliamentary strength is automatically required not merely to accept but actively to support policy decisions which, if they are of great importance, will nearly always have been taken by one man after consultation with a handful of advisers he has picked for the occasion. In Bagehot's day, collective cabinet responsibility meant the responsibility of a group of equal colleagues for decisions taken collectively, after full, free and secret discussion in which all could participate. It now means collective obedience by the whole administration, from the foreign secretary and the chancellor downwards, to the will of the man at the apex of power. This situation has been aptly summarised as follows:

While British Government in the latter half of the nineteenth century can be described simply as Cabinet Government, such a description would be misleading today. Now the country is governed by the Prime Minister who leads, co-ordinates and maintains a series of ministers, all of whom are advised and backed by the civil service. Some decisions are taken by the Premier alone, some in consultation between him and the senior ministers, while others are left to heads of departments, the Cabinet, Cabinet committees or the permanent officials. Of these bodies the Cabinet holds the central position because, although it does not often initiate policy, or govern in that sense, most decisions pass through it or are reported to it, and Cabinet ministers can complain that they have not been informed or consulted. The precise amount of power held by each agency, and the use made of the Cabinet depends on the ideas of the Premier, and the personnel and situation with which he has to deal.[8]

With the coming of prime ministerial government, the cabinet, in obedience to the law that Bagehot discovered, joins the other dignified elements in the constitution. Of course, like the monarchy, the House of Lords and the Commons, it retains very real reserve powers which can on occasion be suddenly and dramatically used for good or for ill. A prime minister, for instance, can be unseated by his colleagues; and it is this fact with which the constitutional purists seek to justify the distinction they still make between presidential and prime ministerial government. A president, we are told, cannot be removed before the end of his term of office; a prime minister can be.

The distinction is valid, provided we observe that a British party leader exerts such power and patronage within the machine that he can never be removed in real life by public, constitutional procedure. The method employed must always be that of undercover intrigue and sudden unpredicted *coup d'état*. The intra-party struggle for power that is fought in the secret committees, and in the lobbies, may suddenly flare up round the cabinet table. But if it does, the proceedings there will only be a ritual, and the real fight will have finished before they begin.

The decline of the cabinet has been concealed from the public eye even more successfully than its rise to power in Bagehot's era. Here was a secret of our modern English constitution which no one directly concerned with government – whether minister, shadow minister or civil servant – was anxious to reveal. Yet, despite the thick protective covering of prerogative and constitutional convention under which our government is still conducted, there must come occasions on which the drapery is whisked aside, and the reality of power revealed. One such occasion was when Sir Winston, shortly after he took office in 1951, announced that the first British A-bomb had been successfully tested. The premier was careful to pay his tribute to his predecessor for making the initial decision and sanctioning the huge expenditures that had never been revealed to parliament. It has since been established that this issue – one of the most important defence problems that has confronted any British government since 1945 – was settled in the Defence Sub-Committee without any prior discussion in full cabinet. Nor was there any cabinet discussion *after* the decision. When the minutes of the particular meeting of the Defence Committee came before full cabinet, the prime minister did not feel it necessary to call attention to this item; and, since no one else had any comment to make, it became cabinet policy without a word being said – and without even being recorded in the cabinet minutes.

So completely had the reality of collective cabinet responsibility been transformed by this date into a myth, that no member of Mr Attlee's government either noticed anything unusual about this procedure or felt aggrieved that he had not been consulted.[9]

Another occasion which showed the new role of the cabinet under prime ministerial government was the Suez crisis. Lord Avon took the decisions and prepared the plans for the Anglo-French attack on Port Said without cabinet consultation, and with the assistance of only a handful of his colleagues and permanent advisers. After the secret was revealed, he was able until he fell ill to enforce collective responsibility on a cabinet only informed of his policy when it was already doomed to failure. He has been blamed for the policy; but no one has suggested that he acted unconstitutionally. Here then it was demonstrated that a British premier is now entitled on really momentous decisions to act first, and then to face his cabinet with the choice between collective obedience or the political wilderness.

It has often been observed that when they were plunged into total war in 1940 the British people readily put their democratic constitution into cold storage, and fought under a system of centralised autocracy. The Nazi totalitarian state was defeated because we were ready to accept a more far-reaching system of voluntary totalitarianism. What is not so often noticed is the extent to which the institutions and the behaviour of voluntary totalitarianism have been retained since 1945. The development of prime ministerial government in Whitehall and Westminster has been accompanied outside by the growth of oligopoly in finance and industry, and by a startling concentration of power in newspapers, television and most recently in publishing, which has enabled a handful of businessmen and executives to manage the new media of mass communications.

In a period of affluence, this rapid concentration of power occurs almost unnoticed by an indifferent electorate, which behaves with that deference Bagehot claimed to be the essential precondition of political stability in a free society. And from these two facts – the passivity of the people below and the concentration far above them of irresponsible power – the conclusion is sometimes drawn that 'grass-roots' democracy is a utopian mirage, and that the modern, highly developed industrial state must be managed on authoritarian lines.

The pessimists may be right. But a postwar decade is too short a period from which to draw firm conclusions. In theory – but also in practice – the British people retains the power not merely to choose between two prime ministers, and two parties, but to throw off its deferential attitude and reshape the political system, making the parties instruments of popular control, and even insisting that the House of Commons should once again provide the popular check on the executive. It is my hope and belief that this will happen. Already there are signs of popular protest against the growing ineffectiveness of parliament and the oligarchic tendencies inherent in our modern two-party machine politics. Perhaps the secret of prime ministerial government discussed in these pages will be as rapidly overtaken by events as Bagehot's *The English Constitution* was when it appeared in 1867.

References

1. Reprinted from Mr Crossman's 'Introduction' to Walter Bagehot, *The English Constitution* (London: Watts, 1964), pp. 37–57, with the permission of the publisher.

2. See H. J. Laski, *Reflections on the Constitution* (Manchester: Manchester University Press, 1951) pp. 104, 108.

3. This is described by M. Ostrogorsky in his *Democracy and the Organisation of Political Parties* (Chicago: Quadrangle edn, 1964).

4. First described by R. Michels, in *Political Parties* (London: Constable edn, 1959).

5. See Lord Morrison, *Government and Parliament* (London: Oxford, 1964), p. 17.

6. On this topic I have closely followed 'The Apotheosis of the Dilettante', by Dr Thomas Balogh, in Hugh Thomas (ed.), *The Establishment* (London: Blond, 1959).

7. See Lord Home, *Observer*, 16 September 1962.

8. See John P. Mackintosh, *The British Cabinet* (London: Stevens, 1962). Mr Mackintosh was asked to produce a third revised edition of Berriedale Keith's *British Cabinet System*. After some months' work he found the book so out of date that it could no longer, after adequate revision, be attributed to Keith. Hence this new book, in which the first attempt is made by a trained political scientist to record the changes in cabinet structure made by the war.

9. I must express my gratitude to the Rt Hon. George Strauss MP for his help in reconstructing precisely what happened on this occasion. In the first edition of this introduction, I had written 'it was common knowledge that this decision had been taken by Mr Attlee without any prior discussion in the cabinet, and that he had not revealed it to any but a handful of trusted friends'. Mr Strauss, who as minister of supply was responsible for the production of the atomic bomb, wrote to the *New Statesman* that this account was unfair and inaccurate. The revised version is the result of the argument which then took place in the correspondence columns of the *New Statesman*. The full text of this correspondence, which extended from 10 May 1963 to 7 June 1963, is worth examining by the curious student of political science, since it shows with unusual clarity both how little is normally revealed of what goes on in the modern cabinet, and how much information is available about these secret proceedings, if only someone who knows the truth can be stimulated to divulge it.

8

The Prime Minister's Power

G. W. JONES[1]

Richard Crossman's theme in the previous chapter was the decline of the cabinet and the growing ascendancy of the prime minister. Crossman's view was (and still is) shared by many others, including John Mackintosh whose study The British Cabinet *remains a standard work on the British system of government at the top. In this chapter, however, written soon after Crossman, Professor George Jones, while not denying that the prime minister of the day has formidable powers at his or her disposal, insists that the prime minister's position is far more constrained than the Crossman analysis allows. Like an American president, Jones maintains, the prime minister is confronted with other holders of political power with whom he or she is forced to do business.*

It has become part of the conventional wisdom expressed by some academics and journalists that the position of the prime minister in the British system of government has altered significantly in recent years. No longer, they assert, is he merely *primus inter pares* or just the leading member of the cabinet, but he has been transformed into something quite new, perhaps a quasi-president, or an elected monarch or even an autocrat. The prime minister's predominance, attained by Churchill during the Second World War, is said to have persisted in peacetime during the administrations of Attlee, Churchill again,

Eden, Macmillan, Douglas-Home and now Wilson. If this view is correct then cabinet government is a dignified façade behind which lurks the efficient secret of prime ministerial power.[2]

It may not be possible to test the validity of these suppositions until the cabinet papers are made available, 50 years after the events they refer to have taken place, and until the politicians and civil servants involved in the process have published their memoirs. But even with the scanty evidence at present before us, there are grounds to argue that the prime minister's power has been exaggerated and that the restraints on his ascendancy are as strong as ever, and in some ways even stronger. The aim of this paper is to consider the argument that the prime minister has become more powerful and to suggest some countervailing factors which seriously inhibit his freedom to initiate and manoeuvre.

The elevation of the prime minister is attributed to many trends. The extensions of the franchise, the growth of nationwide mass parties and the development of the mass media of communications[3] are said to have changed the nature of a general election. From a number of separate constituency contests it has become almost a plebiscite, a gladiatorial contest between the party leaders. On them are concentrated the efforts of the party propagandists and the attentions of the press, radio and television. Their words and nuances of expression are carefully analysed to expose their parties' policies, which they are supposed to embody. This personalisation of political issues and allegiances is said to be essential if most of the electors, who are not very politically conscious, are to be reached, interested and won over. They may not understand or follow debates about policies, but they appreciate a clash of personalities. The leaders appear to be the only significant contestants during the campaign; neither the calibre nor the personal views of the other candidates count for much more than 1,000 votes, since the electoral swing over the whole country or at least regionally at a general election is fairly uniform. Candidates seem to attract or repel voters solely on the basis of which leaders they will support in the House of Commons.

Thus the only mandate given by the electorate to an MP is to support his leader.[4] The prime minister therefore can be sure that his party in the Commons will back him. Obedience to the prime minister, however, rests not just on the commands of the electors. Some commentators claim that the prime minister's power to obtain a dissolution of parliament from the crown deters his supporters from rebellion, since they wish to avoid a costly and arduous election campaign which may jeopardise their seats.[5] Others stress that if MPs voted against their party in the House, their constituency parties would be likely not to readopt them as official candidates, and without party endorsement the former MPs would be defeated ignominiously, like Dr Donald Johnson at Carlisle in October 1964. Party loyalty, feelings of personal attachment to a group of colleagues and fear of letting the other party either damage the standing of his own party or even gain office, are additional pressures on an MP to follow his party's line.

The party policy which the MP has to follow is most likely the prime minister's policy, rather than a collective party policy which all members have helped to form. A prime minister, whether Conservative or Labour, effectively controls his party and is not restrained by it, despite the differences in the formal constitutions of the parties. The limitations which the Labour party's constitution places upon its leader fall away when he becomes prime minister and are superseded by the conventions of the British constitution, which put into his hands the power to choose his colleagues and decide policy. The powers of a Conservative and a Labour prime minister are identical.[6] They have the freedom to choose whom they will to be members of their governments. One appointment in particular is of special importance in sustaining the prime minister's sway over his parliamentary colleagues, and that is the chief whip. And a lord of the Treasury he is directly responsible to the prime minister for the performance of his duties. He lives at 12 Downing Street, close to the prime minister, with whom he can communicate unobtrusively whenever required. They have daily sessions together, called 'morning prayers', when they discuss the state of the parliamentary party. The chief whip has to maintain discipline amongst its ranks, and he does this not just by bullying, but also by explaining and clarifying the prime minister's views to those who are anxious. He also assists the prime minister to dispense a host of honours, awards, decorations, knighthoods and peerages, and of particular significance for the MPs, government offices.[7] MPs are said now to have less scope to make reputations as mere backbenchers.[8] They want government office, and the easiest way for them to earn this reward is to give loyal service to the prime minister and not to appear to him or the chief whip as nuisances. Criticism of the prime minister will bring his disfavour which will block future prospects of advancement. The importance of the power of patronage has increased as the number of government offices has grown. Conservatives have recently attacked Harold Wilson for enabling more MPs to hold government offices, on the grounds that he is reducing the independence of the legislature, by packing it with place men dependent on the executive and his will.[9] Alarm has also been expressed that even parliamentary private secretaries are being regarded as junior members of the government, liable to lose their unpaid offices, if they oppose a government decision.[10] Promotion seems to depend on knuckling under to the prime minister's decisions. Thus the loyalty of the MPs is cemented to the prime minister because the chief whip, who maintains discipline and helps to bestow patronage, is a personal agent of the prime minister, and because the amount of patronage at the prime minister's disposal has increased.

Through his control of his party the prime minister can be certain that the Commons will support his government and accept his measures. His will becomes an Act of Parliament, for the House of Lords is no obstruction to Commons' decisions and the queen's assent is automatic. The courts, too, will not resist a statute. Parliamentary sovereignty means prime ministerial sovereignty. It does not mean cabinet sovereignty, because the prime minister is said to dominate his cabinet through his power to appoint and dismiss its members, to control its operations and even bypass it altogether by the use of cabinet committees and informal conversations with individual ministers.

The prime minister's power of patronage is said to enable him to master his cabinet. Able to hire and fire, to demote and promote and to allocate particular offices to whomever he pleases, he holds the political future of his colleagues in his hands. He can advance the careers of those he favours and check those he dislikes according to the positions he gives them, for some offer the chance to make a good reputation, while others can bring the holder little esteem. Thus a minister who wants to climb is dependent on the prime minister, and the easiest way to earn his gratitude is to serve him loyally. Ministers are not usually keen to retire. Since the cabinet consists of a fairly formal hierarchy of ministers, resignation would take a man out of the queue for higher office. Few want to lose their places, so they stay, often consoling themselves and others with the thought that they can be more influential on future policy inside rather than outside the cabinet. If they do resign, they will be asked to explain why, and if the reason is a disagreement over policy, then the opposition is given an opportunity to damage the party, which injures even more the reputations of those who resigned. The prime minister is strengthened because of his ministers' reluctance to resign. Even when some important ministers do resign, the prime minister can remain secure and laugh the episode off as a little local difficulty. He can dismiss a large part of his cabinet and still stay secure. The famous purge of 12 July 1962, when Harold Macmillan sacked one third of his cabinet, made 24 governmental changes in all and brought 11 backbenchers into the government, is said to indicate the great power of the prime minister and the dependence of his colleagues on his whims. He creates and destroys his cabinet at his pleasure. When he retires, so do all his colleagues; his successor has a free hand in forming his own administration.[11]

Once the cabinet is chosen the prime minister is said to have a free hand in managing its operations. It meets in his house; its members wait outside the door of the cabinet room until he is ready to start. He controls the agenda; his ministers send their papers to the Cabinet Office, whose secretariat prepares the agenda, which the prime minister has to approve. He can therefore keep off the agenda anything he wishes, include what he wants and stop the circulation of any memoranda he objects to. No minister, it is claimed, can get anything discussed at cabinet which is not on the agenda. If he tries to raise such an item, the prime minister as chairman can rule him out of order and even walk out, thus closing the meeting. During the proceedings he guides the discussion, naturally along the lines he wants, and when he is ready, he can end the discussion with his summary and assessment of the sense of the meeting. He may have listened to the cabinet's advice, but the last word is his. Since no votes are normally taken, it is hard for opposition to his views to crystallise, and it is rare for his decision to be challenged.

It is often claimed that the prime minister has scant concern for his cabinet, whose approval of his decisions is a mere formality, or which he can side-step completely. Through informal talks with individual ministers, who are more amenable alone than in cabinet, he can infiltrate his views, influence and even reshape the minister's proposals.[12] At his house, at Chequers, over meals, or through the network of private secretaries,[13] he can arrange with ministers the main outlines of what they will present to the cabinet. Policy will have been settled before the cabinet stage. The prime minister can set up cabinet committees, chaired by himself or a trusted colleague, to watch over certain topics or certain ministers. Here issues can be thrashed out in a thorough discussion and policy proposals agreed. Members of the cabinet not in on these discussions find it very difficult to raise objections in cabinet when these matters arise.[14] They lack knowledge about the problems involved; they would be unlikely to prevail and fear to make fools of themselves through their ill-informed contributions. The crucial policy decisions, it is said, are taken not in the cabinet, but in interdepartmental committees after consultation with the interests concerned, in cabinet committees, or in conversations between the prime minister and an individual minister. This downgrading of the cabinet is said to have been encouraged recently by some new methods introduced by Harold Wilson: working weekends at Chequers for the ministers and officials concerned to discuss defence and economic policies, working dinners at 10 Downing Street for vice-chancellors and exporters, and the meetings between the prime minister and the heads of the aircraft industry. These developments show once again that the prime minister and not the cabinet is the crucial element in the decision making process.

Some commentators have said that an inner cabinet has

emerged, the efficient part, which really directs the formal cabinet's activities. It is said to comprise the prime minister and a clique of his personal cronies. They take the important decisions and get them through the cabinet or else avoid it. Churchill is said to have ruled in this manner; Attlee began the large-scale production of atomic weapons and Eden carried out his Suez policy by means of these techniques of government. The cabinet as a whole and individual ministers are kept very largely in ignorance; a minister may find that a decision is taken concerning his own department without his being consulted. Thus the traditional concept of collective cabinet responsibility applies no longer, or else applies in a new way. Ministers have the choice now if they disagree with the prime minister's decisions either of resigning or of accepting them. The concept of collective responsibility is used to muzzle the opponents of the prime minister in the cabinet. The cabinet has been transformed into a network of committees and individuals, all subordinated to the prime minister who controls them. His personal policy is endorsed automatically as cabinet policy.

The concept of individual ministerial responsibility has also been transformed, since a minister is said now to be the public relations man for his department and the errand boy for the prime minister. This change is supposed to have been revealed in 1962 by the foreign secretary (Lord Home) when he said in an interview: 'Every Cabinet Minister is in a sense the Prime Minister's agent – his assistant. There's no question about that. It is the Prime Minister's Cabinet, and he is the one person who is directly responsible to the Queen for what the Cabinet does . . . If the Cabinet discusses anything it is the Prime Minister who decides what the collective view of the Cabinet is. A Minister's job is to save the Prime Minister all the work he can. But no Minister could make a really important move without consulting the Prime Minister, and if the Prime Minister wanted to take a certain step the Cabinet Minister concerned would either have to agree, argue it out in Cabinet, or resign'.[15]

The civil service is also said to be dominated by the prime minister.[16] As government has expanded its activities, there has been a growing need to centralise and co-ordinate the administration to ensure coherence of policy. Free of departmental entanglements the prime minister is able to survey the whole range of government and to intervene where he likes. He is aided by the Cabinet Office and his own private office, both of which act as his intelligence agencies. Through their work 10 Downing Street is said to be much better informed about the full spread of government business than any other department, and this factor tends to set the prime minister apart from his colleagues: 'In the nervous system of Whitehall, the prime minister's office must be the ganglion'.[17] His control over the civil service is achieved also by his close links with the Treasury. The personnel of the civil service are managed by the establishment division of the Treasury, whose joint permanent secretary, the head of the Home Civil Service, is directly responsible to the prime minister in his capacity as First Lord of the Treasury. He is, therefore, able to decide which civil servants will hold the most important positions in the departments. This patronage is said to enable his will to prevail in Whitehall.

Thus the prime minister controls his party, parliament, the cabinet, and the civil service. But he can also control to a great extent the succession to his position. If he retires in mid-term, he is strongly placed to pass on his office to the man of his choice. This is somewhat easier for a Conservative than a Labour prime minister to do, since the Labour party's constitution lays down that the MPs shall elect a new leader, while the Conservative party uses certain processes of consultation, which allow the outgoing prime minister great scope to gain support for his favourite. It seems that Harold Macmillan's activities helped Sir Alec Douglas-Home to succeed him.[18] A Labour prime minister, however, can smooth the path of his choice and obstruct the course of another through his power to allocate governmental offices. His candidate can be given a position from which to earn a good reputation, while the other can be landed with a difficult assignment unlikely to advance his career.

When the prime minister has finally to face the people at a general election, he does not undergo a severe ordeal. He can decide when to appeal to the country within the statutory limit, and since opinion polls furnish him with a fairly accurate assessment of the likely result, he can pick a favourable time.

For the actual campaign he has many advantages over the leader of the opposition. Publicity is showered on him as prime minister, wrestling with the nation's problems and speaking for the whole country. He can be depicted as more constructive and less partisan than his apparently party-minded and carping opponent. He can turn his whole term of office into a permanent election campaign, using the manipulative techniques of the advertisers and public relations men to create for him a favourable image in the eyes of the gullible public. Prime ministers have rarely lost an election in the 20th century. Sir Alec almost won, and might have succeeded if he had been able to stay on longer.

The prime minister, therefore, is in a position of unrivalled predominance, and one ex-prime minister has been prepared to admit this himself. Lord Avon has said, 'A prime minister is still nominally *primus inter pares*, but in fact his authority is stronger than that. The right to choose his colleagues, to ask for a dissolution of Parliament and, if he is a Conservative, to appoint the Chairman of the party organisation, add up to a formidable total of power.'[19] So powerful has he become that one journalist has advocated that he should give regular press conferences to let 'a window into the Prime Minister's mind'.[20] Apparently he is the only individual who counts. His supremacy was shown in 1963 when the opening of the Commons session was delayed until Lord Home was made a commoner and an MP.

The arguments which have been outlined so far neglect many factors which restrain the prime minister in the exercise of his power. His actual position is not as predominant as has been presented.

Election studies and opinion poll data present no firm evidence for a categorical statement that people vote for or against party leaders.[21] What can be said is that voters are greatly influenced by images they have in their minds of the parties, and the image is not composed just of the leader but it is a compound, whose main component is the record and achievement of the party when it was in the government. The overall performance of the government and not the activity of the leader shapes the image of the party. Other less significant elements of the image consist of the main figures of the party, their views and attitudes, the ways they behave to each other, the history of the party, its traditional and present associations, its past and present policies and its broad ideals. These, however, are not as decisive as the conduct of the party when in office. This creates the impression of the party in the minds of most electors. Elections then are won or lost by governments not by oppositions, and not just by the leaders. If the role of the leaders were as important as some suggest, then it might be expected that the electoral swings in the constituencies where they stand would show significant variations from the regional and national swings. In fact no such divergencies can be shown. The leader is as much the prisoner of the image of his party as the other candidates. Although much of the propaganda of the parties concentrates on the leaders, there is no evidence that it is effective. Studies of the effects of television show that most people display a sturdy resistance to the blandishments of the manipulators. They seem to absorb from a programme only what fits in with their preconceived notions. Their previous attitudes are reinforced, not overturned. The claims that advertisers and public relations men make for their techniques are exaggerated in the face of the dogged obstinacy of the public.[22]

If the leader is not the individual whom the electors vote for or against, then there is no mandate on the MPs to support their leaders.[23] Their obedience to their leader is not based on the wishes of the electorate, nor does it arise because of his ability to call for a dissolution when he likes. The cost of an election campaign is no burden to an MP, since his expenses are paid by his party. The campaign is not very arduous; for most MPs, a three weeks' irritation at worst, while it is more arduous for the leader who is the leading campaigner, having to travel over the whole country. Since the bulk of parliamentary seats, over two-thirds, are safe, few MPs worry that they will lose.[24] Thus dissolution is not a very realistic threat against potential or actual rebels. Indeed, the individual who has most to lose from a dissolution is the prime minister himself, who may lose his government office, his prestige, power and high salary. Further, since he wants to win, he is hardly likely to enter an election campaign wielding the weapon of dissolution against his own party, for the opposition will make much capital out of the splits within his party. If dissolution is the potent device some suggest, then there should be a tendency for rebels to sit for safe seats, immune from the changes of electoral fortune. But there is no correlation between the tendency to rebel against the party leadership and the size of the MP's majority. Thus neither the actual use of nor the threat to use the power of dissolution are the means of enforcing discipline on MPs.[25] They are kept in line by their constituency parties who may not readopt them. But local parties do not penalise their members for all acts of rebellion. MPs can expect trouble from their local parties if they go against their parliamentary party over a period of time by taking up a position close to that of the opposition party. A revolt to the centre will arouse the anger of the local parties far more than a revolt to the extreme wing, farthest from the position of the opposition.[26] A revolt therefore is not completely out of the question.

Parties are not the monoliths depicted by some commentators. Neither inside nor outside parliament are the parties tamely subservient to the will of the prime minister. They are riven with factions, divided over both short- and long-term policy objectives, the claims of various interests and local and regional issues.[27] More commonly in the Labour than in the Conservative party the alignment over one topic persists for a whole range of others, so that more permanent cleavages exist in the Labour party than in the Conservative.[28] The most important factions in both parties are those which coalesce around the main figures in the party. Each of the chief colleagues of the prime minister has a personal following which would prefer to see their man leader rather than the actual leader. There is no loyalty at the top because the prime minister's colleagues are his rivals, eager to replace him, and he is engaged in a constant battle to fend them off. Many attempts were made to displace Mr Attlee, but they collapsed because his *prima donna* rivals failed to unite around a successor.[29] Churchill, it seems, had to retire earlier than he wanted in order to please Sir Anthony Eden and his following.[30] Even before the Suez venture there were serious rumblings against Eden, and if he had not retired through ill-health after the Suez affair, it is most likely that he would have been forced out.[31] Mr Macmillan had to fight hard to remain leader, and but for his operation he too might have been forced out. Sir Alec Douglas-Home became prime minister not because Mr Macmillan or the queen chose him but because his chief rivals tolerated him and led no revolt against him. It is significant that the queen asked him at first only to try to form an administration. He kissed hands as prime minister 24 hours later. These were the crucial hours when he sought to win over Butler, Maudling and Hogg; it was during those hours that he was chosen as prime minister, by his colleagues. Today Harold Wilson is not secure; George Brown's reputation has risen considerably. Some commentators detect opposition to Wilson from within his own party. He has been described as tending 'to look more and more like a Labour Foreign Secretary, with Mr Brown as Prime Minister'.[32] The prime minister is only as strong as his colleagues let him be. Without their support he falls. To become and remain prime minister a man must work hard to retain the support of his main colleagues and not present them with an opportunity to remove him.

Television has enhanced the stature of the prime minister's rivals far more than his own standing. Gladstone and Disraeli, Asquith and Balfour, MacDonald and Baldwin were at the centre of the stage because of the office they held; their colleagues did not have the opportunities to display themselves to their party members and public which the colleagues of a postwar prime minister have. Today television brings into almost every home not just the prime minister, who cannot be on the screen all the time, but also the major ministers, his chief colleagues. They have the chance to win, consolidate and encourage a personal following, which their prewar counterparts never had. They have been strengthened in their relations *vis-à-vis* the prime minister. Thus the significance of the development of television is not that it has elevated the prime minister but that it has contributed to undermining his position. Maudling, Heath, Macleod, Brown and Callaghan are the men who have been helped by television. Even if the prime minister does receive considerable attention from television, it is not necessarily a one-sided blessing. Much depends on his telegenic qualities. Sir Alec Douglas-Home seemed to think that exposure together with Mr Wilson would not help his cause in the 1964 election campaign. The standing of a prime minister can be damaged, if he gives a poor performance, and a skilful interviewer may make him seem very foolish. Thus the case that the prime minister has been strengthened by television is not proven.

The prime minister if he is to remain in office must carry his leading rivals with him. He might withstand a backbench revolt with their support, but if a backbench revolt found a spokesman of leadership calibre, who could win the backing of his other close colleagues, then the prime minister would be in a very insecure position. To avoid this fate he must woo and coax his colleagues and party to support him and his policies. He is engaged in a continual dialogue with his party both inside and outside parliament. The whips act as his eyes and ears, conveying to him through the chief whip the feelings of the parliamentary party. The chief whip's job is to tell the prime minister what the MPs will not stand; he restrains the prime minister as much as the MPs; he mediates between the two, explaining each to the other. The whips are responsible for knowing thoroughly the views of certain groups of MPs divided into the geographical areas of their constituencies and they also attend the specialist party committees in the House. Whenever any policy or tendency of the leadership is found to be creating displeasure then the whips inform the prime minister and try to effect a reconciliation. The whips should not be regarded as the bullying agents of the prime minister.[33] By other means also he keeps in close touch with the feelings of his party, through individual trusted MPs, his private secretaries, his own personal contacts in the House, in its tearoom, dining room, bar and corridors and through more formal meetings with backbench committees. It would be fatal for a prime minister to set himself apart from his parliamentary party. It requires management. So too does the extra-parliamentary party, especially the Labour party which has less of a tradition of loyalty to the leadership than the Conservative party. To keep the outside party conversant with the policy of the parliamentarians, ministers, since the Leyton by-election, are to explain their positions to area conferences of party members all over the country and a liaison committee has been established to mediate between the parliamentary Labour party and the National Executive Committee.[34] The leaders in parliament recognise that the basis of their power would vanish if they alienated their party activists. Thus the prime minister is not the master of his party. Leaders can lose their parties' support and be toppled. They lead only with the sufferance and by the courtesy of their followers. A prime minister is only as strong as his party, and particularly his chief colleagues, let him be.

The prime minister's power of patronage has been exaggerated as a means of keeping his supporters loyal. Careerists can argue with great force that the way to achieve top office is not to give loyal and silent service, but to build up a following, to gain a reputation of having expertise in a certain sphere and to make a nuisance of oneself. The prime minister will then be forced to give the man office to quieten down his attacks, to restrain his following and generally to keep the party contented. But once in government office the man is not necessarily neutralised and muzzled. He will still maintain his following and keep open his informal contacts with them: indeed his stature amongst his faction may be enhanced by his performance in office. Thus he will be able to bring forceful pressure to bear on the prime minister whenever a policy is contemplated that he thinks undesirable. And if the opponent is a leading figure in the party with a significant following, the prime minister will be most reluctant to force the matter so far that he will be faced with a rebellion and resignation which will injure the reputation of his government. The prime minister's power to offer office and promotion to backbenchers and ministers is not a sure-proof device for obtaining their obedience to his wishes. He is seriously checked by his major colleagues who can rally other ministerial and formidable backbench support against him. The MPs then are not mere 'lobby fodder' for the prime minister, nor is the House of Commons just a 'rubber stamp' or 'talking shop'. MPs can bring their views to the notice of the prime minister, individually or collectively, through discussion with the whips in the specialist committees, and by approaching him themselves directly. Since he depends on their allegiance, he will try to accommodate his policies to their wishes.

The prime minister's influence over policy has been exaggerated. Government business has so increased and involves many technical and complex factors that no one man is able to survey the whole field. Policy initiatives come from many sources, not just from the prime minister, but from party policy, from the recommendations of civil servants who have worked out schemes with various interests often before the prime minister knows about them, from administrative necessity, from the sheer pressure of events at home and abroad and from the demands of public opinion channelled upwards in various ways. The House of Commons itself is no negligible factor and even the opposition is influential. On some issues the arguments of the opposition may gain favour with the electorate and then the government party, especially if an election is imminent, will take over some of the opposition's suggestions as its own, so as to blunt the force of its attack. Before the last election the Labour party frequently claimed that its policies had been filched by the government. Debates in the House of Commons, therefore, are not a meaningless charade; they can help shape the government's policy. The prime minister has also to take into account the views of his own party both in and outside the House. Through their specialist committees MPs have opportunities for gaining expertise in the work of particular departments and can therefore keep significant checks on the policy of the government. The coming of independent television indicates that a specialist committee can even impose its policy eventually on a reluctant cabinet.[35] Thus the prime minister is not necessarily able to initiate the policy he wants, nor shape policy as he desires. There are too many political pressures which he has to take account of.

A prime minister has a free hand constitutionally to form his own cabinet, but politically he is limited. He has to include the leading figures in the parliamentary party, and they may be so influential within the party and in the country that they may even dictate which office they will have. His cabinet must represent a cross-section of opinion in the party and contain the main faction leaders. Harold Wilson before the election said that Sir Alec Douglas-Home's cabinet was too large. It revealed, he said, the prime minister's weakness, because he had had to strike a large number of bargains. He promised to form a smaller cabinet.[36] In fact it was exactly the same size, again evidence of the number of powerful figures and interests the prime minister had to conciliate. Moreover, the actual offices to which he allocated the individuals showed very few surprises and suggested that he had not had much freedom to manoeuvre. Most went to offices to which they had already staked a claim, as members of the shadow cabinet, as frontbench spokesmen, and because they had some expertise or interest in the subject.[37] Thus the prime minister has not a free hand in the choice of his colleagues or the allocation of their offices.

Nor has he a free hand in dismissing them. None of the ministers who were dismissed or retired after disagreement with the cabinet in the postwar years were men of sufficient standing in their parties to present a significant challenge to the prime ministers, with the exception perhaps of Aneurin Bevan. No prime minister threw out or forced the resignation of a man who had support enough to displace him.[38] Even in the July purge of 1962 no serious contender for leadership was removed. The prime minister took care to keep in the cabinet his main rivals. His display of butchery illustrated further the limitations on his freedom of action. It did not enhance his position, rather it damaged an already fading reputation. He appeared to be making scapegoats of ministers who had served him loyally and carried out policies he had agreed with. He seemed to be sacrificing them to save his own skin. His actions did not increase confidence in his powers of judgement or timing. He made enemies inside the parliamentary party and inside the Conservative party outside parliament. He did not increase the popularity of the government. He undermined his own position by his purge.[39] The incident also illustrated the point that loyal service is not enough to bring a minister promotion and to prevent dismissal. None of those axed had a reputation for being awkward or nuisances or opponents of the prime minister. They were removed because they were easy targets and appeared to have no significant following among the remaining leading cabinet ministers or the MPs generally. Thus the importance of the prime minister's powers of appointment and dismissal has been grossly overestimated, perhaps most of all by Harold Macmillan.

Although the proceedings of the cabinet follow a formal protocol, the predominance of the prime minister suggested by the customs of cabinet etiquette has been exaggerated. His control over the agenda is not as absolute as has been presented. He may temporarily be able to keep off the agenda an item he dislikes, but he would be unable to prevent permanently a group or even one of his major colleagues from bringing up a matter they wished to discuss. If he did try to obstruct them, he would be acting senselessly, stirring up their opposition and encouraging them to rally support amongst the rest of the cabinet and the MPs against him. It would be very foolish for a prime minister to storm out of a cabinet meeting when one of his leading colleagues brought up an issue which the bulk of the cabinet wished to discuss. To walk out on such an occasion would seriously damage his reputation in their eyes.[40] The actual drawing up of the agenda is not solely dictated by prime ministerial whim. Outside pressures are significant, from his colleagues, departments, the party in and out of parliament, public opinion and events both domestic and external. Nor is he in command of the final verdict of the meeting. His summary and decision cannot go against the sense of the meeting. He cannot impose his own views on a reluctant session, especially if the chief figures in the cabinet oppose him. He may see his ideas modified and even rejected in the give-and-take of discussion.[41] To carry on as leader, the prime minister must retain the confidence of his cabinet, which means that he cannot dictate to it. Just because there is little evidence of revolts against the prime minister within the cabinet, it does not indicate that its members are tamely subservient to him. Most likely it shows that the final decisions are agreed ones, reached after discussion and compromise. Harmony implies not so much obedience to the prime minister's will as general agreement amongst the cabinet members, including the prime minster.

The charge that the prime minister by-passes the cabinet through conversations with individual ministers, cronies, cabinet committees, and experts outside government loses sight of the important fact that any major decisions which such meetings come to have to pass through the cabinet before they can be implemented. Any participant in such sessions with the prime minister, who objects to any decision, can get it discussed and decided at cabinet level, and any member of the cabinet can query any decision of such sessions, get a discussion started and a cabinet decision taken.[42] The doctrine of collective responsibility is still meaningful. By it, ministers are encouraged to take an interest in the work of other departments than their own. It is a myth that a minister is so completely absorbed in the work of his own department that he neglects the other aspects of government policy.[43] Ministers are still members of the House of Commons and members of their party. They have to defend the whole range of government policy and not just that of their department. Moreover they are usually keen on promotion, and thus do not immerse themselves in a single subject to the exclusion of other topics.

It is only sensible for the prime minister to keep on specially close terms with his chief colleagues and major rivals. These are the men with most weight in the cabinet; to square them would be the first stage in getting a policy through the cabinet. This inner cabinet has no formal structure, nor is it a collection of the prime minister's personal friends. He consults them not because he likes their company but because they are the most powerful men in his government. This kind of grouping is quite different from those meetings which Churchill used to hold late at night with some cronies. These were his personal friends with whom he enjoyed discussing matters, using their ideas to stimulate and sharpen his own.[44] The chief men in his cabinet were a different set. The former had not the real influence in government which the latter had, who could block some of Churchill's own objectives.[45]

Harold Wilson's meetings with ministers and officials to discuss particular topics are not innovations. Other prime ministers have had such meetings, and dinners with experts;[46] what is new is the publicity given to them. This is part of the technique of government, creating the impression that the government is active.

The two instances always quoted to show the great scope of prime ministerial power, the decisions to produce atomic weapons and to carry out the Suez venture, have been presented in a very biased way. The decision to produce atomic weapons was taken after thorough discussion in the Defence Committee of the cabinet; it was circulated in the cabinet agenda, but not discussed in cabinet because the decision was accepted by the cabinet ministers; the decision was also announced to parliament, and again no discussion took place because at that time in 1948 there was no significant opposition to the manufacture by Britain of such weapons.[47] The Suez affair was not the personal policy of the prime minister. The policy was discussed and initiated in a committee of the cabinet, comprising the chief men in the cabinet; the full cabinet was kept informed about the committee's decisions, and objections seem to have been raised by a few members; but clearly the majority of the cabinet was behind the policy of the committee.[48] Thus in neither case were these decisions taken solely by the prime minister. He had to carry with him his chief colleagues and the majority of the cabinet.

The standing of the individual minister has not been so depressed as some have suggested. The quotation from Lord Home, as he then was, has been overrated. It may tell us something about his relations with the prime minister, but nothing about Harold Macmillan's relations with other ministers. Some said that Lord Home was appointed foreign secretary because Macmillan wanted a man who would agree with him, performing much the same role as Selwyn Lloyd. In any case it has long been the custom for the prime minister to be virtually his own foreign minister. Only Austen Chamberlain and Ernest Bevin since 1919 were allowed a significant measure of independence by their prime ministers. The Foreign Office has often succumbed to prime ministerial intervention. Thus, since the relations between the prime minister and the foreign secretary are of a special character, any statement about their relations is not a general statement about the prime minister's relations with other ministers. A more apt quotation by a minister about Harold Macmillan's practices comes from Iain Macleod, 'Mr Macmillan set a new standard of competence in the business of forming, controlling and guiding a cabinet. He knew how to delegate to individual Ministers and to leave them alone. It was because the whole Cabinet worked so well and so smoothly that people formed the impression of an absolute personal ascendancy, and the notion grew up that we were changing from a Cabinet to a Presidential system of Government. In fact the reverse was happening. Mr Macmillan by his skill, restored a great deal of vitality to the Cabinet as a body'.[49] And Sir Alec Douglas-Home in a later interview in the *Observer*, when he was prime minister, said 'A good Prime Minister, once he had selected his Ministers and made it plain to them he was always accessible "for comment or advice", should interfere with their departmental business as little as possible'.[50] Harold Wilson has described the task of a prime minister as 'conducting an orchestra and not playing the instruments oneself'.[51] The only postwar prime minister who claimed that he was more than *primus inter pares* and acted as such by for example interfering and fussing with ministers and their departments was Sir Anthony Eden.[52] His activities did not gain him the support of his colleagues, and he can hardly be called one of the more successful prime ministers of Britain.

The prime minister is at a serious disadvantage with his colleagues. Unlike most of them he has no department to keep him informed and to brief him. He is not able to check the information flowing to him from the departments and their ministers. Without alternative sources of information he cannot easily evaluate their advice.[53] He is especially weak in that he cannot involve himself in the 'germinating stage' of a policy,[54] when the civil servants and ministers are mulling over some proposals. He is most likely brought in when discussions are completed, and opinions have solidified. His private office and Cabinet Office are not comparable to the departments behind his ministers, nor do they approach the large number and expertise of the advisers of the American president.[55] Harold Wilson, before becoming prime minister, expressed the view that the prime minister needed to be served by a briefing agency to ensure that he was as fully informed as a departmental minister, and that the prime minister should come in on policy discussions at an early stage.[56] Harold Wilson's sessions at Chequers, which he claims are a return to the methods of Churchill and Attlee, are attempts to bring the prime minister into this early stage, and his attaching to the Cabinet Office of certain academics and civil servants, economists, scientists and technologists in particular, is an attempt to provide himself with new sources of information and advice. He has not added them to his private office, which has remained very much the same as before, but to the Cabinet Office. It is, however, not just the servant of the prime minister; it has a collective loyalty to the cabinet and its prime function is to serve that body, not a single man. Indeed Wilson's refusal to turn his private office into a strong central intelligence service for himself indicates some limits on his power. If he had done so he would have irritated his ministers and civil servants.[57] To avoid their displeasure he had to strengthen the Cabinet Office. But far from enhancing the position of the prime minister above his colleagues the Cabinet Office has served to sustain the doctrine of collective responsibility, since it has been loyal to its function of serving the cabinet as a whole.

Even if he had established a stronger private office, it is unlikely that it would have prevailed against older and larger departments. They have usually triumphed over small *ad hoc* teams of civil servants attached to new-fangled ministries with lofty aims and no traditional establishment. Non-departmental ministers and prime ministers have had little success when fighting the entrenched departments, who remain impervious to takeover bids.[58] The civil service consists of a number of departments, each possessing a strong *esprit de corps*. It is not as centralised and monolithic as some have suggested and therefore not so easily amenable to prime ministerial control. His power over appointments is not such that he can put exactly whom he wants in any position he likes. He has to defer to the advice of the joint permanent secretary to the Treasury and the consensus amongst the top echelons of the civil service about who should fill the major posts. Even if a personal choice is put in charge, there is no guarantee that he will remain a loyal servant of the prime minister. He will most likely become the spokesman of his department's view, defending its interests against all comers.

It is hard for an individual minister to know all that is going on in his own department, and therefore even harder for a prime minister to know all that is going on in the whole machine of government. If on one item he does exert himself to influence the course of a decision, he will have to expend much energy and effort, and in so doing will naturally neglect other aspects of policy. If he does prevail in one area, he fails in others, because he cannot influence everything at once.[59]

The prime minister has no executive powers vested in him. To achieve anything he must work with and through his ministers who have executive power vested in them.[60] These men have powerful and independent departments to brief them and possess significant followings in their party who hope to see their man one day leader. To become and remain prime minister a man must carry these major colleagues, who are his rivals, with him. He cannot dictate to them, but must co-operate, consult and negotiate with them and even at times defer to them. Cabinet government and collective responsibility are not defunct notions. Shared responsibility is still meaningful, for a prime minister has to gain the support of the bulk of his cabinet to carry out his policies. He has to persuade it and convince it that he is right. Its meetings do not merely follow his direction. Debate and conflict are frequent. It cannot be by-passed and he cannot be an autocrat. To attempt to become one presages his political suicide.

The prime minister is the leading figure in the cabinet whose voice carries most weight. But he is not the all-powerful individual which many have recently claimed him to be. His office has great potentialities, but the use made of them depends on many variables, the personality, temperament, and ability of the prime minister, what he wants to achieve and the methods he uses. It depends also on his colleagues, their personalities, temperaments and abilities, what they want to do and their methods. A prime minister who can carry his colleagues with him can be in a very powerful position, but he is only as strong as they let him be.

References

1. Reprinted from *Parliamentary Affairs*, xviii (Spring 1965), pp. 167–85, with the permission of A. D. Peters & Co and the Hansard Society for Parliamentary Government.
2. R. W. K. Hinton, 'The Prime Minister as an Elected Monarch', *Parliamentary Affairs*, xii (Summer 1960), pp. 297–303.

   D. J. Heasman, 'The Prime Minister and the Cabinet', *Parliamentary Affairs*, xv (Autumn 1962), pp. 461–84.

   R. H. S. Crossman, 'Introduction' to Walter Bagehot's *The English Constitution* (London: Watts, 1964), pp. 51–7.

   B. Crick, *The Reform of Parliament* (London: Weidenfeld & Nicolson, 1964), pp. 34–9.

John P. Mackintosh's *The British Cabinet* is often quoted as supporting this argument, but the book contains serious inconsistencies, noted in D. N. Chester, 'Who Governs Britain?', *Parliamentary Affairs*, xv (Autumn 1962), pp. 519–27. However, Mr Mackintosh clearly supported this argument in an ITV broadcast on 10 January 1965: 'Power in Britain'.

A. Sampson, *Anatomy of Britain* (London: Hodder & Stoughton, 1962), pp. 330–3.

P. Johnson, *New Statesman*, 14 February 1964.

P. Worsthorne in the *Sunday Telegraph* quoted by John P. Mackintosh, *British Cabinet*, p. 437 and Professor M. Beloff (in the *Daily Telegraph*, 2 August 1960), quoted by A. Sampson, *Anatomy of Britain*, p. 330.

3. 'Radio and television bring him more frequently than any other politician into the homes of the people, who therefore see in his personality the embodiment of the party and, in times of emergency, the trustee of the national cause': J. Harvey and L. Bather, *The British Constitution* (London: Macmillan, 1964), p. 224.

4. W. G. Andrews, in 'Three Electoral Colleges', *Parliamentary Affairs*, xiv (Spring 1961), describes a general election as conferring imperative mandates for the designation of the prime minister (p. 182) and as 'an indirect way of voting for prime ministerial candidates' (pp. 184–5).

5. Harvey and Bather, *British Constitution*, p. 224.

6. R. T. McKenzie, *British Political Parties*, 2nd edn (London: Heinemann, 1963).

7. P. G. Richards, *Patronage in British Goverment* (London: Allen & Unwin, 1963).

8. Because of the declining interest in parliament and politics. Mackintosh, *British Cabinet*, p. 389.

9. Parliamentary Debates, House of Commons, vol. 702, cols. 671–2 (19 November 1964) and vol. 703 cols. 1839–42 (10 December 1964).

10. *The Economist*, 27 May 1961.

11. 'The prime minister expresses his changes and emphasis by changing his colleagues, they themselves being given scant opportunity to modify their own positions': D. J. Heasman, 'The Prime Minister and the Cabinet', p. 479. 'The uncertainty among ministers resulting from frequent changes and dismissals consolidated his power': H. Daalder, *Cabinet Reform in Britain, 1914–1963* (London: Oxford University Press, 1964), p. 125.

12. See, for example, Lord Hill of Luton, *Both Sides of the Hill* (London: Heinemann, 1964), pp. 236–7. Junior ministers are said to have to give the prime minister reports on progress in their departments: *New Statesman*, 23 January 1965.

13. A. Sampson describes this network as 'the bush-telegraph of Whitehall', *Anatomy of Britain*, p. 334.

14. When discussing Harold Macmillan's chairmanship of the cabinet, Lord Hill of Luton said, 'If I have a criticism it is that, now and again, the cabinet was consulted at too late a stage in the evolution of some

important line of policy; he seemed to forget that many of us had not been present at the cabinet committee concerned with the topic'. Hill, *Both Sides of the Hill*, p. 235.

15. *Observer*, 16 September 1962.
16. R. H. S. Crossman, op. cit. pp. 49–51, says that the prime minister is the 'apex not only of a highly centralised political machine, but also of an equally centralised and vastly more powerful administrative machine', and that in both 'loyalty has become the supreme virtue'.
17. A. Sampson, *Anatomy of Britain*, p. 331.
18. Iain Macleod, 'The Tory Leadership', *Spectator*, 17 January 1964. R. S. Churchill, *The Fight for the Tory Leadership* (London: Heinemann, 1964), pp. 94–139.
19. Sir Anthony Eden, *Full Circle* (London: Cassell, 1960), p. 269.
20. P. Worsthorne, *Sunday Telegraph*, 5 May 1963.
21. J. Blondel, *Voters, Parties and Leaders* (Harmondsworth: Penguin, 1963), pp. 81–4.
22. J. Trenaman and D. McQuail, *Television and the Political Image* (London: Methuen, 1961); A. H. Birch, *Representative and Responsible Government: An Essay on the British Constitution* (London: Allen & Unwin, 1964), pp. 171–88.
23. On the 'mandate' see A. H. Birch, *Representative and Responsible Government*, pp. 114–30.
24. C. O. Jones, 'Inter-Party Competition in Britain – 1950–1959', *Parliamentary Affairs*, xvi (Winter 1963–64), pp. 50–64.
25. On the power of dissolution see W. G. Andrews, 'Some Thoughts on the Power of Dissolution', *Parliamentary Affairs*, xiii (Summer 1960), pp. 286–96.
26. L. D. Epstein, 'British MPs and their Local Parties: The Suez Cases', *American Political Science Review*, liv (June 1960), pp. 374–90.
27. R. Rose, 'Parties, Factions and Tendencies in Britain', *Political Studies*, xii (February 1964), pp 33–46.
28. S. E. Finer, H. B. Berrington and D. J. Bartholomew, *Backbench Opinion in the House of Commons 1955–59* (London: Pergamon Press, 1961).
29. L. Hunter, *The Road to Brighton Pier* (London: Arthur Barker, 1959) and Hugh Dalton, *High Tide and After* (London: Muller, 1962).
30. McKenzie, *British Political Parties*, p. 581, especially note 2. R. S. Churchill, *Rise and Fall of Sir Anthony Eden* (London: MacGibbon & Kee, 1959), p. 192. Lord Dalton in an obituary of Sir Winston Churchill said that 'his younger colleagues pushed him overboard', *New Statesman*, 29 January 1965.
31. McKenzie, *British Political Parties*, pp. 582–6. R. S. Churchill, *Rise and Fall*, p. 309. Lord Hill said that Eden was made a scapegoat for Suez; *Both Sides of the Hill*, p. 179.
32. *Spectator*, 8 January 1965. A *Times* leader noted that 'the word is going round that he [Mr Wilson] has not got a good backbone' (19 January 1965).
33. On the role of the whips see 'The Commons in Action', an interview

with M. Redmayne, *The Listener*, 19 December 1963 and 26 December 1963. Lord Hill said that 'A chief whip's job is to listen and to learn, to gather up the scraps of gossip, to assess other people's opinions. He is the prime minister's ears and eyes in the smoking room and the lobby'. *Both Sides of the Hill*, p. 242. See also *The Economist*, 15 July 1961.

34. *The Times*, 28 January 1965.

35. H. H. Wilson, *Pressure Group: the Campaign for Commercial Television* (London: Secker & Warburg, 1961).

36. Harold Wilson, *Whitehall and Beyond* (London: BBC Publications, 1964), p. 26.

37. R. M. Punnett, 'The Labour Shadow Cabinet, 1955–64', *Parliamentary Affairs*, xvii (Winter 1964–65), especially p. 70 where he says 'On the whole there was very little change in the allocation of senior responsibilities in the transition from opposition to power, and the ministerial duties are very largely based on the allocation of responsibilities that applied in the 1963–64 session'.

38. Attlee never threw out Bevin, Cripps or Morrison.

39. Even Crick points out (*Reform of Parliament*, p. 39) that by-election reverses continued; opposition in his own party was brought out into the lobbies when 70 backbenchers held a protest meeting against the dismissal of Selwyn Lloyd, and it led to the revolt of October 1963.

   See also Lord Hill, *Both Sides of the Hill*, pp. 246–8 and Lord Kilmuir, *Political Adventure* (London: Weidenfeld & Nicolson, 1964), pp. 322–4; Reginald Bevins said that 'In July 1962 Harold Macmillan committed political suicide more certainly than if he had himself resigned'. *Sunday Express*, 17 January 1965.

40. Enoch Powell said 'A minister clearly has a right to bring a matter to his colleagues if he wants to. The very nature of collective responsibility implies that if a man wants his colleagues' assent or advice he can have it': *Whitehall and Beyond*, p. 59.

41. Lord Hill said of Macmillan that 'if he found himself in a minority he accepted the fact with grace and humour': *Both Sides of the Hill*, p. 235.

42. Mr Wilson in the ITV broadcast on 'Power in Britain' said that it was open to any member of the cabinet to question any of the assumptions of the cabinet committees, and ministerial meetings at Chequers which he said were like cabinet committees: 10 January 1965. Also see *The Times*, 11 January 1965.

43. See Enoch Powell's view on this point in *Whitehall and Beyond*, p. 48.

44. Lord Kilmuir noted that Macmillan refused to have an inner cabinet: *Political Adventure*, p. 309; Mackintosh, *British Cabinet*, p. 343. Lord Woolton points out, p. 377–8, that this was not government by cronies.

45. Mackintosh, *British Cabinet*, p. 435, especially note 2.

46. Harold Wilson claimed to be returning to the practices of Attlee and Churchill: *Whitehall and Beyond*, p. 26.

47. See the correspondence between R. H. S. Crossman and G. R. Strauss

in *New Statesman*, 10 May 1963, 17 May 1963, 24 May 1963, 31 May 1963 and 7 June 1963, and in *Encounter*, June 1963 and August 1963.

48. Mackintosh, *British Cabinet*, pp. 435–6, Anthony Eden, *Full Circle*, p. 432.

49. *Spectator*, 14 February 1964. Lord Kilmuir noted that 'Macmillan's approach to cabinet business was businesslike and firm; all important issue [*sic*] would be dealt with by the cabinet, to remove the very real possibility that some unconsidered independent action by a junior minister might damage the government as a whole': Kilmuir, *Political Adventure*, p. 308.

50. *Observer*, 13 September 1964.

51. In the ITV broadcast 'Power in Britain', 10 January 1965 and in *The Times*, 25 January 1965. The political correspondent of the *New Statesman* said, 'The Labour leadership is composed of a full (if at times discordant) orchestra, rather than a one-man band', 29 January 1965. Earlier he had claimed that Harold Wilson showed a readiness to delegate responsibility. *New Statesman*, 22 January 1965.

52. Mackintosh, *British Cabinet*, p. 435; Dalton, *High Tide and After*, p. 20. Kilmuir points out that Eden annoyed Macmillan by interfering in his department (*Political Adventure*, pp. 243–4) and that Macmillan interfered far less than Eden 'Unless he judged that they [departmental matters] merited cabinet consideration' (ibid., p. 308).

53. Because he is so weak in this respect there have been suggestions that he should have a department of his own, a prime minister's office: *The Economist*, 8 June 1963, or Lord Shawcross in *The Times*, 11 October 1963; *Guardian*, 26 February 1964.

54. Lord Bridges and Harold Wilson have noted the restraints on the prime minister's power because he was absent at the 'germinating stage': *Whitehall and Beyond*, pp. 26, 68–9.

55. R. Rose, *Politics in England* (London: Faber, 1965), p. 195. Sampson, *Anatomy of Britain*, pp. 334–5. G. Smith, 'The Political Prisoner', *Sunday Times Colour Magazine*, 18 September 1963. Interview with Sir Alec Douglas-Home, *Observer*, 13 September 1964. Interview with R. Neustadt, *Sunday Times*, 8 November 1964.

56. *Whitehall and Beyond*, p. 26.

57. Interview with R. Neustadt, ibid.

58. *The Economist*, 13 August 1960.

59. Daalder, *Cabinet Reform*, p. 248.

60. G. C. Moodie, *The Government of Great Britain* (New York: Thos. Crowell, 1964), p. 85.

9

The Case for a Constitutional Premiership

TONY BENN[1]

Tony Benn is no academic radical. He served in the governments of Wilson and Callaghan and has been a member of parliament, with only one short interruption, since 1950. His analysis starts where that of Richard Crossman in chapter 7 left off. Mr Benn believes that British government is indeed prime ministerial government, that this is a bad thing and that something should be done about it. In the course of suggesting what is wrong and how the institution of the prime ministership might be reformed, Mr Benn emphasises a number of elements of prime ministerial power in addition to those mentioned by Crossman. Mr Benn also raises, albeit implicitly, the question of whether the idea of a 'constitutional prime ministership' is one that should appeal only to members of the Labour party or whether it should also be taken seriously by supporters of other parties. This chapter was written soon after Labour left office in 1979.

The Argument in Outline

My argument can be very simply summarised. The wide range of powers at present exercised by a British prime minister, both in that capacity and as party leader, are now so great as to encroach upon the legitimate rights of the electorate, undermine the essential role of parliament, usurp some of the functions of collective cabinet decision making and neutralise much of the influence deriving from the internal democracy of the Labour party. In short, the present centralisation of power into the hands of one person has gone too far and amounts to a system of personal rule in the very heart of our parliamentary democracy. My conclusion is that the powers of the prime minister, and party leader, must be made more accountable to those over whom they are exercised, so that we can develop a constitutional premiership in Britain. To transform an absolute premiership into a constitutional premiership would involve making some fundamental changes in its functions comparable to those made over the years, when the crown was transformed from an absolute monarchy to a constitutional monarchy.

One advantage of looking at the top of the tree for the causes of some of Britain's political problems, rather than at the electorate as a whole, is that it makes a welcome and healthy change from the theory that Britain is afflicted with a national malaise, so serious that even a succession of wise leaders have been unable to bring the nation to its senses. I have never found that analysis very convincing. Even if it were true, I could not accept the only remedy on offer: to limit the democratic process and hand even more power to the people at the top. Democracy means that the electorate can remove their government, not that political leaders can take over power from the electors because they are disappointed with their performance in exercising responsibility for their own affairs. Power and responsibility must necessarily go together and it is my argument that, if the people are supposed to lack responsibility, it may be because they have too little power and that the true remedy lies in decentralising power by moving it down from the top, instead of shifting more of it to the top. That is the basic case for democracy and it needs to be restated in this generation, beginning with a very critical look at the premiership, where so much power now lies.

Britain's political history has been marked by a long series of struggles to wrest powers away from the centre and redistribute them to a wider group of interests. From the truly absolutist monarchy of William the Conqueror, there was a succession of bitter battles from which the monarchy emerged with its powers trimmed, first by the feudal barons at Runnymede, then by the House of Lords itself and, later still, by the revolution of the gentry at the time of Cromwell. The growing power of the House of Commons after 1688, and the development of cabinet government in the century that followed, led to the situation under which the crown's own ministers were required to command a majority in the elected chamber. After the 1832 Reform Act the processes of extending the franchise were carried to the point which we have reached today, when ministers are accountable to a House of Commons chosen following an election at which all adults may vote. Under this textbook version of the development of our constitutional monarchy, within a parliamentary democracy, the powers of the prime minister can be seen as a great achievement because they have been wrested away from the throne, and are now only exercised at the will of the electorate – but the analysis leaves out of account the impact that the powers of the prime minister may have on the rights of those in parliament, in the political parties and on the electorate as a whole. The establishment of an 'elected monarch' may reproduce, in a significant sense, the very system of personal rule which earlier struggles were intended to end. Indeed, it is quite legitimate to ask whether we have not, accidentally, made a very good job of reproducing feudalism, complete with a whole new generation of barons, who owe their positions of power to a new 'monarch' dispensing power and status of a much more significant kind, as well as the old honours. This is not to suggest that all the very real achievements of British democracy have been eroded by these tendencies. The ultimate power of the House of Commons to topple a prime minister remains unaffected, as does the even greater power of the voters to get rid of both governments and the MPs who support them: the very fact that this power is there operates to restrain the exercise of all powers by prime ministers and their ministers. Within that broad framework of public and parliamentary consent, however, there has certainly been a greater centralisation of personal power in the hands of one man or woman than outward appearances would suggest.

To complete the background, it is necessary to look at the growth of the party system. The labour movement in the 19th century saw itself as representing working people before they had the vote, and campaigned with the Chartists to extend the franchise. The trade unions then saw the need for working men to be put up as candidates to represent their class and the Labour party was born out of the Labour Representation Committee. Its constitution of 1918 has as its first purpose 'To organise and maintain in parliament and in the country a political Labour Party'. The whole basis of the deep commitment of the Labour party to the parliamentary system lies in the fact that it believes that, by the adoption of candidates who are pledged to policies agreed at annual conference, the rank and file can, subject to the will of the electors in a general election, win a majority to carry through those policies in a peaceful and democratic way. Thus the link between the party in the country and Labour MPs lies at the very root of the party's concept of how parliamentary democracy would work. A whole range of issues bearing upon that relationship are up for discussion at this moment but here it is the link between the party and the party leader that is most relevant. The Labour party in parliament was the first party to have any sort of election for its leader. Indeed, the very idea of MPs of any party electing their leader was seen as revolutionary not so very long ago, when it was widely believed that the crown had retained the prerogative right to ask anyone it chose to form a government. Now that all three main parties elect their leaders, the crown accepts that its choice of prime minister will be made for it by the majority party in parliament. Only in very exceptional circumstances would it have any discretion and that would only occur in a hung parliament. The reason that this is such a sensitive political issue for the Labour party is that the whole existence of, and justification for, the party depends upon it being able to rely upon the Labour prime minister of the day being the last link in the process by which its policies get implemented, after they have been hammered out at conference and have won approval at a general election. Of course, the leader also has a very important role to play in, and on behalf of, the party, even when a Labour government is not in power and this raises the same questions of democratic accountability.

The Powers of the Party Leader in Opposition

Though the parliamentary committee of 12 people is elected by the whole parliamentary Labour party (PLP) when the party is in opposition, the leader, at present, chooses which elected MP is to shadow which department – and he or she can reshuffle his or her team at any time without consulting either the parliamentary committee or the MP. This power is based upon the practice of appointing, or reshuffling, ministers when a Labour government is in office. The main difference is that no MP elected to the parliamentary committee can actually be removed by the leader and for that reason their relationship is quite different from the relationship of ministers to the prime minister. Even so, the allocation of these shadow portfolios is very important in that it amounts to real patronage – carrying, as it does, at least a hint of what office a person might expect to hold if a government was formed. Moreover, any person chosen to speak for the party from the front bench will find that his pronouncements carry great weight and can actually blank out the policy decided by the party nationally. In the case of MPs who are unsuccessful in winning a place on the parliamentary committee the leader of the party has an unrestricted right to appoint them to shadow for a department as the principal, or secondary, spokesman. Such non-elected spokesmen, now numbering 45 (excluding the whips), are in a different position from their elected fellows: their places are entirely at the disposal of the leader, and to this extent they are much more dependent upon his wishes. (Admittedly, they have a certain freedom from 'shadow cabinet responsibility' on any subject other than the one which they speak about from the front bench, while for the full members of the parliamentary committee there is an expectation that they will follow the line agreed by it.)

It had long been the custom of the prime minister of the day to offer the leader of the opposition the right to nominate people for peerages to 'strengthen the opposition in the House of Lords'. This became institutionalised when life peerages were started in 1958 and it became a habit to put an asterisk against the names of persons whose nomination came from opposition party leaders. Whatever the justification for this development, it started a very important new source of much-prized patronage in the hands of the leader of the Labour party, whether in office, or out of office. A peerage carries with it a seat in parliament for life, daily attendance allowances and – in the case of former MPs – the much-valued right to use the facilities of the House of Commons, save only the right to enter the chamber. (Many Labour peers work very hard indeed watching the passage of every bill and putting up opposition to those the party has opposed in the Commons: nothing is intended to be a criticism of their work.)

The problem of patronage, however, is really a problem that begins long before the honour has been awarded. Stemming from the relationship that is set up between the party leader – as donor – and those who may wish – as applicants – to receive the award, it extends the influence of patronage far beyond the number of people who, in the event, actually receive an honour. For every Labour peer who is created, there may be many more who hope that they will be: thus, at any one time, there may be dozens of Labour MPs – or others – who want what only the leader can give them and some of these would be less than human if the knowledge that their heart's desire could only be realised by their remaining in favour with the leader, did not in some way affect their conduct on issues upon which the leader had very definite views or interests. This is how patronage can shift the interests of a person away from representing constituents or the party, to the quite different one of pleasing the leader. And it follows that, in such cases where these very human reactions take place, the leader gains voting strength and influence in the PLP from the hopefuls, which could possibly be used to frustrate the policies of the party outside. The argument does not imply any criticism of leaders who exercise this power, or of the recipients of his patronage, but that the system of patronage – whether in the appointment of ministers or peers – is absolutely inseparable from the flows of political power that are an integral part of the whole system.

The leader of the party is not directly elected by conference but elected by the PLP and his place on the NEC is *ex officio*;

thus when he attends conference he is not meeting his 'constituents' but is there as a representative of the PLP. It is in that capacity that his influence over the manifesto is exercised. Though the party constitution provides that the manifesto shall be drawn up by the NEC and the parliamentary committee sitting together, the power of the leader is greater than the formal constitutional position suggests. For he is a permanent member of the NEC and does not have to wait to use his power until the actual manifesto meeting takes place. In the past, the leader has also argued that there is a formal veto which he can exercise over the manifesto, or any part of it, which he is not prepared to agree should be put to the electorate.

The leader's consent is also needed before any joint meeting between the NEC and the parliamentary leaders to draft the manifesto can be arranged. In this way he can effectively block early work and defer the discussion and agreement until the general election is imminent. This power of timing is crucial to the content of the manifesto and its role in the campaign. If it is drawn up early, free from the pressure of an impending campaign, the NEC is in a much more favourable position to press for conference policies to be included; and if the draft can actually be published as a campaign document before the election is announced, the party has much more time to get its proposals across to the electorate. This happened in 1974 when a campaign document was issued under the authority of the joint committee and the voters knew, well in advance of the election, what policies Labour candidates would be advocating. If, however, the manifesto is left to the last minute, as happened in 1979, as the leader can insist that it is, then there can be no real certainty as to what commitments can be included in it before the campaign has begun.

Moreover, since the natural desire for unity within the party is at its peak at the beginning of a campaign, the leader's veto is absolute and unchallenged. He only has to hint that, if a certain pledge were included, he would feel obliged to resign for all pressure for that pledge to subside at once at the terrible prospect of the party losing its leader at such a critical juncture. In this way his wishes are complied with as a simple matter of confidence in him on the eve of the battle. By extension, the leader can, in effect, actually set aside any draft prepared by the

NEC and substitute one of his own, insisting that the meeting address itself to his draft manifesto instead of to the NEC draft.

The Powers of the Prime Minister in Office

All the powers enjoyed by a party leader in opposition are, of course, retained when he becomes prime minister and, indeed, are reinforced by virtue of that office. In addition, he acquires a formidable battery of new powers which are so numerous as to make it difficult to compress the list down to manageable proportions. For the sake of simplicity I have divided them into groups. Of all these, the power to appoint and dismiss ministers without any constitutional need for approval by parliament or the party is the most decisive for it is by its use, or threat of use, that all the other powers described below fall into the hands of the prime minister alone.

This power derives from the formal constitutional position that the crown entrusts the task of forming an administration to an individual who is then solely responsible for nominating his cabinet and all other ministers. The number of ministerial appointments by seven prime ministers from 1945 to 1976 was 1,494, made up of 309 cabinet and 1,185 non-cabinet ministers.

The power to create peers, too, derives from the general right to advise the crown on the use of its prerogative. From 1945–76, 568 hereditary and life peers were created on the advice of seven prime ministers. Each peer is a member of parliament: for comparison, it takes 40 million electors to elect 635 members of the House of Commons. (Though a political honours scrutiny committee examines these nominations, this process cannot be said to involve any real accountability.) The prime minister has, of course, considerable powers of a much wider range of honours included in the new year and queen's birthday and special lists; 118 baronetcies, and 264 knighthoods were created during that period.

The prime minister expects to be consulted, personally, on appointments of all chairmen of nationalised industries and in effect enjoys the right to insist upon the appointment of the person he wishes to go forward. These chairmanships – of which there were some 65 – confer real power in that the nationalised industries account for about 20 per cent of the nation's output, employ about 1¾ million people and have an aggregate turnover of over £14 billion a year. In addition, during the same period 35 chairmen of Royal Commissions were appointed. So far we have identified 2,564 major appointments or patronage awards made by seven men over a 31-year period. The scale of it all is breathtaking and no medieval monarch could compare with it, either in numbers or in importance. But there is more to come, since prime ministers also appoint permanent secretaries, ambassadors, chiefs of staff and the heads of the security services – MI5 and MI6. They can obviously have an influence, if they choose to use it, over the names of all those put forward for the 31 public boards listed in 1977 or the 252 fringe bodies, which themselves employ 184,000 people and spent £2,367 million a year as recorded in the Civil Service Department Record of 1978. On the not unreasonable assumption that there are two or three hopefuls for every successful candidate for an honour or an appointment, the seven postwar prime ministers extended their influence over between 5,000 and 7,000 would-be ministers, lords, knights and chairmen.

Each new prime minister issues a personal minute of procedure for ministers which lays down a whole range of requirements for ministers, governing everything from collective cabinet responsibility through the need for Number 10 to authorise all broadcasts and the banning of articles in the press. Even memoirs are covered. These minutes, which began as a guide to the conduct of government business, are never submitted in draft for cabinet approval. While the 1945 version issued by Mr Attlee, and now released under the 30-year rule, consisted of four pages and 23 paragraphs, the 1976 version ran to 27 printed pages, in 132 paragraphs, under 14 main sections and 51 sub-sections. A further minute, confined to travel, ran to six pages and a schedule – making a total of 33 printed pages, 17 sections and 156 paragraphs. Although parliament, the public and the party are entitled to know what restrictions are placed upon ministers, these rules are classified as confidential. As a recent parliamentary answer made clear, the prime minister regards the application, or non-application, of the rules of collective cabinet responsibility as being entirely within his own personal discretion. His power to secure compliance with them rests upon his power to dismiss those who breach them.

A prime minister's second greatest power, after patronage, lies in his complete personal control of the conduct of government business as it is carried out by ministers and officials. He determines which items of business are to be discussed in cabinet and which are to be excluded. He has the power to set up cabinet committees, appoint their members and keep their existence secret from the public, from parliament and even from other members of the cabinet. There were 23 standing committees of the cabinet and probably 150 *ad hoc* committees set up over the last five years. The prime minister has the power to circulate, or not to circulate, papers written by cabinet ministers for cabinet and the same power to withhold cabinet committee papers from other members of the cabinet who do not serve on that committee. He has the power to instruct the civil service on the conduct of its business through the appointment of interdepartmental official committees and to commission papers from them even on matters that primarily concern the responsibilities of a departmental minister. The prime minister is thus able to use the government to bring forward the policies which he favours and to stop those to which he is opposed, including policies deriving from Labour policy or the manifesto. To complete these powers, he can refuse his consent to joint meetings of the cabinet and the NEC to discuss matters of common concern, including the preparation of the next election manifesto. To this extent the conduct of government business can be said to reflect a personal and autocratic, rather than a collective and democratic, spirit.

A prime minister is also in a unique position to control the flow of information about the work of the government. Alone among ministers he has the power to inform parliament, or the public, directly on any matter relating to the government's policy or activity which he believes it to be in the government's interest should be known. In addition he can arrange for unofficial briefings of the press or trusted correspondents on any matter which he decides should be handled in that way; and under the 'lobby rules' the prime minister may decline to confirm or deny that any such briefings have taken place. He has the power to classify any documents to any level, and to establish a leak inquiry to be undertaken by a minister, or an official, into any suspected disclosure of information which he, as prime minister, believes should not have been disclosed: and may withhold the results of that inquiry from the cabinet even when cabinet ministers have been questioned. His personal responsibility for the security services entitles him to have any person – including ministers – put under surveillance and to withhold knowledge both of the fact and its outcome from anyone he chooses.

A prime minister may use the royal prerogative to secure the adherence of the United Kingdom to treaties which bind parliament without any requirement for its formal ratification by parliament. He may enter into binding commitments in respect of the European Communities – personally or through ministers – which have legal force in the United Kingdom without prior approval of parliament or the cabinet. He also enjoys special responsibilities for the conduct of the armed forces through the secretary of state for defence.

The prerogative powers of the crown, which in this case have to be exercised with proper caution, because of the sensibilities of the monarch, also confer two final powers upon the prime minister. He can advise, and normally expects to secure, a dissolution of parliament before the end of its natural life-span, even in the absence of a defeat in the Commons. He can also terminate the life of the whole government by the simple procedure of tendering his own resignation to the sovereign, which automatically carries with it the resignation of all his colleagues. The prime minister is not constitutionally required to consult the cabinet about his decision on either of these matters but his real power flows from his ability to threaten to resign or to dissolve parliament if the cabinet will not support him. Thus votes of confidence, even within cabinet, can achieve results when persuasion may have failed.

Prime Ministerial Powers and Their Use

It is essential for government to be able, in the national interest, to respond quickly and effectively to situations, at home or abroad, which require immediate decisive action, perhaps under the tightest veil of secrecy. In such circumstances it may well be neither practicable nor desirable for that action to be delayed to allow consultations to be arranged even within the cabinet, and for these purposes the prime minister must be accepted as the proper person to initiate such action, to arrange for it to be implemented, and to be ready to justify his actions afterwards. But the existence of some situations which call for the exercise of his personal authority should not be used as an excuse for acting in this way when it is not strictly necessary to do so. It is obviously tempting for a prime minister to argue that other decisions he takes fall into this category of 'action in the national interest' and then require support as a matter of confidence in him. Not only is this unacceptable, but where decisions could be anticipated, a previous policy discussion could lead to guidelines being agreed in cabinet beforehand and this should also be arranged.

It is desirable that as many government policy decisions as possible should be reached after consultations with those whose interests are likely to be affected. Policies arrived at in this way are more likely to be effective, to be acceptable and to endure. Secrecy makes this consultation difficult, if not impossible, and it is therefore very important that the formulation of policy should not be shrouded in secrecy unless it is absolutely necessary to do so. Where consultation does take place, it must always include MPs generally and the Labour party in particular. Committees of the House are naturally angry if they discover that bills they are discussing have been drafted to reflect agreements reached in bilateral discussions between the government and interest groups which then cannot be varied. The same argument applies with special force to Labour MPs and the Labour party which regularly experienced exclusion from the consultative process. Although some ministers made it their business to keep in close contact, the party often thought it was treated more like a normal external pressure group and was denied the special relationship with its ministerial colleagues which it believed would have been more natural. The tension arising from this discontent reached new levels during the 'Lib–Lab pact', when Liberal MPs were brought into a formal consultative relationship with ministers, thus underlining the exclusion of the party and Labour MPs. During this period ministers were expected to discuss their policy proposals with their Liberal counterparts before bringing them to colleagues: neither Labour MPs, even when organised in specialist groups, nor the NEC policy committees ever enjoyed such rights. What is wanted is a permanent 'Lib–Lab pact' whenever a Labour government is in power and the institution of arrangements which would guarantee its effectiveness, best achieved by developing greater accountability by the prime minister and ministers to backbench MPs and the party. Such arrangements would in no way weaken the authority of the House of Commons, which would retain precisely the same rights to approve or disapprove government policies, just as the electorate would retain its power to re-elect or dismiss the government, but the policy presented in parliament, and to the voters, would emerge from a very different consultative process that took greater account of the interdependence of the parliamentary leadership with the party which secures its election and sustains it in power.

One of the unfortunate side effects flowing from the excessive secrecy of government, and from the centralisation of power within the cabinet into the hands of the prime minister, is that the public, the House of Commons, Labour MPs and even the cabinet itself may find themselves faced more and more often by *faits accomplis* which cannot be changed. Some of these may involve a policy change of quite a fundamental character that could, and should, have been the subject of proper consultation. If that consultation has not taken place, the only choice that is left is to accept what has happened or to repudiate the decision and the prime minister who made it. Since no political party wants to repudiate its own elected leader, or to damage the party's interest by being seen to do so, there is a strong pressure to rally to what has been done: prime ministers know this very well and may be tempted to make everything they do into a vote of confidence. This is inherently unsatisfactory because it personalises politics, substituting loyalty for the consideration of issues and downgrades the role of MPs to that of 'lobby fodder'. The problem can only be resolved if the personal power of the prime minister is diminished by giving others, including the cabinet and Labour MPs, a greater say in the issues discussed before they have been decided and any question of confidence arises. There will be circumstances in which a vote of confidence takes place, but they should be very much the exception and not the rule.

The attitude of the Labour party towards its leader is always a complex one. Unlike the Conservative party, whose leader is treated with elaborate personal respect and then disposed of as soon as he or she is thought to have failed, the Labour party feels free to be critical of everything the leader says and does but retains a fierce personal loyalty against all outside criticisms, and this will last until the leader dies or chooses to retire. Of the two attitudes, the Labour approach is much the best, but since Labour prime ministers depend so much upon that underlying loyalty, it must not be taken for granted, nor tested beyond what is reasonable, by trying to use it to reject policies the party wants or to implement policies the party has rejected. The Common Market, incomes policy and *In Place of Strife* are examples where this has been tried and failed.

In most of the discussion about the Labour party conducted in the mass media, three supposed 'conflicts' are highlighted. The first is the 'conflict' between the 'left wing' and the 'moderates', the second is between the PLP on the one hand and the NEC and annual conference on the other, the third involves the role of the trade unions. And to simplify the situation even more, the PLP is seen as 'moderate' while the NEC and annual conference are projected as being dominated by the 'left'. The trade union contribution to conference decisions is variously described according to how their votes are cast: if they vote with the 'moderates', their vote is seen as being 'responsible' and 'democratic'; if they vote with the 'left', then the 'brute force of their block votes' is blamed for the outcome. The reality is, however, quite different and must be rescued from under the mass of half-truth and deliberate distortion with which it is overlaid.

First, the use of the adjectives 'moderate' and 'left wing' merit some examination. The Labour party, being avowedly socialist in its aims, is itself left-wing and so are all its members, as compared to Conservatives and Liberals. Moreover, the term 'moderate' is equally confusing: by any world standard of socialism, the entire party is exceptionally moderate, offering, even in its supposedly 'full-blooded' manifestos in the past, the most modest proposals for changes in the structure of wealth and power, all to be achieved firmly within the framework of parliamentary democracy, complete with regular and free elections. The main characteristic of the 'left wing' of the party is that it may be more analytical and philosophical in its approach, and more committed to carrying through the policies agreed at conference once they have been endorsed by the electorate and a Labour government is in power. By contrast, some of the self-proclaimed 'moderates' in the past have ended up in other political parties. Whatever else it turned out they were, they were not moderate socialists but committed Conservatives or Liberals. Thus the labelling now in general use is not very accurate in describing the wide spread of opinion within the party and the spirit of tolerance to be found among people of differing views.

The second 'conflict' is also most misleading for, whatever may be said in the media, the attitude of the PLP on the issues of the day may not differ as sharply from the attitude of the NEC and the conference as it is made to appear. The plain fact is that there is hardly ever a vote about policy among Labour MPs at meetings of the PLP and their collective view cannot be ascertained. There were no votes at PLP meetings before the cabinet decided to accept the renegotiation of Common Market terms, before key parts of the industrial policy were abandoned, before the cuts in public expenditure were approved or before the 5 per cent pay limit was announced. In each case the cabinet reached its view in private, announced it and then called upon MPs' support as 'a matter of confidence'. Faced with the alternative of appearing to repudiate a Labour prime minister (and risking the defeat of a Labour government), they quite properly gave their support to what had already been announced, but it is anyone's guess whether they would have endorsed these policies if they had been asked before the cabinet had reached its view and committed its public reputation. Certainly, in respect of some of those issues we know for a fact that the PLP agreed with the NEC and conference and disagreed with the cabinet: at no time from 1975–79 did a majority of the PLP vote for cabinet policy in recommending the nation to accept the renegotiated terms for the EEC or for the legislation to hold direct elections, nor can we be at all sure that the PLP would have supported the cuts in public expenditure or the 5 per cent pay policy. The real problem facing Labour MPs does not arise from pressure on them from the NEC, the annual conference or their own constituency activists, but stems directly from the excessive powers of the prime minister, who is able to secure compliance by the carrot of patronage and the stick of threatened dissolutions. Unless they insist upon democracy within the PLP, they can never reach a position in which their own view is known and can be made effective in influencing their leader.

The role of the trade unions is also very different in practice from the public presentation of it. First, the trade unions already have the greatest say in determining the composition of the NEC: of 29 elected members of the NEC, the trade unions directly elect 12, while their votes are decisive in choosing the treasurer and the five members of the women's section, making 18 in all. The PLP elect the leader and the deputy leader, making 20, leaving only seven constituency representatives, one from the socialist, co-operative and professional organisations and one Young Socialist. The supposed 'left wing' domination of the NEC by constituency activists, therefore, does not stand up to a moment's examination. Next, it should be made clear that without trade union support no policy statement presented by the NEC has any chance of being endorsed. The 1974 manifesto policies for industry were overwhelmingly carried by conference with trade union support; the TUC economic and industrial policies in recent years have followed the lines first set out by the NEC and were pressed upon the Labour government by the TUC even more strongly than by the NEC: during the winter of 1978–79 it was the trade union membership, and not the NEC, which secured a modification of the 5 per cent pay policy. Finally, it should be added that the relationship between the TUC and the Labour government was much closer than the relationship between Labour ministers and either the NEC or the PLP. Everyone in the party welcomed this close government–TUC contact which constituted the real extra-parliamentary role of the labour movement.

The real tension within the party, then, does not only stem from the 'conflicts' above but to a great extent from the tension that exists between the dominating power of the party leader, especially when he is prime minister, and the rest of the labour movement, Labour MPs, the NEC, conference and the trade unions. Unless this power balance is redressed by the introduction of more democracy within the party and the movement, we shall never resolve the pressures which have built up and the nature of which it is so easy to misrepresent. The Labour party and its affiliated trade unions are united in wanting to make real socialist reforms through the agency of parliamentary democracy and are quite open in spelling this out in resolutions and in manifestos. If the electorate vote for a Labour government, the party expects its MPs to implement this policy. At present, the main barrier to the realisation of that hope seems to be the use of the power of the leader and not Labour MPs as a body. The only possible criticism that can be levelled against the latter is that they have accepted the situation which only they have the power to correct. Unless this problem is dealt with by greater party democracy, there is a risk that the pent-up pressure for real economic, industrial and social change, now so evident inside the labour movement, may seek expression outside the Labour party and outside parliament and thus damage the role of the party as the main democratic instrument of working people and their families and its capacity to win elections to advance those interests. Indeed, I can visualise an even greater danger. If the perspective of peaceful change by democratic means were to get blocked within the Labour party, it would not just be the party but parliamentary democracy itself that might be undermined.

Towards a Constitutional Premiership

Having emphasised the immense concentration of power in the hands of the prime minister, it is now necessary to consider ways and means by which the exercise of that power could be made more accountable to those in parliament, party and country over whom it is now exercised. The real problem is not that the power is grossly abused or grossly misused. If either were to happen, a prime minister would be overthrown by his cabinet colleagues through collective resignation or by Labour MPs through a withdrawal of support in the Commons

– either of which would precipitate a change of leader or a general election in which case the decision of the voter would be final. The real problem lies in the full exercising of power that is now held to be legitimate and established in such a way as to create a centre of power so great that the fine balance of the constitution is disturbed to the public disadvantage. All systems of government ultimately depend upon the good will and common sense of those occupying positions of responsibility and require a degree of trust by those who are governed in those who govern them. Mechanistic solutions cannot replace the need for this common sense and this trust, but our history has taught us that even good kings were not good enough to make an absolute monarchy acceptable – and even good prime ministers can never be good enough to make the present concentration of power in their hands acceptable either. Some countervailing democratic influences need to be developed if we are to move toward a constitutional premiership more in keeping with the tenets of democracy. It is to these reforms that I now turn.

The abolition of the House of Lords, to which the Labour party is firmly committed by an overwhelming conference vote, would dispense with the need to nominate peers. The party does not support the idea of an elected second chamber and nor do I, but were one set up it would also end all prime ministerial power to place people in a second chamber and the argument about the end of this form of patronage is therefore common to those who do not believe in unicameral government.

Were a system to be instituted under which all cabinet ministers were elected by the PLP and the allocation of portfolios were put to Labour MPs for approval before their nomination to the crown, there would be a real sharing of power that would greatly strengthen the role of the government's supporters, without diminishing in any way the power of the House of Commons as a whole over a government thus constructed in that it could still overthrow that government if a majority was available for that purpose.

Further development of the Commons select committee system should include the right to summon ministers and would open up the workings of government in a way that no other method could achieve. Effective select committees would probably do more to set up countervailing power to the power of the executive than any other single reform.

A parliamentary confirmation system for major public appointments should be instituted. With departmental select committees now about to be established, it should be open to them to recommend to the House whether or not ministerial appointments, chairmen of nationalised industries and Royal Commissions, or even top ranking civil servants, should be confirmed by the Commons as a whole.

A Freedom of Information Act conferring the statutory right of access to government papers, save those in a clearly defined narrow category involving defence and security or commercial or personal files, would greatly reduce the powers of the prime minister to the advantage of the public, parliament and the party. The process of consultation would be revitalised by such a change and accountability would be much easier.

Lawmaking powers should be returned from Brussels to parliament. Since so much of the lawmaking in Britain now flows from ministerial decisions taken at private meetings of the council of ministers in the European Communities without the express authorisation by the House of Commons, and since these powers are exercised by the prime minister through a combination of the royal prerogative and Section 2 of the 1972 European Communities Act, effective means of restoring House of Commons power over the executive powers of the prime minister are needed to deal with this problem.

An examination of the ways of redressing the balance between the prime minister and the rest of the constitution would turn out to involve a strengthening of the parliamentary Labour party, rather than a weakening of it as the media always suggest. The PLP has a very important role to play within the Labour party of which it forms an integral part. Like all individual members of the party, Labour MPs have a responsibility to advocate, and to implement, the policies of the party as agreed at annual conference, and they have the opportunity to do so in the House of Commons. The party meeting made up of all Labour MPs should be seen as the main forum of debate within the PLP and the final authority on all matters concerning the day-to-day working of the party in the House of Commons, within the framework of conference policy.

It should have the right at all its meetings to discuss all recommendations relating to the handling of parliamentary business, or to propose amendments of all kinds, which should in every case be put to party meetings for approval. This, combined with the election of frontbench spokesmen, approval of the allocation of shadow portfolios and a greater role for the subject groups of the PLP, would go a long way to redress the present imbalance in the power relationships betweeen MPs and the party leader. There should also be regular meetings between the parliamentary committee and the NEC, which should have the last word on the manifesto, to discuss any matter relating to the work of the party that anybody may wish to raise. This whole clutch of simple reforms should remain in force when a Labour government is in office.

The recommendations made involve the greater use of three tried and tested constitutional principles that we used to extend democratic accountability in the past. The first is greater disclosure, the second is the replacement of patronage by election or confirmation procedures, the third is the emphasis on truly collective decision making as opposed to personal rule.

In arguing for this approach, there is one factor to be taken into account that greatly strengthens the case. Not only has the prime minister's power over the government greatly increased over the years, but the role of government itself has also greatly increased: the prime minister thus exercises greater personal power over a much more formidable array of state powers and the case for greater accountability is, as a result, much stronger. This growth of state power is necessary to protect the citizens against the even greater growth of extra-parliamentary centres of power – many of them now international – in finance and industry and in the international organisations, including the EEC, which now controls so much of our legislation, trade, economic and military policy. To seek a remedy to the problem I have described by trying to reduce the role of government, rather than by trying to bring it under greater democratic control, would only expose our people to greater domination by those extra-parliamentary forces against which they have no means of redress at all. We need a strong government to protect us; and those who see that need must also be most vigilant in seeing that it is, itself, fully democratic in character. The trend to centralisation of power is there for all to observe worldwide. We cannot allow it to grow here, even in .Downing Street, and least of all under Labour party auspices. Strong leadership there must be, but it must be open, collective, and accountable, and must learn to exercise its necessary powers by persuasion and, above all, through the development of a constitutional premiership.

Reference

1. This article is based on a talk given to the Study of Parliament Group in January 1979 and a lecture at Bristol in July 1979, reprinted from 'The Case for a Constitutional Premiership', *Parliamentary Affairs*, XXXIII (Winter 1980), pp. 7–22.

10

Strength at the Centre – The Case for a Prime Minister's Department

KENNETH BERRILL[1]

Although Tony Benn on the whole avoids the language of 'strengthening' and 'weakening', he clearly believes that the position of the prime minister should be weakened vis-à-vis the cabinet, the Labour party and the British people as a whole. Sir Kenneth Berrill in this chapter holds that, on the contrary, the tasks that any prime minister has to perform are not matched by adequate staff resources. The centre of British government is too weak vis-à-vis the periphery. In making out the case for the creation of a new prime minister's department, Sir Kenneth, who served as head of the Central Policy Review Staff (abolished since he gave this lecture), takes issue with both Tony Benn and George Jones.

The title of this lecture is 'Strength at the Centre – The Case for a Prime Minister's Department'. It stems from my last seven years' experience in Whitehall, and I chose to speak on this subject partly because it is an issue of some importance and partly because, in contrast to some other countries, here in the United Kingdom the subject has excited comparatively little public interest or debate. In this respect perhaps the greatest contrast is with the United States where the presidential form of government means that the head of government has many direct and legal responsibilities placed on his shoulders which in our system are borne by individual cabinet ministers. It is not surprising, therefore, that the past 40 years should have seen study after study on the theme 'What help does the president need, and how should it best be organised?'. The work load on the president can only be described as awesome and the support system almost equally so, for in the White House and the Executive Office of the President we are talking of a cast of literally thousands all working to support the president in his executive role, including men of great power as presidential aides able to transmit what they interpret as the president's wishes to the departments and bureaux.

Washington is indeed a very different world from Whitehall and in what I have to say about the role of our prime minister in the United Kingdom and the need for support in that role I am not confusing our system with a presidential one. Unlike in the United States, our cabinet ministers are senior elected members of the legislature in their own right, with major responsibilities for which they are directly answerable to parliament and to the courts. I am well aware that it would be quite inappropriate for us to try to emulate Washington in the support system which we provide to our head of government.

As I have said, given the United States presidential system, it is not surprising that the organisation of the White House and the Executive Office of the President should have been fairly continuously in the public eye. What is more surprising, to me at any rate, is the contrast between the United Kingdom and a number of other countries with a prime ministerial cabinet system of government such as Canada, Australia or Germany. In those countries there has been considerable public analysis both of the role of a prime minister in the world today and the extent and type of support which that role demands. In the United Kingdom there have indeed been writings on the role of prime minister – by academics and by politicians such as Patrick Gordon Walker, Richard Crossman, notably in his Godkin Lectures, and by John Mackintosh. But in contrast to say Germany and Australia the support system has excited comparatively little attention.

It might be thought that one reason for this is the traditional low profile and confidentiality of those who work at Number 10 and the Cabinet Office. I do not myself regard this low profile and confidentiality as vitiating discussion of the prime ministerial support system, but perhaps I should make it clear that nothing I will say tonight will add to the facts which have already been set forth by politicians such as Gordon Walker, Crossman or Mackintosh or more recently the Whitehall correspondent of *The Times*.

It may be, however, that lack of public discussion is due to a general acceptance of John Mackintosh's view that the present arrangements are wholly adequate. As he put it 'Harold Wilson (notoriously a fast reader) found that Number 10 and the Cabinet Office provided all the material he could cope with, so it is agreed that there is sufficient advice and support'. The more fundamental question is not whether the *volume* of advice presented to a prime minister is adequate but the depth of work and knowledge behind that advice.

But before I turn to the support system let me first speak about the role of prime minister in Britain today. This has been well enough analysed by others. A prime minister has immense powers of patronage; the power both to form an administration and to decide when to end it; the power to appoint ministers and the power to drop some of them in what is euphemistically called a reshuffle.

Parallel to these powers of appointment are the powers to decide on the machinery of government – the organisation and reorganisation of ministries and particularly the organisation of the business of cabinet and cabinet committees. As is now well known, the weekly meeting of cabinet concentrates on foreign affairs, forthcoming business in parliament and major issues such as a public expenditure review. The bulk of discussion and decision in all areas is necessarily delegated to cabinet committees. The prime minister decides the membership of those committees and who should be chairman of those committees not chaired by the prime minister.

As we all know, to be chairman of any committee can be a position of great strength. The prime minister (or the senior minister appointed as chairman of the cabinet committee) approves the agenda.

A cabinet minister can always decide that he would like to bring a matter before his colleagues and if it involved legislation would always do so. But the prime minister (or chairman) can always insist that he does so and ask for the necessary papers to be circulated – perhaps after interdepartmental consultation. Clearly it is important for the chairman to have a good idea of all the issues which are stirring in the area covered by the committee, and one task of a support system is to constitute eyes and ears in this respect.

As well as deciding on the agenda and seeing that the necessary papers are circulated, the prime minister (or chairman) controls the order of speakers, decides if further work is called for and how it should best be undertaken and, finally, sums up the 'consensus' of the meeting on the basis of the discussion. That 'summing up of the consensus' is vital for it appears in the minutes circulated next day throughout Whitehall and forms the operating instructions for implementation of the decisions.

In addition to the formal business of cabinet and cabinet committees there is a large volume of interministerial correspondence on important issues, the great bulk of which is seen by the prime minister, who can intervene with a query, express an opinion or pull the matter more closely into the Number 10 orbit by calling in the minister for a talk, setting up a working group or whatever. The system of cabinet, cabinet committee and interministerial correspondence means that there are few issues being argued between ministers of which the prime minister is not *au courant* and on which therefore the staff at Number 10 and the Cabinet Office may be asked to give advice.

The power of a prime minister to intervene in any field at any time is clear enough (and prime ministerial intervention is a significant force indeed). The more interesting question is, why they should feel the need to do so? There are a number of reasons and taken together they seem to me both to explain the increase in the role of the head of government in most industrial democracies and to suggest that this increase will continue inexorably.

The first and perhaps the most powerful reason for prime ministerial intervention can be expressed in the form 'The centre is the guardian of the strategy and the prime minister is the mainstay of the centre'. In opposition, shadow cabinets can spend a considerable amount of time working out their strategy for putting the country to rights when they get back to power. Each member of the shadow cabinet has a department he is shadowing but since he is not actually in charge its problems do not preoccupy his mind. Inevitably things are different when the shadow cabinet becomes the real cabinet and each member moves into his department, for the basis of the departmental system is that each 'fights its own corner'. The regional departments (Scotland, Wales, Northern Ireland) fight for the interests of their areas. Defence, Industry, Transport, Education, Health, etc. do the same. Their job is to fight for their own programmes, their own public expenditure, their own share of the legislative timetable. Inevitably they come to see the world and any proposed action in terms of the possible effect on their particular interests and objectives. So much so that after a year or two's experience at the centre one can predict with a high degree of certainty each department's arguments and views on any topic on the agenda.

It is also a well-observed fact that the longer ministers have held a particular portfolio the more likely they are to see the country's problems increasingly through the eyes of their department and less in terms of the strategy of the government as a whole. Of course this is never universally true, but it would be strange if it were not usually so, given the very long hours they spend immersed in the details of their department's affairs and the continual batterings they get on those affairs in the media, in parliament and from the ever more professionally organised pressure groups.

But the sum of spending departments' interests can be a long way from adding up to a coherent strategy and no one is more aware of this than a prime minister. A prime minister knows only too well that the government will be judged at the next election more on its overall performance than on its success or failure in particular departmental areas. Prime ministers know too that time is not on their side. In the 35 years since the end of the Second World War we have had nine different prime ministers – an average period in office of around four years each. The longest anyone has achieved was Sir Harold Wilson with eight years and that was split into two separate periods. So a prime minister has to think in terms of a four-year time horizon in which the government strategy has to be seen to be working sufficiently well to achieve re-election. Hence the importance of sufficient 'strength at the centre' to hold the balance in any decision between the requirements of the strategy and the crosspulls of the interests of the different spending departments.

It is, of course, not just the prime minister who has the task of trying to maintain this balance. The 'centre' is the 'troika' of the prime minister, the chancellor of the exchequer and his ministerial team and the foreign secretary and his team. The cohesion of this troika is crucial yet even these three elements do not always pull naturally in quite the same direction for the Treasury and the Foreign and Commonwealth Office too have their departmental preoccupations. The Treasury is liable to approach every decision concerned mainly with the effect on the balance of the domestic economy and the Foreign and Commonwealth Office preoccupied mainly with the effects on our relations with other countries. The troika may at any time have the support of certain spending ministers who continue to put adherence to the strategy over departmental considerations. But in general terms the troika is the centre and the centre has to hold. It was Richard Crossman who said that 'perhaps the biggest task of a prime minister is to stop the fragmentation of the cabinet into a mere collection of departmental heads'. It is this task of preserving the balance between strategy and departmental interests which provides the first, crucial reason for the width of involvement of a prime minister across the business of government.

The second reason for widespread prime ministerial concern and involvement is less basic but is a powerful influence nonetheless. It is the tendency of the media and the public to hold the government responsible for virtually any problem that arises in both the public and the private sectors and to identify the government's reaction to the problem with the persona of the prime minister. Internationally as well as domestically governments are expected to have a view, a policy, a programme of action for virtually everything. The policies have to be both positive and 'caring'. Statements along the lines of 'there's little we can do about it' or 'yes, it is unfortunate and unfair but a lot of life consists of rather rough justice' are not popular.

This wide public expectation of the role of government is allied to the increased personalisation of government which I believe stems mainly from television and parliament. The television camera peering, oh so closely, at every flickering emotion across a politician's face gives the public the belief that they know him as a person, can judge his character and how he will act. In a presidential system the powers of the head of government are so immense that this approach to voting may have more merit. It is obviously less so in a prime ministerial system and more weight is indeed given by the public to the persona of cabinet ministers. But at bottom the media and the public think and talk of Margaret Thatcher's government or Mr Callaghan's. They lay the ultimate responsibility for virtually every act or omission by the government at the door of the prime minister who must expect to be attacked on any of them and be ready to answer in any interview and at question time in parliament. Small wonder then that a prime minister should feel the need to try to keep an eye on everything and be tempted into fire-fighting intervention on issues which look like causing political difficulties.

The first two reasons for very wide prime ministerial involvement are then (1) the need for the centre to keep the balance on every decision between departmental objectives and strategic objectives and (2) the need to be ready to answer to the media and parliament for virtually every government action. The third reason, and in recent years it has become one of ever-increasing weight, is the growth in personal contact between heads of government, to such an extent that we expect to read daily in our newspapers of personal visits by one head of government to another.

These contacts take place at formal 'summits' in a variety of different fora (EEC, Commonwealth, major OECD countries, etc.), by bilateral visits and through unpublicised messages and telephone conversations. To take the EEC: we are all very much aware that the founding fathers greatly underestimated the part that would be played in the operation of the Community by the various councils of ministers (Agriculture, Energy, Finance, etc.). We are all aware too that very major issues, such as the UK contribution to the EEC budget, have to be hammered out by heads of government personally often through a complex package of measures involving many departments of state. Preparation for these summit meetings, be they bilateral or multilateral, has therefore to be over a wide canvas. For even if there is a previously agreed agenda this is usually wide enough in all conscience. But there may well be non-agenda items which we on our side would like to raise if the occasion is ripe, and we have to be prepared for anything the other side may raise. These issues may be political, military, economic or social. They may be raised in general terms or in considerable detail, particularly in bilateral discussions. A head of government cannot always have the relevant cabinet minister by his side or leave it to him to do all the talking. The head of government must know the facts and have views on the objectives, the strategy and the tactics across a very wide range of issues in their international context. The importance of this preparation and briefing hardly needs stressing for if heads of government come to an understanding, even an informal one, that is bound to have a major influence on policy.

No matter what his priorities, in today's world it is just not open to a head of government to devote himself very largely to his country's domestic problems. In a country like Britain the prime minister is involved every week and sometimes every day in international visits and contacts, and the frequency seems continually to rise. This international involvement provides the third powerful force which is moulding the role of head of government towards a wider and more interventionist role.

So far in this lecture I have been concerned with the role of a prime minister and with the forces which, as I see it, are moulding and expanding that role in most major parliamentary democracies. That role and those forces constitute the case for what I have called 'strength at the centre'. The centre clearly cannot leave all industry issues to the Department of Industry, agriculture to the Ministry of Agriculture, etc. There must be some degree of parallel competence in the expenditure divisions of the Treasury and in the Foreign Office. But what of the prime minister? What kind of support system does a prime minister need, and has this system developed adequately in parallel with the degree and width of prime ministerial involvement?

Well, there has been little development inside the cramped confines of 10 Downing Street. Television has made the entrance to Number 10 the most famous front door in the country – a sharp contrast from before the First World War when Margot Asquith complained that no taxi driver could find it. Number 10 is a surprise in many respects, particularly to overseas visitors used to the much grander looking offices of other heads of government. The narrowness of the street, the absence of armed guards at the door, the closeness of the public to the arriving visitors. The small terraced house facing Downing Street conceals of course the much bigger house joined on behind which looks out on Horse Guards. But in administrative terms the impression from Downing Street *is* the correct one. The prime minister's staff at Number 10 remains as it always has been, very small indeed. If we want to look for changes in the support system it is through the door at the back of Number 10 into the Cabinet Office that we need to look.

Here there has indeed been organisationally almost continuous change. The creation of a European Unit to co-ordinate Whitehall's approaches to Brussels; the creation and then dissolution of a constitution unit to handle devolution to Scotland and Wales; the creation of a CPRS and then later the creation of an Advisory Council for Applied Research and Development serviced by the CPRS and the incorporation of the Cabinet Office Scientific Unit into the CPRS.

I realise that it is difficult for an outsider to see how the shape of the Cabinet Office may be changing for its constituent parts must seem so amorphous. For what has the large Central Statistical Office (CSO) in common with the small CPRS, the assessment staff with the European Unit, the secretariat with the Civil Contingencies Unit, etc.? And how far are each of these units a support system for the prime minister rather than for the cabinet generally? Perhaps this very difficulty of identification is part of the explanation of the lack of public discussion in the United Kingdom of this support system question.

Other countries have equally been in a state of flux over the organisation of their support system for prime minister and cabinet, but usually with more public discussion. In the years in which I was head of the CPRS there was a stream of visitors from other capitals looking at how we in the CPRS did things.

They asked very pertinent questions, too. In what sense were we non-political? Could we really move immediately from being very close to the prime minister of one administration to a head of government from another political party? Did the departments starve us of the vital facts? Did we have a rough time if we disagreed openly with a senior cabinet minister? How far did we work on the things we were told to look at, or did we initiate work for ourselves? How much work was strategic and long-term, and how much short-term and tactical? How much of our product went to the prime minister personally and how much to ministers collectively? How much of what we did was made public?, etc.

All good questions, asked against a different political and administrative background in each capital. It was clear that many of our arrangements were just not transplantable to the other places and vice-versa. Each country was working out a slightly different solution. In particular no two places brigaded the same functions into the equivalent of our Number 10 and Cabinet Office.

But one general impression remained, which was that none of the countries with a prime ministerial system gets to anything like the size of the White House and the Executive Office of the President; but several countries which one might reasonably compare with the United Kingdom have settled for a prime minister's department and Cabinet Office complex which runs towards the 500 staff mark. In the United Kingdom our numbers are boosted by the inclusion of the CSO, but this apart almost every visitor to the CPRS I entertained commented on the small numbers we employed.

The Australian prime minister's department and Cabinet Office is interesting as an example of a country where there have been a number of reorganisations and considerable public debate and where the publication of an annual report gives a fairly up-to-date picture of size and functions. The size is around 450 staff, organised in divisions, which cover parliamentary affairs, external relations, trade and industry, resources and development, welfare, prime minister's correspondence and a priorities branch with a function somewhat akin to the CPRS. For the record the annual report has them servicing in the year 470 meetings, processing 1,424 papers and submissions and 3,046 decisions. The United Kingdom is certainly not less complex in this respect than Australia.

The task of a prime minister's department and Cabinet Office needs perhaps some analysis for at first sight there is an ambiguity as to whether its task is to serve the prime minister or the cabinet as a whole. There is indeed such an ambiguity, for the same officials may be performing one function in the morning and another in the afternoon.

The first function is the traditional and fairly straightforward one of providing a secretariat for the cabinet committee system – preparing the forward programme of meetings and agendas, ensuring that the right papers are circulated, servicing the meetings, following up the decisions. To say that this secretariat function is traditional and fairly straightforward in no way implies that it is unimportant or routine. Quite the reverse. The best laid forward programmes are swiftly overtaken by new domestic and international events. Very quick footwork is necessary to see that the papers and meetings keep up. The very functioning of government depends on this staff work being well organised and the operational orders which emerge from the meetings being prompt and clear. In this respect the British Cabinet Office is quite superb. Nor is the work undemanding. The load is a shifting one depending on international and domestic events. A series of international meetings which require parallel action in Whitehall can put a heavy secretarial load on particular sections of the Cabinet Office. On the domestic front, continual interministerial meetings on, say, the details of incomes policy can work another section almost into the ground.

The second function is to provide neutral (i.e. nondepartmental) chairmen and secretaries of interdepartmental committees and working groups of officials. Departments look for a neutral chairman because the very disparate nature of their interests means that they are reluctant to trust one of the other spending departments in the powerful position of chairmen. In principle any one of the central departments might perform the function but as time goes by the task seems to fall more and more to the Cabinet Office.

Providing neutral chairmanship for an interdepartmental committee of officials can be, as I know only too well, a frustrating task. The object is to obtain for ministers an agreed report with clear conclusions and recommendations all in as brief a compass as possible. Each departmental representative on the committee is fighting not only for the interests of his department but for the inclusion in the text of particular points or reservations which seem important where he comes from, if to no one else around the table. The result is often a reasonably short report with an unreasonable number of appendices to sweep up the departmental points.

This function of supporting the work of the cabinet committee system by providing a good secretariat and neutral chairmanship of official committees is important and non-controversial. In the past there have been some who believed that this was basically all that was needed. It was argued in Australia that if ministers were well chosen and departments well organised (including the Treasury and the Foreign Office playing their role at the centre) then the role of a Cabinet Office should be almost entirely secretarial and co-ordinating and a prime minister needed little in the way of a parallel advice system.

I doubt if this picture ever really held true – at least not for many years. Prime ministers have long expected advice from their permanent secretary – the secretary to the cabinet – and the briefs for the chairman of any cabinet committee have long contained analyses and advice on the issues raised on the agenda. But whatever happened in years gone by the position today is clear enough. For the reasons which I have outlined in this lecture the role of head of government has necessarily become increasingly activist and interventionist over a wide spectrum. For very good reasons, which I have also described, the centre cannot just accept the analysis of the spending departments. The need for a parallel capacity to monitor, analyse and advise has always been present and has grown stronger. But where in the centre should it be?

Traditionally it is located in the ministry of finance (the

Treasury) with something much slimmer in the Foreign Office. Why does there need to be anything additional in the prime minister's office? Partly because, as I have said, the Treasury and the Foreign Office although part of the centre look at things from their own special points of view; the Treasury tends to be preoccupied with the effects on the balance of the domestic economy – particularly with the short-term effects on public expenditure.

No. Prime ministers need and expect an advice system of their own to help in the work of cabinet and cabinet committees, in their reaction to issues raised in ministerial correspondence, in their relations with other heads of government – not least because of the time factor. Briefs for cabinet committees, reactions to ministerial correspondence, etc., often have to be prepared at considerable speed. It would be a very great handicap indeed if the back-up for all this was situated in another central department. More frequent contacts between heads of government has increased the extent to which the offices of the prime ministers in the different capitals are necessarily in frequent telephone contact. Indeed there is now the standing group of personal representatives of the heads of government who help prepare the way for the next summit (hence the term Sherpas). Here in the United Kingdom our Sherpa is the secretary to the cabinet. All this reinforces the need for a parallel advice system in Number 10 and the Cabinet Office.

There is, of course, good advice and bad. As John Mackintosh said, a prime minister certainly gets plenty to read and the question is which advice to accept and which to reject? Or as Machiavelli put it 'Good advice depends on the shrewdness of the Prince who seeks it and not the shrewdness of the Prince on good advice'.

Nevertheless, if advice is to be proferred at a point as sensitive and influential as a prime minister or to a cabinet committee, then that advice needs to be based on knowledge and study of reasonable depth, and that takes time and people.

Certainly I found that in the CPRS. Our work consisted of a mixture of short-term tactical issues on today's problems and today's agenda, and longer-term studies which could take many months to complete. Those long-term studies were the capital on which we lived. Several months' work on a subject, seeing people up and down the country and perhaps overseas, meant that you knew the problems in some depth, knew what you thought about the issues and, almost equally important, got to know people you could contact for a quick update. Then when problems in that area come before ministers again some time later at fairly short notice one can second-guess the sponsor department from a basis of some strength.

As I have already said, here in Britain the Cabinet Office has adapted continuously and fluidly to the changing circumstances and the changing need of ministers (the EEC unit, the devolution unit, the switch from a science unit to a council on applied research and development). The CPRS is a good example of this flexibility and pragmatism. Its workload has shifted continuously between work for the prime minister personally and work for ministers collectively, and the balance between areas of work has moved with the interests of different administrations. In the early and mid-1970s it was deeply involved in the macro-balance of the economy, in public expenditure issues and above all in the details of incomes policy. That last preoccupation obviously declined sharply after the 1979 election. A heavy deployment of resources on social policy issues and relations with developing countries shifts to industrial issues, and so on. By the end of the 1970s the CPRS had been involved at some time or another in virtually the whole spectrum of government policy – shifting partly with its own appreciation of what was likely to become important in the period ahead and partly with the changing concerns and interests of the prime minister and cabinet.

The staff of Number 10 and the Cabinet Office works long hours to try to meet the needs of the prime minister and the cabinet collectively. In my view it copes remarkably well with its mixture of roles, and it copes well too with the shifts in the workload from one area to another. It achieves this in part by hard work, partly because it is a hand-picked group of very high fliers and partly by great flexibility and team effort, which is all the more remarkable in that it is a revolving team all on secondment for a couple of years or so.

It really is a team effort from the front door of Number 10 round through the Cabinet Office, with no false pride of authorship and everyone prepared to help the man struggling to prepare a brief on a cabinet committee item at very short notice. I have no doubt that it is a good service. The question I ask is: is it good enough? Do we put into it the resources it deserves given the trends in the role of prime minister and the importance of advice at such a potentially powerful point?

I have little doubt that if prime ministers past or present were asked if they were satisfied with the service they receive the answer would be 'yes' – partly because it is a good service, and partly because if the answer were 'no' the first supplementary would be 'Well, why didn't you do more about it?'. Prime ministers may indeed be satisfied with the service they have received, but working for years, as I have, on the servants' side of the green baize door gives one a different perspective.

My thesis is a simple one. In today's world the support system for the head of government is a subject of increasing importance. Our competitors have, by and large, faced this issue and come to some structured solutions which have put rather more resources into the area than we have been prepared to do. We have preferred to keep a very small staff at Number 10 and rely on incremental changes in the Cabinet Office and on the flexibility of those who work there.

If there were to be a more public discussion, my own argument would not be for massive change. Britain is a prime ministerial democracy, not a presidential form of government. I would not envisage a prime minister taking more day-to-day involvement even in those departments to which they are nominally connected – Treasury and Civil Service Department. The prime ministerial load is already too heavy to take on yet more detailed responsibilities. What in my view is at issue is whether a prime minister should have a support system with time to work on problems in some depth across the width of government activities. At present the advice is given, and very presentably too, but the depth is inevitably patchy.

An across-the-board support system for a prime minister of adequate depth seems a simple enough issue and one where the expense involved is tiny in relation to the issues involved. A simple question, but it raises many issues. Would these extra staff just be added to the Cabinet Office secretariat and work both for the prime minister and cabinet or would they work for the prime minister alone? Would they all be drawn from the public service or from outside? Would they be political or non-political appointments?, etc. I am also aware that, though the cost of such an improved support staff would be tiny in relation to the issues involved, any suggestion for increased numbers is an anathema at present and no prime minister could increase staff while everyone else was being expected to cut back.

But this is a long-term question which, if I am right, will not go away but get sharper with the developing role of heads of government. It is also a question which is better discussed in opposition than in government, for in government time is always pressing, a prime minister's support system raises delicate issues of the balance of power between prime minister and members of the cabinet, and there are enough difficulties which have to be faced so why disturb something which is working as well as is the Cabinet Office?

It may be considered when in opposition, but even then the issue of a prime minister's department is a sensitive one for a number of prospective members of the cabinet could well fight shy of strengthening the hand of a future prime minister. This would be a gloomy note on which to end a lecture, so I will end on a more positive note. The CPRS was a significant change in the system at the centre and that was conceived by the Conservative party in opposition. Of one thing I am sure: we *do* need strength at the centre if as a nation we are to find a way out of our troubles. The role of a prime minister at the centre has increased, is still increasing and will not be diminished. We will be foolish if we do not face up to that fact and structure our arrangements adequately.

Reference

1. Reprint of the Stamp Memorial Lecture for 1980 (London: University of London, n.d.).

Bibliography

Most books on British politics and government contain some references to the prime ministership; but, as was pointed out in the Introduction, the volume of academic literature focused directly on Number 10 is small. Would-be students of the prime ministership are therefore forced to do a good deal of digging for themselves. The following bibliography is intended to facilitate that task. It falls into four parts. The first consists of books and articles on the prime ministership itself. The second lists memoirs and biographies of postwar prime ministers. The third sets out the most important books and articles on Margaret Thatcher and her period of office so far. The fourth consists of case studies of British politics that throw light on the prime minister in action. All four parts of the bibliography should be read in conjunction with the references at the end of the chapters in this volume.

Prime Ministership

Alderman, R. K., 'The Prime Minister and the Appointment of Ministers: An Exercise in Political Bargaining', *Parliamentary Affairs*, xxix (Spring 1976), pp. 101–34.

Alderman, R. K. and Cross, J. A., 'The Prime Minister and the Decision to Dissolve', *Parliamentary Affairs*, xxvii (Autumn 1975), pp. 386–404.

Barber, James, 'The Power of the Prime Minister', in R. L. Borthwick and J. E. Spence (eds), *British Politics in Perspective* (Leicester: Leicester University Press, 1984).

Benemy, F. W. G., *The Elected Monarch: The Development of the Power of the Prime Minister* (London: Harrap, 1965).

Benn, Tony, 'The Case for a Constitutional Premiership', *Parliamentary Affairs*, xxxiii (Winter 1980), pp. 7–22.

Berkeley, Humphry, *The Power of the Prime Minister* (London: George Allen & Unwin, 1968).

Berrill, Kenneth, *Strength at the Centre – The Case for a Prime Minister's Department*, The Stamp Memorial Lecture for 1980 (London: University of London, n.d.).

Berrington, Hugh, 'The Fiery Chariot: Prime Ministers and the Search for Love', *British Journal of Political Science*, 4 (July 1974), pp. 345–70.

Blake, Lord, *The Office of Prime Minister*, Thank-Offering to Britain Fund Lectures (London: Oxford University Press for the British Academy, 1975).

Brown, A. H., 'Prime Ministerial Power', Parts I and II, *Public Law* (Spring and Summer 1968), pp. 28–51, 96–118.

Campbell, Colin, *Governments under Stress: Political Executives and Key Bureaucrats in Washington, London, and Ottawa* (Toronto: University of Toronto Press, 1983).

Carter, Byrum E., *The Office of Prime Minister* (London: Faber & Faber, 1956).

Cockerell, Michael, Hennessy, Peter and Walker, David, *Sources Close to the Prime Minister: Inside the Hidden World of the News Manipulators* (London: Macmillan, 1984).

Cornford, James, 'The Fiery Chariot', *British Journal of Political Science*, 5 (October 1975), p. 509.

Cosgrave, Patrick, 'The Weakness of the Prime Minister' in W. J. Stankiewicz (ed.), *British Government in an Era of Reform* (London: Macmillan, 1976), pp. 211–14.

Crossman, Richard, *Inside View: Three Lectures on Prime Ministerial Government*, The Godkin Lectures for 1970 (London: Jonathan Cape, 1972).

Crossman, Richard, 'Introduction' to Walter Bagehot, *The English Constitution* (London: Watts, 1964).

Dowse, Robert E., 'Reflections on a Fiery Chariot', *British Journal of Political Science*, 5 (October 1975), pp. 507–9.

Heasman, D. J., 'The Monarch, the Prime Minister and the Dissolution of Parliament', *Parliamentary Affairs*, xiv (Winter 1960–61), pp. 167–85.

Heasman, D. J., ' "My Station and Its Duties" – The Attlee Version', *Parliamentary Affairs*, xxi (Winter 1967–8), pp. 75–84.

Heasman, D. J., 'The Prime Minister and the Cabinet', *Parliamentary Affairs*, xv (Autumn 1962), pp. 461–84.

Heath, Edward and Barker, Anthony, 'Heath on Whitehall Reform', *Parliamentary Affairs*, xxxi (Autumn 1978), pp. 363–90.

Hinton, R. W. K., 'The Prime Minister as an Elected Monarch', *Parliamentary Affairs*, xiii (Summer 1960), pp. 297–303.

Hudson, John, 'Prime Ministerial Popularity in the UK: 1960–81', *Political Studies*, xxxii (March 1984), pp. 86–97.

Iremonger, Lucille, *The Fiery Chariot: British Prime Ministers and the Search for Love* (London: Secker & Warburg, 1970).

Jennings, Ivor, *Cabinet Government*, 3rd edn (Cambridge: Cambridge University Press, 1959).

Jones, G. W., 'Development of the Cabinet' in William Thornhill (ed.), *The Modernization of British Government* (London: Pitman, 1975).

Jones, G. W., 'Harold Wilson's policy-makers', *Spectator*, 6 July 1974, pp. 12–13.

Jones, G. W., 'The Prime Minister's Advisers', *Political Studies*, xxi (September 1973), pp. 363–75.

Jones, G. W., *The Prime Minister's Aides*, Hull Papers in Politics No. 6 (Hull: Department of Politics, University of Hull, 1980).

Jones, G. W., 'Prime Ministers and Cabinets', *Political Studies*, xx (June 1972), pp. 213–22.

Jones, G. W., 'The Prime Minister and Parliamentary Questions', *Parliamentary Affairs*, xxvi (Summer 1973), pp. 260–73.

Jones, G. W., 'The Prime Minister's Power', *Parliamentary Affairs*, xviii (Spring 1965), pp. 167–85.

Jones, G. W., 'The Prime Minister's Secretaries: Politicians or Administrators?', in J. A. G. Griffith (ed.), *From Policy to Administration: Essays in Honour of William A. Robson* (London: George Allen & Unwin, 1976).

Lee, J. M., ' "Central Capability" and Established Practice: The Changing Character of the "Centre of the Machine" in British Cabinet Government', in Brian Chapman and Allen Potter (eds), *WJMM: Political Questions: Essays in Honour of W. J. M. Mackenzie* (Manchester: Manchester University Press, 1974).

Mackintosh, John P., *The British Cabinet*, 3rd edn (London: Stevens, 1977).

Mackintosh, John P., 'The Prime Minister and the Cabinet', *Parliamentary Affairs*, xxi (Winter 1967–68), pp. 53–68.

Madgwick, P. J., 'Resignations', *Parliamentary Affairs*, xx (Winter 1966–67), pp. 59–76.

Margach, James, *The Abuse of Power: The War Between Downing Street and the Media from Lloyd George to James Callaghan* (London: W. H. Allen, 1978).

Margach, James, *The Anatomy of Power: An Enquiry into the Personality of Leadership* (London: W. H. Allen, 1979).

9 & 10 Geo. 6, *Ministers of the Crown (Transfer of Functions) Act* 1946, Ch. 31.

Moodie, G. C., 'The Monarch and the Selection of a Prime Minister', *Political Studies*, v (February 1957), pp. 1–20.

Morrison, Lord, *Government and Parliament*, 3rd edn (London: Oxford University Press, 1964).

Neustadt, Richard E., interviewed by Henry Brandon, '10 Downing Street: Is It Out of Date?', *Sunday Times*, 8 November 1964.

Neustadt, Richard E., 'White House and Whitehall', *The Public Interest*, 2 (Winter 1966), pp. 55–69.

Petrie, Sir Charles, *The Powers behind the Prime Minister* (London: MacGibbon & Kee, 1958).

Rose, Richard, 'British Government: The Job at the Top', in Richard Rose and Ezra N. Suleiman (eds), *Presidents and Prime Ministers* (Washington, D.C.: American Enterprise Institute, 1980).

Rush, Michael, *The Cabinet and Policy Formation* (London: Longman, 1984).

Walker, Patrick Gordon, *The Cabinet*, 2nd edn (London: Jonathan Cape, 1972).

Wilson, Harold, interviewed by Norman Hunt, in *Whitehall and Beyond* (London: BBC Publications, 1964).

Wilson, Harold, interviewed by Kenneth Harris, 'Mr Wilson's Job', I and II, *Observer*, 24 and 31 October 1965.

Wilson, Harold, interviewed by Norman Hunt, 'The Prime Minister and the Machinery of Government', I and II, *Listener*, 6 and 13 April 1967.

Wilson, Harold, *The Governance of Britain* (London: Weidenfeld & Nicolson and Michael Joseph, 1976).

Zulueta, Philip de, 'The Power of the Prime Minister', *Swinton Journal*, 12 (Autumn 1966), pp. 37–43.

Memoirs, Biographies, etc.

Thal, Herbert von (ed.), *The Prime Ministers*, vol. II, *From Lord John Russell to Edward Heath* (London: George Allen & Unwin, 1975).

ATTLEE

Attlee, Clement R., *As It Happened* (London: Heinemann, 1954).

Attlee, Lord, 'The Art of Being a Prime Minister', *The Times*, 15 June 1958.

Attlee, Lord, 'In the Driver's Seat', *Observer*, 18 October 1964.

Harris, Kenneth, *Attlee* (London: Weidenfeld & Nicolson, 1982).

Williams, Francis, *A Prime Minister Remembers: The War and Post War Memoirs of Earl Attlee* (London: Heinemann, 1961).

CHURCHILL

Earl of Birkenhead, *The Prof in Two Worlds: The Official Life of Professor F. A. Lindemann, Viscount Cherwell* (London: Collins, 1961).

Broad, Lewis, *Winston Churchill: The Years of Achievement* (London: Sidgwick & Jackson, 1964).

Harrod, R. W., *The Prof* (London: Macmillan, 1959).

Moran, Lord, *Winston Churchill: The Struggle of Survival, 1940–65* (London: Constable, 1966).

Seldon, Anthony, *Churchill's Indian Summer: The Conservative Government 1951–55* (London: Hodder & Stoughton, 1981).

Pelling, Henry, *Winston Churchill* (London: Macmillan, 1974).

Stansky, Peter, (ed.), *Churchill: A Profile* (London: Macmillan, 1973).

EDEN: LORD AVON

Avon, Lord (Anthony Eden), *Full Circle* (London: Cassell, 1960).

Aster, Sidney, *Anthony Eden* (London: Weidenfeld & Nicolson, 1976).

Broad, Lewis, *Sir Anthony Eden: The Chronicles of a Career* (London: Hutchinson, 1955).

Carlton, David, *Anthony Eden: A Biography* (London: Allen Lane, 1981).

Churchill, Randolph, *The Rise and Fall of Sir Anthony Eden* (London: MacGibbon & Kee, 1959).

Campbell-Johnson, Alan, *Sir Anthony Eden* (London: Robert Hale, 1955).

Rees-Mogg, William, *Sir Anthony Eden* (London: Rockliff, 1956).

MACMILLAN

Evans, Harold, *Downing Street Diary: The Macmillan Years 1957–63* (London: Hodder & Stoughton, 1981).

Egremont, Lord, *Wyndham and Children First* (London: Macmillan, 1968).

Fisher, Nigel, *Harold Macmillan: A Biography* (London: Weidenfeld & Nicolson 1982).

Macmillan, Harold, *Riding the Storm: 1956–1959* (London: Macmillan, 1971).

Macmillan, Harold, *Pointing the Way: 1959–61* (London: Macmillan, 1972).

Macmillan, Harold, *At the End of the Day: 1961–63* (London: Macmillan, 1973).

Sampson, Anthony, *Macmillan: A Study in Ambiguity* (London: Allen Lane, 1967).

HOME

Dickie, John, *The Uncommon Commoner: A Study of Sir Alec Douglas-Home* (London: Pall Mall, 1964).

Home, Lord, *The Way the Wind Blows: An Autobiography* (London: Collins, 1976).

Home, Lord, interviewed by Kenneth Harris, 'A Conversation with Lord Home', *Observer*, 16 September 1962.

WILSON

Falkender, Marcia (Marcia Williams), *Downing Street in Perspective* (London: Weidenfeld & Nicolson, 1983 (see also Marcia Williams).

Foot, Michael, *Harold Wilson: A Pictorial Biography* (Oxford: Pergamon, 1964).

Foot, Paul, *The Politics of Harold Wilson* (Harmondsworth: Penguin, 1968).

Haines, Joe, *The Politics of Power* (London: Jonathan Cape, 1977).

Noel, Gerard Eyre, *Harold Wilson: A Biographical Study* (London: Gollancz, 1964).

Roth, Andrew, *Sir Harold Wilson: Yorkshire Walter Mitty* (London: Macdonald & Jane's, 1977).

Smith, Dudley, *Harold Wilson* (London: Robert Hale, 1964).

Smith, Leslie, *Harold Wilson: The Authentic Portrait* (London: Hodder & Stoughton, 1964).

Williams, Marcia (Marcia Falkender), *Inside Number 10* (London: Weidenfeld & Nicolson, 1972) (see also Marcia Falkender).

Wilson, Harold, *The Labour Government 1964–1970; A Personal Record* (London: Weidenfeld & Nicolson and Michael Joseph, 1971).

Wilson, Harold, *Final Term: The Labour Government 1974–1976* (London: Weidenfeld & Nicolson and Michael Joseph, 1979).

HEATH

Hurd, Douglas, *An End to Promises: Sketch of a Government 1970–4* (London: Collins, 1979).

Hutchinson, George, *Edward Heath: A Personal and Political Biography* (London: Longman, 1970).

Laing, Margaret, *Edward Heath: Prime Minister* (London: Sidgwick & Jackson, 1971).

Roth, Andrew, *Heath and the Heathmen* (London: Routledge & Kegan Paul, 1972).

CALLAGHAN

Kellner, Peter and Hitchens, Christopher, *Callaghan: The Road to Number Ten* (London: Cassell, 1976).

Margaret Thatcher

Arnold, Bruce, *Margaret Thatcher: A Study in Power* (London: Hamish Hamilton, 1984).

Aughey, Arthur, 'Mrs. Thatcher's Philosophy', *Parliamentary Affairs*, 36 (Autumn 1983), pp. 389–98.

Burch, Martin, 'Mrs Thatcher's Approach to Leadership in Government: 1979–June 1983, *Parliamentary Affairs*, 36 (Autumn 1983), pp. 399–416.

Cosgrave, Patrick, *Margaret Thatcher: Prime Minister* (London: Arrow Books, 1979).

Economist, 'Britain's Foreign Office', 27 November 1982, pp. 25–9.

Economist, 'Denting the contraption: How Mrs Thatcher goes about strengthening and denting Britain's constitution', 10 March 1984, p. 20.

Economist, 'Machinery of government: No other gods but Mrs T', 10 March 1984, pp. 27–30.

Economist, 'Thatcher steps out', 7 July 1984, pp. 11–12.

Gardiner, George, *Margaret Thatcher* (London: William Kimber, 1975).

Greenaway, J. R., 'Bureaucrats under Pressure: The Thatcher Government and the Mandarin Elite' in Lynton Robins (ed.), *Updating British Politics* (London: Politics Association, 1984).

Hoggart, Simon, 'The invisible man at Number 10', *Guardian*, 12 November 1979, p. 15.

Hoggart, Simon, 'The Thatcher Phenomenon', Parts 1 and 2, *Observer*, 2 January 1983, p. 41; 9 January 1983, p. 41.

Jenkins, Peter, 'Matriarch with a sense of mission', *Guardian*, 1 August 1979, p. 11.

Jenkins, Simon, 'The fall and rise of Margaret Thatcher', *Economist*, 21 April 1979, pp. 39–42.

Jenkins, Simon, 'The Thatcher Style: The trials and triumphs of a party ideologue', *Economist*, 21 May 1983, pp. 29–33.

Jones, Michael, 'Inside Number 10', *Sunday Times Magazine*, 27 April 1980, pp. 54–7.

Junor, Penny, *Margaret Thatcher: Wife, Mother, Politician* (London: Sidgwick & Jackson, 1983).

Kavanagh, Dennis, 'Margaret Thatcher: The Mobilizing Prime

Minister' in A. Clarke and Moshe M. Czudnowski (eds), *International Yearbook for Studies of Leaders and Leadership* (De Kalb, Ill.: Northern Illinois University Press, forthcoming).

Keegan, William, *Mrs Thatcher's Economic Experiment* (London: Allen Lane, 1984).

Leach, Robert F., 'Thatcherism, Liberalism, and Tory Collectivism', *Politics*, 3 (1983), pp. 9–14.

Lewis, Russell, *Margaret Thatcher: A Personal and Political Biography*, 2nd edn (London: Routledge & Kegan Paul, 1983).

Murray, Tricia, *Margaret Thatcher* (London: W. H. Allen, 1978).

Pym, Francis, *The Politics of Consent* (London: Hamish Hamilton, 1984).

Raphael, Adam, 'At the court of Queen Maggie', *Observer*, 7 October 1979, p. 11.

Raphael, Adam, 'Our gutsy Iron Lady is a warrior, not a healer', *Observer*, 27 April 1980, p. 8.

Riddell, Peter, *The Thatcher Government* (Oxford: Martin Robertson, 1983).

St John-Stevas, Norman, *The Two Cities* (London: Faber & Faber, 1984).

Stephenson, Hugh, *Mrs Thatcher's First Year* (London: Jill Norman, 1980).

Thatcher, Carol, *Diary of an Election: With Margaret Thatcher on the Campaign Trail* (London: Sidgwick & Jackson, 1983).

Times, 'Mrs. Thatcher's mid-term report', 9 October 1981, p. 11.

Wapshott, Nicholas, and Brock, George, *Thatcher* (London: Futura, 1983).

Young, Hugo, and Righter, Rosemary, 'Britain's Foreign Policy: Who's in Charge?', *Sunday Times*, 9 January 1983, p. 17.

Case Studies

Brandon, Henry, *In the Red: The Struggle for Sterling 1964–66* (London: Deutsch, 1966).

Brittan, Samuel, *Steering the Economy: The Role of the Treasury* (London: Secker & Warburg, 1969).

Bruce-Gardyne, Jock, and Lawson, Nigel, *The Power Game: An Examination of Decision Making in Government* (London: Macmillan, 1976).

Camps, Miriam, *Britain and the European Economic Community 1955–63* (London: Oxford University Press, 1964).

Dorfman, Gerald A., *British Trade Unionism Against the Trades Union Congress* (London: Macmillan, 1983).

Dorfman, Gerald A., *Government Versus Trade Unionism in British Politics Since 1968* (London: Macmillan, 1979).

Gowing, Margaret assisted by Lorna Arnold, *Independence and Deterrence: Britain and Atomic Energy 1945–52*, vols. 1 and 2 (London: Macmillan, 1978).

Hastings, Max, and Jenkins, Simon, *The Battle for the Falklands* (London: Michael Joseph, 1983).

Holmes, Martin, *Political Pressure and Economic Policy: British Government 1970–1974* (London: Butterworths, 1982).

Howard, Anthony, and West, Richard, *The Making of a Prime Minister* (London: Jonathan Cape, 1965).

Jenkins, Peter, *The Battle of Downing Street* (London: Charles Knight, 1970).

Mitchell, Joan, *Crisis in Britain 1951* (London: Secker & Warburg, 1963).

Ovenden, Keith, *The Politics of Steel* (London: Macmillan, 1978).

Ross, George W., *The Nationalisation of Steel* (London: MacGibbon & Kee, 1965).

Thomas, Hugh, *The Suez Affair* (London: Weidenfeld & Nicolson, 1967).

Index